Microsoft's Official Excel 2000 Expert Exam Objectives

Excel 2000 MOUS
Study Guide

Excel 2000 MOUS
Study Guide

Gini Courter
Annette Marquis

San Francisco • Paris • Düsseldorf • Soest • London

Associate Publisher: Amy Romanoff
Contracts and Licensing Manager: Kristine O'Callaghan
Acquisitions and Developmental Editor: Sherry Bonelli
Editor: Emily K. Wolman
Technical Editor: Don Meyers
Book Designer: Bill Gibson
Graphic Illustrator: Tony Jonick
Electronic Publishing Specialist: Franz Baumhackl
Project Team Leader: Lisa Reardon
Proofreader: Carrie Bradley
Indexer: Rebecca Plunkett
Cover Designer: Design Site

based upon final release software whenever possible. Portions of the manuscript may be based upon pre-release versions supplied by software manufacturer(s). The author and the publisher make no representation or warranties of any kind with regard to the completeness or accuracy of the contents herein and accept no liability of any kind including but not limited to performance, merchantability, fitness for any particular purpose, or any losses or damages of any kind caused or alleged to be caused directly or indirectly from this book.

Photographs and illustrations used in this book have been downloaded from publicly accessible file archives and are used in this book for news reportage purposes only to demonstrate the variety of graphics resources available via electronic access. Text and images available over the Internet may be subject to copyright and other rights owned by third parties. Online availability of text and images does not imply that they may be reused without the permission of rights holders, although the Copyright Act does permit certain unauthorized reuse as fair use under 17 U.S.C. Section 107.

Library of Congress Card Number: 99-64119
ISBN: 0-7821-2513-1
Manufactured in the United States of America

10 9 8 7 6 5 4 3 2 1

November 1, 1997

Dear SYBEX Customer:

Microsoft is pleased to inform you that SYBEX is a participant in the Microsoft®
Independent Courseware Vendor (ICV) program. Microsoft ICVs design, develop,
and market self-paced courseware, books, and other products that support Microsoft
software and the Microsoft Certified Professional (MCP) program.

To be accepted into the Microsoft ICV program, an ICV must meet set criteria. In
addition, Microsoft reviews and approves each ICV training product before
permission is granted to use the Microsoft Certified Professional Approved Study
Guide logo on that product. This logo assures the consumer that the product has
passed the following Microsoft standards:

- The course contains accurate product information.
- The course includes labs and activities during which the student can apply
  knowledge and skills learned from the course.
- The course teaches skills that help prepare the student to take corresponding
  MCP exams.

Microsoft ICVs continually develop and release new MCP Approved Study Guides.
To prepare for a particular Microsoft certification exam, a student may choose one or
more single, self-paced training courses or a series of training courses.

You will be pleased with the quality and effectiveness of the MCP Approved Study
Guides available from SYBEX.

Sincerely,

Holly Heath
ICV Account Manager
Microsoft Training & Certification

MICROSOFT INDEPENDENT COURSEWARE VENDOR PROGRAM

To all those pioneering souls who have already become Microsoft Office User Specialists.

Acknowledgments

When Microsoft first introduced the MOUS program, it was uncertain whether the program would take off. Sherry Bonelli, our acquisitions and developmental editor par excellence, saw the exciting potential of this program and made sure Sybex was taking a lead in providing the highest quality books for their readers. Thank you, Sherry, for having faith in the project and recognizing the importance of expanding Sybex's offerings as the program grows.

Hats off to Emily Wolman, who worked diligently as our editor, and Don Meyers, who offered his valuable field experience as technical editor. We are always amazed at how much better our writing is when our editors have had a crack at it.

We are lucky to have hired a trainer and found that she is also a writer. We cannot begin to extend our appreciation and admiration for the hard work and skills of Karla Browning. Karla stepped in, picked up, followed through and made sure this book got out the door. Karla, we think you are the greatest!

Thanks also to Franz Baumhackl, electronic publishing specialist, for creating the typeset pages; to Lisa Reardon, project team leader, for seeing the manuscript through the production cycle; and to proofreader Carrie Bradley and indexer Rebecca Plunkett.

Every Sybex book is the result of a coordinated team effort, and we know there are many members of the team we never even hear about. We hope you feel appreciated, too, and know that we could not do this without you.

Contents at a Glance

Table of Contents

Introduction

The *Excel 2000 MOUS Study Guide* is designed to prepare you for the Microsoft Office User Specialist exams and, in the process, make you a more knowledgeable Excel user. Most Excel users use less than 15 percent of the program's features—they only learn what they need to know to accomplish a particular task. Chances are, however, that the methods they use are neither the most efficient nor the most effective. Hidden in Excel's menus and toolbars is an incredible array of tools designed to help you make financial projections, track data, and analyze results.

Knowing how to delve more deeply into Excel's features is what sets a competent user apart from the rest. By the time you finish this book, you will be well equipped to impress your colleagues (and maybe even your employer) with your ability to tackle any project with confidence and skill.

About This Book

This book is a study guide organized around the MOUS objectives published by Microsoft. Refer to Appendix A for more information about the MOUS exams and what you need to do to prepare. It's a good idea to start by reviewing the objectives for both the Core and Expert exams so you will know what you're aiming for.

NOTE   Visit the Microsoft Certification site, www.mous.net, for the most current information about the MOUS exam guidelines.

This book covers each of the activities listed in the Excel 2000 MOUS exam guidelines. The certification map in the front of this book guides you to the page number where each activity is presented. Although each objective is covered somewhere in the book, they are not presented in order. As experienced trainers who work with beginning and advanced students on a regular basis, we are confident that you'll find it easier to learn the required skills in the order presented here. After you have finished learning each skill, you can go back through the list in order and make sure you are comfortable completing each of the required activities.

To prepare for an exam, work through one chapter at a time. At the beginning of each section related to a specific MOUS activity, you'll find an icon that looks like this, indicating the objective number listed in Appendix A.

Objective XL2000.1.1

SEE ALSO Not all sections relate to specific objectives. We included some additional topics that we think are important for you to know, even if you will not be tested on them (isn't that just like a teacher!). These topics help round out your understanding of a specific objective and provide the background you need to move ahead.

Throughout the chapter, you'll find summaries of the steps to accomplishing the tasks described in the previous section. Use summaries like the one shown here to review your knowledge and practice the steps involved in completing a task.

Embedding or Linking a File

1. Open the destination document and place the insertion point where the object is to be inserted.

2. Choose Insert ➤ Object from the menu. Click the Create From File tab.

3. Browse to select the file you want to embed or link.

4. Click the OK button to embed the file, or choose Link To File, and then click OK to link the file.

After each major topic or group of topics, Hands On sections give you a chance to apply what you've learned. If you can complete these exercises *without* help from the book, you should be in pretty good shape for the exam. We've included the objectives that the exercises relate to, so you can refer to the text if you need assistance.

Hands On

Objectives XL2000E.2.1, E.2.2, E.2.3, and E.12.1

1. Use another of the templates (such as Expenses) included with Excel 2000. Customize the template with your company's information. Save the customized template.

2. Create a template that calculates and totals gross pay, taxes, and net pay for 10 employees based on information entered by the user. Users should enter the following information for each employee: social security number, last name, first name, hourly rate, tax rate (as a percentage), and hours worked.

Special Icons

Throughout the book, you'll find additional comments about the material in the form of notes, tips, and warnings.

NOTE   Notes provide additional information about a topic.

TIP   Tips offer another way of doing something or a shortcut to completing a particular task.

WARNING   Warnings suggest possible problems you may encounter when completing a task or things to look out for along the way.

We hope that each of these extra comments will help you to more fully understand Excel so you can apply your skills to even more complex Excel applications.

Additional Help on the Web

Although we recommend that you create your own workbooks to practice the skills in this book, the sample workbooks we used as examples are available for download at www.sybex.com; to find them on the site, just navigate to this book's page. If you get stuck on how to set up a particular workbook, these examples will help you figure it out.

On this Web site, we have also included additional practice exercises and important links to other resources to help make your preparation for the MOUS exams even easier.

A Final Check

When you complete an entire chapter, review the objectives once again and see if there are any topics that you are uncertain about. Go back and review those sections in the text, and try the Hands On exercises a second time using different documents. If you still have difficulty, go on to the next topic and return later. Working on related topics sometimes causes the topic with which you're struggling to fall into place.

When you've finished all the topics, you're ready to take the MOUS exam. Do the best you can—you can always take it again if you find out the first attempt was only a practice round.

We'd Love to Hear from You!

We've provided you with a variety of tools to help you on your path to certification. We hope that you'll find them useful, challenging and fun as you improve your Microsoft Office skills. If you'd like to let us know about your experiences with this book and with taking the exams, we'd love to hear from you. Good luck!

Annette Marquis and Gini Courter
c/o Sybex. Inc.
1151 Marina Village Parkway
Alameda, CA 94501
E-mail: authors@triadconsulting.com

NOTE   If you're interested in contacting the publisher directly, Sybex welcomes reader feedback on all of their titles. Visit the Sybex Web site, www.sybex.com, for book updates and additional certification information. You'll also find online forms to submit comments or suggestions regarding this or any other Sybex book.

CHAPTER

1

Working in Office 2000

Microsoft Office 2000 is a toolkit jam-packed with powerful tools including Excel 2000, the leading spreadsheet application in the world. Whether you work for a multinational corporation or run your own small business, Excel's top-of-the-line tools will help you work smarter and more efficiently.

This chapter will familiarize you with the features in Office 2000, focusing on basic skills you'll need to work in Excel. If you've used Excel 95 or Excel 97, a lot of this will be old territory, but you should still quickly work through the chapter, particularly if you came to Windows 95/98 from Windows 3.1 or the Mac. The newer 32-bit versions of Windows (Windows 95, Windows 98, and Windows NT)—which we'll simply refer to as Windows throughout this book—and Office 2000 have some subtle time-savers, like the ability to manage files in standard dialog boxes. So whatever your prior experience, we recommend that you skim *Working in Office 2000*; you're sure to pick up one or two new concepts that you'll use over and over again.

Office Pro 2000

Microsoft Office Professional 2000 features some of the most popular and powerful software programs around. The suite includes 32-bit versions of six applications:

- Word: word processing program
- Excel: spreadsheet software
- Access: database software
- PowerPoint: presentation software
- Outlook: desktop information manager
- Publisher: design and layout software

These are the latest, most powerful versions of Microsoft's award-winning office productivity tools. There are various versions of Office 2000 (Office Standard, for example), and each contains different combinations of these applications. But all versions of Office 2000 contain Excel, the business standard for spreadsheets.

Office 2000 programs support better integration than ever before: between applications, between yourself and other users, and with the Internet and intranets. All of the applications include the Office Assistant, an active Help feature that offers timesaving advice to help you work more efficiently.

Office Professional 2000 also includes a number of smaller tools:

- WordArt: a text-graphics program
- The Clip Gallery: an archive of clip art, sounds, and video

Office also features applets that are available within all the major applications, so you can add line art, graphic representations of numeric data, or text-based logos to any Office document.

Exploring Common Features in Office

One of the best things about Office 2000 software is that each application has several useful features in common. If you want to save a letter in Word, a database in Access, or a spreadsheet in Excel, the Save button not only looks the same in all three programs, but you can locate it in approximately the same place. Working in Windows applications is like déjà vu—you will see certain features and tools again and again.

This section gives you a general introduction to some of Office's universal, commonly used features. You'll get more detailed, Excel-specific information in upcoming chapters, which address specific skills.

Launching the Shortcut Bar and New Excel Files

Typical of Windows applications, you have more than one way to get Excel 2000 up and running: click a New Document button on the Microsoft Office Shortcut Bar, use the Start menu to open a New Office Document, or navigate through the Programs menu to open Excel.

The Microsoft Office Shortcut Bar does not automatically appear the first time you launch Windows after installation. To open it, click the Start button and choose Programs ➤ Microsoft Office Tools ➤ Microsoft Office Shortcut Bar. You'll be asked if you want it to open automatically when you launch Windows, and then the Shortcut Bar will appear in its default position along the right side of the screen.

The Office Shortcut Bar opens vertically by default. However, as with all of Office's toolbars, you can position the Shortcut Bar anywhere you like on your screen: on the left or right, along the top or bottom, or as a free-floating palette of tools. Simply "grab" the bar by clicking and holding on the gray line at the top/beginning of the toolbar and reposition the mouse to the new location, such as against any edge of the screen.

Clicking the Excel button on the Shortcut Bar is, obviously, the easiest way to launch Excel. If you elect not to show the Shortcut Bar on your Desktop, try one of these other two ways to start a new spreadsheet:

1. Click the Windows Start button to open the Start menu:

2. Choose New Office Document from the top of the Start menu.

3. For brand-new, blank documents, Office 2000 presents you with a host of choices in the New Office Document dialog box—everything from memos and legal briefs to blank presentations and Web pages. Simply choose Blank Workbook and click OK. (More about work-books below.)

Or, if you prefer to launch Excel directly to a blank workbook:

1. Choose Programs from the Start menu. Excel appears as an individual choice on the Programs menu, along with the other Office 2000 applications you have installed.

   2. Click Start ➣ Programs ➣ Microsoft Excel to launch it.

Objective XL2000.2.5

After you've launched Excel, Click the New button on the Standard toolbar (or press Ctrl+N) to open another new workbook. If you want a new template instead, choose File ➣ New from the menu bar to open the New dialog box with templates for commonly used spreadsheet documents like purchase orders and expense statements.

The Office Assistant

Objective XL2000.2.8

The *Office Assistant* (see Figure 1.1) is Microsoft's social help interface for Office 2000. The Office Assistant crosses all applications and provides help for specific features of each. You can choose from several Assistants in the Assistant shortcut menu. Each has its own "personality," including Rocky the power puppy, Mother Nature symbolized as a globe, and an animated Genius with a definite resemblance to Albert Einstein.

F I G U R E 1.1: Office Assistant Clippit offering help

Getting Help

The Office Assistant displays tips that guide you to better ways to complete a task. The Assistant will offer help the first time you work with a feature or if you have difficulty with a task. Sometimes the offer is subtle—Clippit will blink, Rocky wags his tail, or the Genius produces a lightbulb. Other times the Assistant can be entertaining; in Office 2000, the Assistant icon animates during certain basic tasks like saving or running a spell check. Yet offers of help also can be a bit intrusive. If, for example, you open a Wizard, the Office Assistant pops up to ask if you'd like help with the feature.

When you need help, simply click the Assistant to activate it and open a search window. Then type a word or phrase that describes what you need help with ("Change text size," for example) and click Search. The Office Assistant displays a list of topics related to the word or phrase you typed. Choose one of the topics by clicking the blue button preceding it. A Microsoft Excel Help window opens displaying steps to follow to complete the task you chose from the list of topics. Close the Help window when you're through, and click anywhere in your worksheet to proceed.

Getting Less Help

After you've worked with Excel 2000 for a few days, you might decide that you'd like a little less help from your eager Assistant. To change the Assistant's options, right-click the Assistant, and then choose Options from the shortcut menu to open the Office Assistant dialog box. Click the Options tab to display the Options page, shown in Figure 1.2.

F I G U R E 1.2: The Office Assistant dialog box

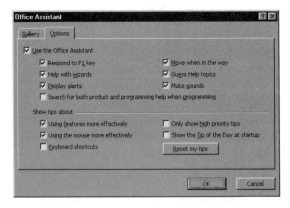

NOTE The Office Assistant is shared by all the Office 2000 programs. Any options you change affect the Assistant in all the Office programs, so if you choose a decreased level of assistance with Excel, you get the same decreased level of assistance with Word.

When you're ready to go it alone, you can close the Assistant window to return it to the Standard toolbar. If you start to get lonely, just click the Office Assistant button to invite the Assistant back into your office.

TIP For help with any dialog box, click the dialog box Help button (with the question mark), then click the dialog box control you want help with.

Hands On

Objective XL2000.2.8

1. Browse the gallery of Office Assistants and choose one you like.

   a) Set up the Office Assistant's options for the level of help you need.

   b) Hide the Office Assistant.

   c) Retrieve the Office Assistant.

2. Use the Office Assistant to search for help on using Cut and Paste. Close the Help window when you're through.

Using the Excel 2000 Interface

The Office 2000 applications share a common user interface. This means that once you're familiar with the *application window* in Excel (see Figure 1.3), for example, getting around in the application window in Word will be a piece of cake.

F I G U R E 1.3: The Excel application window

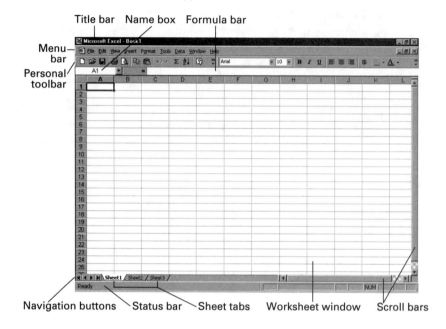

The Excel application window includes the standard title bar and command bars. Below the command bars is a strip that contains the *name box* and the *formula bar*. The Excel status bar displays information about current selections, commands, or operations. The right end of the status bar displays NUM if the keyboard's Num Lock is on.

At the top of the Excel application window is a *title bar* that contains three buttons: Minimize, Maximize or Restore, and Close. Use these buttons to change the size of your window or to close the window itself. When you're working in Excel, you'll usually want to maximize the window.

TIP Before you switch to another application or window, minimizing Excel will free up system resources, making more memory available to the active application.

When a window is maximized, the Restore button is displayed.

When it is restored, the Maximize button is displayed. Even with the application window maximized, the Windows Taskbar shows all open applications, so you can easily switch between open Office 2000 applications by clicking an application's Taskbar button. Clicking the Close button (the X) on the title bar closes the application, returning you to the Windows Desktop or to another open application.

The Worksheet Window

In Excel, your work area is known as the *worksheet window*. Here you're surrounded by the tools you need to get the job done: *scroll bars* to move the display, a *status bar* to keep you informed of an operation's progress, and the *command bars* at the top of the screen to access all of the program's features.

You'll use two types of command bars: the menu bar and toolbars. The *menu bar* organizes the features into categories: File, Edit, Help, and so on. Clicking any of the categories opens up a list of related features for you to choose from. Many of the menu bar options open dialog boxes that allow you to set several options at once related to the feature you choose—all the print options, all the font settings, and so on.

Toolbars are the command bars with graphical buttons located below the menu bar. Toolbars make many of the most commonly used features only one click away. Use toolbars when you want a shortcut to a common feature and the menu bar when you want to see *all* the options related to a feature.

In Excel 2000, the Personal toolbar, comprised of the Standard and Formatting toolbars of previous versions, uses one row to conserve space in the application window. If a toolbar button you want to use is not available, click the down arrow to the right of either toolbar and choose the button from the list. This button replaces a less frequently used button from your toolbar.

NOTE If the Personal toolbar option does not suit you, you can display full menus and view the complete Standard and Formatting toolbars on separate rows by choosing View ➤ Toolbars ➤ Customize and clearing the first three checkboxes on the Options tab.

ScreenTips provide additional help with commands. If you're uncertain which toolbar button to use, point to the button and hover for a moment; a ScreenTip will appear, showing the button's name.

Excel 2000 menus are personalized to the features you use most commonly. If a pull-down menu has more than a handful of commands, Microsoft has "folded up" less commonly used features. When you see a set of small, double arrows at the bottom of a pull-down menu, click them to reveal all the menu commands, or wait a few seconds, and the menu will "unfold"—you don't even need to click the mouse. For example, Excel's Edit menu offers this window:

Zooming In and Out of Worksheets

Objective XL2000.5.4

When you are working with a large worksheet, you may find that it would be nice if you could see more of it than is currently visible in the worksheet window. The Zoom button can adjust the size of the worksheet so you can make it smaller—or bigger. Click the arrow on the Zoom button and choose 200%, 100%, 75%, 50%, 25%, or Selection. To use Selection, select some cells before clicking the Zoom arrow.

NOTE   Zooming does not affect the size of a printed worksheet—it's only to help you see it better.

Workbooks and Worksheets

Objective XL2000.5.5

When you launch Excel, the Excel application window opens with a new Excel *workbook* (as shown earlier in Figure 1.3). A workbook is a multi-page Excel document. Each page in the workbook is called a *worksheet*, and the active worksheet is displayed in the document window. At the left end of the horizontal scroll bar are *sheet tabs* and *navigation buttons*. Use the sheet tabs to move to another worksheet and the navigation buttons to scroll the sheet tabs.

Each worksheet is divided into columns, rows, and cells separated by *gridlines*, as shown in the Payroll worksheet in Figure 1.4. The first column is column A, and the letter A appears in the *column heading*; the rows are numbered. Each worksheet has 256 columns (A through IV) and 65,536 rows—plenty of room to enter all of your numbers!

F I G U R E 1.4: Payroll worksheet

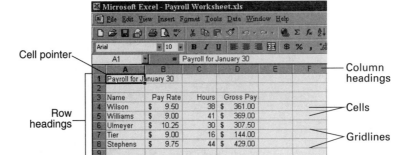

A *cell* is the intersection of a row and a column. Each cell has a unique address composed of the cell's column and row. For example, take a look at Figure 1.4. The cell in the upper-left corner of the worksheet, with the text **Payroll for January 30**, is cell A1. Even though some of the text appears to run over into cell B1 in the next column, it is really entered in cell A1.

The *active cell*, A1, has a box around it called the *cell pointer*, and the headings in the active cell's column (A) and row (1) are outdented, or "lit up." When you enter data, it is always placed in the active cell.

Moving the Cell Pointer

To move the pointer one cell to the left, to the right, up, or down, use the keyboard arrow keys. Table 1.1 shows other frequently used keyboard commands.

T A B L E 1.1: Keystrokes to Move the Cell Pointer

Key(s)	To Move
PgDn	Down one screen
PgUp	Up one screen
Home	To column A in the current row
Ctrl+Home	To cell A1

To activate a cell with the mouse, simply click the cell. If you want to see other areas of the worksheet, use the scroll bars. To scroll up or down one row, click the up or down arrow at the ends of the vertical scroll bar. Use the arrows at either end of the horizontal scroll bar to scroll one column to the left or right. To move up, down, left, or right one window, click the empty space above, below, or to the left or right of the scroll bar's scroll box, respectively:

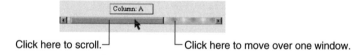

Click here to scroll.⌐   └Click here to move over one window.

Drag the scroll box to scroll more than a couple of rows or columns. As you drag, a *ScrollTip* shows the location you are scrolling over. Note that scrolling doesn't change the active cell; scrolling lets you view other parts of the worksheet, but the active cell is wherever you left the cell pointer. To scroll large distances, hold the Shift key while dragging the scroll box, and Excel will scroll farther for each movement of the mouse.

Navigating to a Specific Cell

Objective XL2000.1.5

If you are working with a large worksheet and know the cell address of where you want to go, you can get there much more easily than by scrolling. Choose Edit ➤ Go To, enter the cell address to which you want to move in the Reference box, and click OK. You'll be taken directly to the cell you specify.

Entering Text and Numbers

Objective XL2000.1.3

You can enter three types of data in a worksheet: numbers, formulas, and text. *Numbers* are values you may want to use in calculations, including dates. Dates are often used in calculations to determine, for example, how many days to charge for an overdue video or how many months of interest you have earned on a deposit. *Formulas* are calculations. *Text* is any entry that isn't a number or a formula.

To enter data in a cell, first activate the cell, and then begin typing the data. As soon as you begin entering characters from the keyboard, three things happen: an insertion point appears in the cell, the text you are entering appears in the cell and the formula bar, and the formula bar buttons are activated:

If you make a mistake while you are entering data, click the Cancel button (the red X) to discard the entry you were making and turn off the formula bar buttons. You can also cancel an entry by pressing the Esc key on the keyboard. Clicking the Enter button (the green check mark) finishes the entry and turns off the formula bar buttons. Pressing the Enter key on the keyboard is the same as clicking the Enter button, except the Enter key also moves the cell pointer down one cell.

The AutoComplete Feature

Excel has an *AutoComplete* feature that keeps track of text entered in a column and can complete other entries in the same column. For example, if you have already typed **Jones** in cell A1 and then enter the letter **J** in A2,

Excel will automatically fill in **ones** to make **Jones**. If **Jones** is the correct text, simply finish the entry by pressing Enter, by moving to another cell, or by clicking the Enter button. If it is not correct, just continue entering the correct text to overwrite the AutoComplete entry. AutoComplete resets each time you leave a blank cell in a column.

Working with Files

One of the great things about Office 2000 is that the dialog boxes used for common file functions are similar in all of the applications. That means when you save a file in Excel, you already know how to save a file in Word—the dialog box is identical for both applications.

Saving a File

Objective XL2000.2.1

When you're finished working with a document or have completed a sizable amount of work and want to store it before continuing, choose File ➤ Save from the menu bar (or press Ctrl+S), or click the Save button on the Standard toolbar to open the Save As dialog box, shown in Figure 1.5.

F I G U R E 1.5: Excel's Save As dialog box

The Save As dialog box opens to your default *folder* (directory), but clicking in the Save In text box opens a drop-down list of accessible drives:

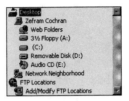

Select a drive, and the folders on the drive are displayed in the pane below the list. Double-clicking a folder opens it so that you can view the files and folders it contains.

When you have located the proper drive and folder, enter a filename in the File Name text box at the bottom of the dialog box. With Windows, filenames can be up to 256 characters long, use uppercase and lowercase letters, and contain spaces. However, they can't contain punctuation other than underscores, hyphens, and exclamation points. And, unlike filenames on the Macintosh, they are not case-sensitive: *MY FILE* and *My File* are the same filename. Make sure the name of the current drive or folder appears in the Save In text box, then click the Save button to save the file.

WARNING   All of the Office 2000 program dialog boxes locate documents based on file *extension*—the three characters following a period in a filename. For example, Excel documents have the .xls extension. Don't create your own extensions or change the extensions of existing documents. If you do, the Office 2000 applications will have trouble finding your files—and that means so will you!

Creating a New Folder

Objective XL2000.2.4

When you're saving a file, you may decide to create a new folder to house it. Click File ➤ Save like you normally would to begin the Save process. Use the Save In drop-down list to navigate to the drive or folder within which you want to create the new folder. Click the New Folder button on the toolbar in the Save As dialog box. Type the name for the folder (no punctuation) and press Enter. Be sure to select the new folder with a double-click before you name the file and click Save.

Using Save As

▶ *Objective XL2000.2.2*

After you've saved a file once, clicking Save saves changes to the file without opening the dialog box. If you want to save a previously saved file with a new name or save it in another location, choose File ➢ Save As from the menu bar to open the Save As dialog box. The Save As feature is particularly useful if you are using an existing document to create a new document and want to keep both the original *and* the revised document.

If you share files with people using other programs, or older versions of Excel, they may not be able to open your Excel 2000 files. You can, however, save your file in a format they can open. In the Save As dialog box, scroll through the Save As Type drop-down list and select an appropriate file format.

Closing a File

To remove a workbook from the application window, choose File ➢ Close or click the Close button on the right end of the menu bar, directly below the Close button on the title bar.

Opening an Existing File

▶ *Objective XL2000.2.3*

You can open an existing Excel 2000 document in three ways. If the file was created recently, click the Windows Start button and open the Documents menu. If the workbook appears there, you're in luck—you can open it directly from the menu.

If you have already launched Excel, click the File menu and see if the workbook you want to retrieve appears at the bottom. If so, you can open it by clicking it.

If you're already working in Excel and want to open a file that doesn't appear at the bottom of the File menu, click the Open button on the Standard toolbar to open the Open dialog box (see Figure 1.6). Use the Look In drop-down list to locate the proper folder and file.

F I G U R E 1.6: The Open dialog box

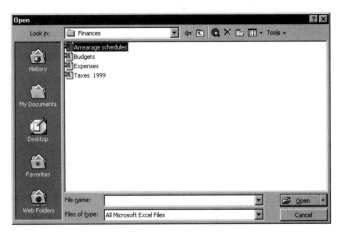

Hands On

Objectives XL2000.1.3, 1.5, 2.1, 2.2, 2.3, 2.4, 2.5, 5.4, and 5.5

1. In a new workbook, create the worksheet shown here. (Don't worry about typographical mistakes right now. You'll learn how to correct them in Chapter 2, *Editing Excel Worksheets*). Save the workbook as **Cyclops Proposal**.

	A	B	C
1	Cyclops Database Proposal - Draft		
2	Hardware		
3			
4	Item	Quantity	Price
5	PCs	19	1565
6	Server	1	4175
7	Scanners	2	685
8	Printers	4	499

2. In the Cyclops Proposal workbook, click Sheet 2 and create the second worksheet shown below. Resave Cyclops Proposal before closing it.

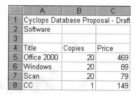

	A	B	C
1	Cyclops Database Proposal - Draft		
2	Software		
3			
4	Title	Copies	Price
5	Office 2000	20	469
6	Windows	20	89
7	Scan	20	79
8	CC	1	149

3. Start a new blank workbook and type a short sentence into cell A1.

   a) Save this file to the My Documents folder and name it **Practice 1**.

   b) Press Enter on the keyboard to move to cell A2 and type another sentence. Use the Save As command to create a separate workbook from it. Name this file **Practice 2** and save it to My Documents also. Close both documents, and close Excel.

4. Open Cyclops Proposal using the Documents menu. Close Cyclops Proposal.

5. Retrieve Practice 1 using the Open button on the toolbar.

6. Change the Zoom setting to 75 percent.

7. Enter five numbers in the first column, pressing Enter between each number. Use Save As to save Practice 1 into a new folder named **Practice Docs**. If you wish, you can use this new folder to house all the exercises you do in this book.

8. Practice using Go To by moving to cell I45, to J257, and then to A3. Close Practice 1.

9. Click File ➢ New and choose the Spreadsheet Solutions tab of the dialog box. Select a template to use as boilerplate for a new workbook and click OK. View the template, then close it without saving changes.

Sending Files Using E-Mail

Objective XL2000.2.7

Every Office 2000 application—Word, Excel, PowerPoint, Outlook, Access, and Publisher—has two new standard features to help you send files via e-mail. You can either send your file as an e-mail message, or you can attach it to an existing e-mail message. You can use either feature by simply choosing one File menu option: Send To. Doing so will give you the following choices:

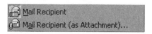

To send an Excel workbook as an e-mail message, open the file and choose File ➤ Send To ➤ Mail Recipient. A space appears at the top of the document where you can fill in the e-mail address(es) and send it on its way.

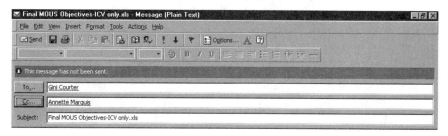

If you prefer to send the document as an attachment, choose File ➤ Send To ➤ Mail Recipient (As Attachment). A separate e-mail window appears, showing the document as an icon in a window at the bottom, with space for you to type a message before you send it out.

A Quick Look at Spelling

Objective XL2000.5.6

Misspelled words automatically cast doubt on the accuracy of the rest of a worksheet. Excel includes two tools to help you correct spelling errors. *AutoCorrect* automatically fixes common typos, and *Spelling* checks all the text in a worksheet to ensure that it is error-free. (Of course, you still need to examine all the numbers in a worksheet to verify that you've entered data and formulas correctly.)

 Check your spelling by clicking the Spelling button on the Standard toolbar. Office reviews your worksheet, flags possible misspelled words, and opens the Spelling dialog box (see Figure 1.7).

If you are not in the home cell when you begin the spelling check, Excel checks from the cell pointer to the end of the worksheet, and then asks if it should return to the top of the worksheet and finish checking. When Spelling is complete, Excel notifies you that it has finished checking the entire sheet.

FIGURE 1.7: Excel's Spelling dialog box

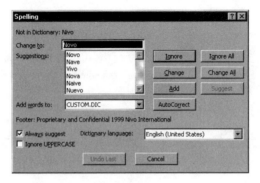

The Spelling And Grammar dialog box gives you several options for handling potential errors. Here you can choose to Ignore All occurrences of the word or to Change All occurrences to the correct spelling. You can also enter the correct spelling. All of the Office applications share a custom dictionary, so words you add in Excel aren't seen as potential spelling errors in Word.

Finding and Replacing Text

Objective XL2000.1.8

When you are working with a large worksheet, one of the fastest ways to make repetitive changes to a document is through Find and Replace. *Find* helps you locate a text string, and *Replace* substitutes new text for the existing string.

Using Find

To locate a word or phrase, click Edit ➤ Find from the menu (or press Ctrl+F) to open the Find Dialog box:

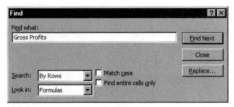

Enter the text you want to locate in the Find What text box. You can search by rows or by columns, and you can have Excel look in formulas, values, or comments. You can also search for words that are in the same case as you entered by checking the Match Case checkbox.

When you have entered your Search options, click the Find Next button to identify the first occurrence of the text string. Click Find Next again to search for additional occurrences of the text string.

Using Replace

Replace allows you to replace one or all occurrences of a word or phrase with different text. Click the Replace button in the Find dialog box to open a Replace With field; this is where you can enter replacement text. When Excel locates the text string you entered in the Find What field, you can click the Replace button to enter the replacement text in that cell, or click Replace All to replace all occurrences of the text string with the replacement text. Close the dialog box when you're through.

Finding and Replacing Text

1. Click Edit ➤ Find on the menu to open the Find dialog box.

2. Enter the characters you want to search for in the Find What text box. Choose whether to search by rows or columns, then set your Look In, Match Case, and Entire Cell options. Click Find Next to locate the first occurrence of the text string.

3. Click Find Next again to search for additional occurrences of the text string.

4. To replace text, click the Replace button in the Find dialog box and enter the text you want in the Replace With field.

5. Click Replace to replace the selected occurrence of the text.

6. Click Replace All to complete the replace operation in one step. If you want to review each replacement, choose Replace. Click Find Next to locate the next occurrence. You may need to reposition the dialog box to see the text. Click Replace until you have made all the replacements.

Selecting, Moving, and Copying

Whether you are correcting mistakes or shuffling your whole document around, the first step is knowing how to select part of your worksheet. Once cells are selected, they can be moved, copied, formatted, deleted, aligned, or resized.

Selecting Cells

In Excel, at least one cell is always selected: the active cell. A group of cells is called a *range*. To select a range, move to the first cell in the range (check to be sure the mouse pointer is the large cross used for selecting), hold down the mouse button, and drag to the last cell you want to select before releasing the mouse button. To deselect cells, click anywhere in the document.

To select all the cells in a column or row, click the column heading or row heading. To select multiple columns or rows, select one heading, then drag to select the others. When you point to row or column headers to select them, be sure that your mouse pointer looks like the fat selection cross as you do this, not a thinner black cross. To select the entire worksheet, click the Select All button, the gray rectangle at the upper-left corner of the worksheet above the row headings.

If the cells, columns, or rows you want to select are noncontiguous (not next to each other), select one of the ranges you want to select, and then hold down the Ctrl key while selecting the others.

Moving and Copying Text

Objective XL2000.1.7

Now that you can select cells, you can move and copy them. When you *move* a selection, the original is placed in a new location. *Copying* text leaves the original in place and creates a copy in a new location.

When you cut a block of cells, they are flagged for deletion and copied to the *Clipboard*. The Clipboard is part of the computer's memory set aside and managed by Windows. The Clipboard can hold only one piece of information at a time, but that piece of information can be text, a graphic, or even a video clip. All the moving and copying techniques work with pictures or other objects just as they do with text and numbers.

You can move text by cutting it from its current location and pasting it in a new location. Once you paste the cut cells, they are removed from the original location. Copying cells moves a copy to the Clipboard without deleting the original.

Moving or Copying Text

1. Select the cells you want to move or copy.

Moving or Copying Text *(continued)*

  2. Click the Cut or Copy button on the Standard toolbar.

3. Click where you want the cells to appear.

 4. Click the Paste button.

TIP   Cut, Copy, and Paste are standard Windows functions, and as a result, they have corresponding shortcut keys that you can use. Select the text or object and press Ctrl+X to cut, Ctrl+C to copy, or Ctrl+V to paste.

Pasting Multiple Items

A new feature of Office 2000 is Collect and Paste, which lets you copy up to 12 items and save them to a temporary Clipboard where you can select and paste them all at once. This makes it easier to move several items from one place to another, without forcing you to scroll up and down or split the screen.

To select items for collecting and pasting, choose your items in order by pressing Edit ➤ Copy (or Ctrl+C) or Edit ➤ Cut (or Ctrl+X), and the Clipboard toolbar appears.

After you move to the new location in the document where you want to paste the items, select them one by one from the Clipboard by double-clicking them to paste.

Hands On

▶ *Objectives XL2000.1.7, 1.8, and 5.6*

1. Open the Cyclops worksheet you created earlier, or another worksheet of your own.

a) Use Spell Check and correct spelling errors you may have made.

    b) Use the drag technique to select all the numbers in the worksheet.

    c) Select all the text in the worksheet.

    d) Select columns A and C only.

    e) Select rows 1 and 3 and column C.

2. Start a new workbook, and type the word **Monday** in A1.

    a) Press Enter to move to A2, and type **Tuesday**. Press Enter to move down one cell, and type **Wednesday**.

    b) Select all three cells by dragging over them with the cell selection pointer.

    c) Cut and paste them to another place on the worksheet.

    d) Select the cells and copy/paste them to another location.

    e) Use Find and Replace to search for "Monday" and replace it with "Friday."

    f) Close this workbook without saving it.

Adding Pizzazz

One of the primary benefits of using Windows applications is the ease with which you can give your documents a professional appearance. The right combination of fonts, font styles, sizes, and attributes can make your words or numbers jump right off the page.

Fonts and Font Styles

Objective XL2000.3.1

Selecting the right font can mean the difference between a professional-looking spreadsheet and an amateur effort that's tedious to read. Fonts are managed by Windows, which means that a font available in one application is available in all Windows applications.

You can access fonts and many of their attributes right from the Formatting toolbar. Excel's Formatting toolbar is shown in its entirety in Figure 1.8. Remember, Excel 2000 makes use of the Personal toolbar feature that places the Standard and Formatting toolbars on one line, collapsing some of the buttons on each toolbar. If you want to see the formatting toolbar as shown here, turn off the Personal toolbar (see "The Worksheet Window" earlier in this chapter).

FIGURE 1.8: Excel's Formatting toolbar

Arial is the default font for Excel. To change the font, select some cells and click the drop-down arrow next to the font name. All Windows True Type fonts (designated by the TT in front of them) are *scalable*, which means that you can make them any size by entering the desired size in the Font Size text box. Of course, you can also select from the sizes listed in the drop-down list.

To turn on **Bold**, *Italics*, or <u>Underline</u>, click the corresponding button on the toolbar. Remember that you must select existing text before you can change the font or font style.

For all of the available font options, choose Format ➤ Cells to open the Format Cells dialog box, and click the Font tab:

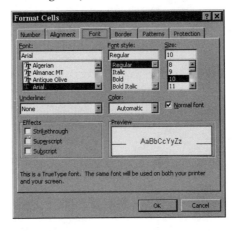

Here you can see what the fonts look like in the Preview window. You can also choose from several underline options such as <u>Single</u> or <u>Double Accounting</u> and apply a number of different effects to your text such as ~~Strikethrough~~, Superscript, and Subscript.

With all the color printers around today, being able to add colors to text is an important feature. Font Color is available from the Formatting toolbar as well as from the Font dialog box.

Copying Existing Formats

▶ *Objective XL2000.3.6*

Once you have formatted a range of cells just the way you like it, there is no need to re-create it for other text that you want formatted the same way. You can easily copy that format to other text in your document using the Format Painter.

Select the cell or cells with the format you want to copy and click the Format Painter button on the Standard toolbar. Your mouse pointer changes shape to a cell selection pointer with a paintbrush next to it.

Drag your mouse over some existing cells, and they will be reformatted to look just like the cells you copied. Once you've applied the format, the Format Painter turns off automatically. If you need to copy the formatting more than once, select the cells you want to copy and double-click (instead of single-clicking) the Format Painter button. When you are finished, click the Format Painter button again to turn it off.

NOTE The Format Painter not only copies fonts and font attributes but other formatting such as line spacing, borders and shading, indents, and number formats. See Chapter 2 for more information about formatting cells.

Hands On

▶ *Objectives XL2000.3.1 and 3.6*

1. Start a new workbook and type your favorite holiday in A1. Press Enter to move to A2, and type another of your favorite holidays. Repeat this two more times.

   a) Select the first holiday and make it bold.

   b) Select the second holiday and make it 20-point.

   c) Select the third holiday. Italicize and underline it.

   d) Select the fourth holiday and use the Font dialog box to make it 14-point Arial blue.

   e) Use the Format Painter to copy the formatting on the fourth holiday to all the others. Close this document without saving.

CHAPTER

2

Editing Excel Worksheets

In this chapter, you'll learn how to work with numbers in Excel, how to change worksheet layout and apply other formatting, and then how to print your worksheets. You'll also learn to create and edit basic formulas.

Throughout this chapter, we use Excel practice worksheets to illustrate concepts. If you would like to use the practice worksheets, you can create them based on the illustrations in the text, or you can download them from the Sybex Web site: www.sybex.com.

You may also choose to practice these skills using your own worksheets, immediately applying the skills to your own work.

Entering and Editing Cell Entries

In Chapter 1, you learned how to create a basic spreadsheet by entering text and numbers in rows and columns. Since you're only human, you probably made a mistake or two when you entered your data. Luckily, it's an easy job to fix errors early on.

Correcting Mistakes

You'll find Excel 2000 to be very forgiving. You are able to correct mistakes you just made or mistakes you made several steps ago. When you're working with numbers and formulas, however, it's a good idea to be very cognizant of your actions so you can undo mistakes right away before you've added components that make use of bad data.

Undo and Redo

Objective XL2000.1.1

The Undo button on the Standard toolbar lets you reverse an action or a whole series of actions you have taken.

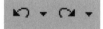

The Undo button dims when you have reached the last action you can undo.

To reverse multiple actions in one step, click the drop-down arrow next to the Undo button and scroll down the history. If you change your mind again, clicking the Redo button reverses the last undo.

Revising Text and Numbers

Objective XL2000.1.4

If you can't undo your mistake, there are two ways you can change an entry in a cell. If you activate the cell and type the new entry, the old entry is replaced. This is the easiest way to change a number (for example, 15 to 17) or to replace text with a short word.

If the original entry is long and requires only minor adjustment, you might prefer to edit it. To do so, click the cell and edit the entry in the formula bar, or double-click the cell to open it and edit directly in the cell. Use the mouse or the keyboard to edit the entry. When you are finished, you must press Enter or click the Enter button to complete the entry. Although you can simply click a new cell to complete a text entry, this creates problems when you're editing a cell that contains a formula. It's better to get into the habit of pressing Enter.

TIP Another way to switch into edit mode is to click the cell you want to edit and press the F2 key.

Clearing a Cell

Objective XL2000.1.2

To delete the contents of a cell completely, first activate the cell. Then press the Delete key on the keyboard, or right-click and choose Clear Contents from the shortcut menu.

WARNING Don't choose Delete from the Edit menu to clear a cell you've selected—that deletes the entire cell, not just the entry in the cell.

Working with Numbers and Formulas

You already know how to type numbers into a worksheet. However, certain numbers in a spreadsheet must be calculated, and you won't just type those in. You use a *formula* every time you want to perform a calculation in Excel, so you'll appreciate some of the formula features built into Excel 2000. Formulas are what make a spreadsheet a spreadsheet; they are the driving force behind the magic of Excel.

Excel uses standard computer operator symbols for mathematical and logical operators, as shown in Table 2.1.

T A B L E 2.1:   Mathematical and Logical Operators

Operation	Operator Symbol
Addition	+
Subtraction	-
Multiplication	*
Division	/
Exponentiation (to the power of)	^
Precedence (do this operation first)	enclosed in ( )
Equal to	=
Not equal to	< >
Greater than	>
Less than	<

Creating Formulas

Objective XL2000.6.2

You can create formulas in a number of ways, but some are more efficient than others. We'll begin with simple formulas that have one math operation. For example, the following *Second Hand News* Payroll worksheet needs a formula to multiply Wilson's pay rate by the hours worked in order to calculate his gross pay.

Payroll for January 30

Name	Pay Rate	Hours	Gross Pay
Wilson	$ 9.50	38 $	361.00
Williams	$ 9.00	41 $	369.00
Ulmeyer	$ 10.25	30 $	307.50
Tier	$ 9.00	16 $	144.00
Stephens	$ 9.75	44 $	429.00

You can approach this formula in two different ways. The first method is the highly reliable point-and-click method for which Excel is known.

Entering a Point-and-Click Formula

1. Activate the cell where you want the result to appear.

2. Type =.

3. Click the first cell you want to include in the formula.

4. Type an operator (+, -, \, or *).

5. Click the next cell in the formula.

6. Repeat steps 4 and 5 until the entire formula is entered.

7. Finish the entry by pressing Enter or clicking the Enter button on the formula bar.

WARNING When you have finished entering the formula, don't just move to another cell—or Excel will include it in the formula!

The other method of entering a formula is the traditional spreadsheet approach: typing in the formula using the cell addresses of each cell you want to include in the formula. This is the least desirable way to create a formula; no matter how well you type, this is the most error-prone method. It's much too easy to glance at the wrong column or row, even when you're only working with a few numbers. When you have thousands of numbers in the middle of a worksheet, the chance of error increases. If you need to reference widely disparate cells, consider naming the cells (see "Naming Ranges" in Chapter 3, *Beyond Excel Basics*) and then referring to the names.

NOTE   Excel 2000 allows you to use labels in formulas, such as =pay rate * hours. To activate this feature, formerly referred to as Natural Language Formulas, choose Tools ➤ Calculations and check the Accept Labels In Formula checkbox.

Whatever formula construction method you use, you can use the *Formula Palette* to view the progress of your formula as it's being constructed. To activate the Formula Palette, click Edit Formula (the = sign button) in the formula bar rather than press the equal (=) key on the keyboard. For more about the Formula Palette, see Chapter 3.

WARNING   Formulas are dynamic, so the results automatically change each time the numbers in the underlying cells are revised. Typed-in numbers don't change unless they are edited. This is the reason for the first of two very important Excel rules: *Never* do math "in your head" and type the answer in a cell where you or other users would reasonably expect to have a formula calculate the answer. (Read on for very-important-Excel-rule number two.)

Complex Formulas

Complex formulas involve more than one operation. For example, you might have separate columns for hours worked in the first week of a pay period and hours worked in the second. You'll want to add the hours together before multiplying by the pay rate: = (Hours Week 1 + Hours Week 2) * pay rate. When you have more than one operation in a formula, you'll need to know about the Order of Operations.

The *Order of Operations* is a short set of rules about how formulas are calculated:

- Formulas are calculated from left to right; 15/3+2 is 7, not 3.

- Multiplication and division are always done before any addition or subtraction. Excel will make two left-to-right passes through the formula above and do the multiplication on the first pass. Then it will come back through and add the hours worked in the first week to the gross pay for second week. Calculating the gross pay this way would not make your employees happy.

- Any operation in parentheses is calculated first. If you want the hours for the two weeks added together first, just throw a set of parentheses around the addition part of the formula. Note that you never need to include parentheses if you're only doing one operation; they only kick in when you need to tell Excel how to order two or more operations.

Using Autofill to Copy Formulas

Objective XL2000.1.10

Now that you understand formulas, you may be tempted to quickly create all the other gross pay formulas from our example. Don't—there's a much faster way. The formula for each employee's gross pay is the same: hours * pay rate. Since you've already created one working formula, all you need to do is to use *Autofill* to fill the series to the other cells.

The square box in the lower-right corner of the cell pointer is called the *fill handle*. As you move the mouse toward the cell pointer, the mouse pointer changes shape to a black cross to let you know that you can use the mouse for a fill operation.

The mouse pointer assumes several shapes as you move it around the worksheet. When the mouse pointer is a large cross, you can use it to activate or select cells.

If you move the mouse toward the border of the active cell, the mouse pointer will change to an arrow. As such, you can use the pointer to move the cell (you'll learn more about moving cells later in this chapter).

TIP   You'll want to look at the mouse pointer frequently while working in Excel. A mouse movement of 1/32 of an inch can mean the difference between selecting, moving, and filling a cell.

Filling is a kind of copying. Begin by activating the cell that has the formula you want to copy. Move the mouse pointer toward the fill handle until the mouse pointer changes to the fill pointer shape:

Press the mouse button and drag the fill handle down to select the cells you want to copy the formula to. Release the mouse button, and the formula will be filled to the other cells.

Filling a Formula

1. Select the cell that contains the formula you want to copy to other cells.

2. Drag the fill handle to select the cells where you want the formula copied.

3. Release the fill handle to fill the formula.

NOTE A common mistake that users make when they're new to fill operations is to include the wrong cells in the initial selection. At this point in your fill career, if all the selected cells don't include formulas, you've selected incorrectly.

Totaling Columns and Rows

Objective XL2000.6.5

Σ

Excel has a one-step method for creating row and column totals using the AutoSum button on the Standard toolbar. Begin by selecting the cells that contain the numbers you want to total; you can include the empty cell that should contain the total in the selection. Then click the AutoSum button. Excel adds a formula to the empty cell (whether or not you selected it) and calculate the total. If you would like a blank row before the totals, simply select two extra cells. Excel always places the total in the last empty cell selected.

If you want to create totals for multiple rows or columns and a grand total, select all the numbers before clicking AutoSum, as shown in the Tickets worksheet in Figure 2.1. In this example, Excel creates formulas in row 9 and column E for each selected row and column. In cell B9, the formula is =sum(B5:B8), telling Excel to sum (total) the values in the range of cells B5 through B8.

FIGURE 2.1: Using AutoSum to total rows and columns

	A	B	C	D	E
1	Vacation Meisters Ticket Sales				
2	First Quarter				
3					
4	Destination	January	February	March	
5	Detroit	17	21	36	
6	Miami	119	101	89	
7	Phoenix	75	77	61	
8	Reno	93	87	90	
9					

Using AutoSum to Total Rows and Columns

1. Select the cells that contain the numbers you want to total and a blank row and/or column to hold the totals.

2. Click the AutoSum button on the Standard toolbar.

Revising Formulas

Objective XL2000.6.3

There are two reasons why you might want to revise a formula: You entered an incorrect formula, or you've added new data and need to change the formula to reflect the new entries. And there are two ways to revise a formula: You can move to the cell that contains the formula and create a new formula, thus overwriting the original formula, or you can edit the existing formula.

To edit a formula, double-click a cell with a formula to open it for editing. When you do this, Excel paints each cell address or range address in the formula a different color and places a border of the same color around the cell or range. The border is called a *Range Finder*. In this example, B10 in the formula and in the Range Finder around cell B10 are blue, and green is used for C10:

Objective XL2000.6.1

Excel's Range Finder makes it easy to see whether a formula refers to the correct cells. If you want to change the formula reference to C10 so that it refers to another cell, you can use either the keyboard or the Range Finder.

To use the keyboard, select C10 in the formula, and then either click the cell you want to replace it with or type the replacement cell's address. If the formula you're revising uses row labels instead of cell addresses, select the column or row label and type the correct label to replace the original entry.

To use the Range Finder, grab the border of the Range Finder and move it to the correct cell. (You're moving the Range Finder, so the mouse pointer should be an arrow.) If you need to include additional or fewer cells in a range, drag the selection handle at the lower-right corner of the Range Finder to extend or decrease the selection; the pointer will change to a fill pointer. When you are finished editing the formula, press Enter or click the Enter button.

WARNING   If the cell reference you want to change is a range, the reference will include the first cell in the range, a colon, and the last cell in the range, like this: B10:B15. To revise this reference in a formula, select the entire reference. Then move into the worksheet and drag to select the cells for the new formula, or move and then extend the Range Finder.

Unions and Intersections   Unions and intersections are two special types of ranges. A *union* is all the cells in two separate ranges. If you want, for example, to add a group of numbers in C2 through C8 and those in C20 through C28, the ranges would be (C2:C8,C20:C28). By using a comma to separate the two ranges, you're indicating that you want all cells from both ranges.

An *intersection* is just what it sounds like: a place where two ranges come together or overlap. For an intersection, use a blank space instead of a comma. The intersection (C2:C10 A10:J10) refers to just one cell: C10, where the two ranges overlap.

Formatting Numbers

Excel lets you present numbers in a variety of formats. *Formatting* is used to identify numbers as currency or percentages and to make numbers easier to read by aligning decimal points in a column.

When you format a number, you change its appearance, not its numeric value. The default format for numbers, General, doesn't display zeros that don't affect the actual value of the number. For example, if you enter

10.50, 10.5 has the same numeric value, so Excel doesn't display the extra, or *trailing*, zero.

You can format selected cells using the Formatting toolbar, the Format Cells dialog box, or the shortcut menu.

Using the Formatting Toolbar

To format cells with the Formatting toolbar, first select the cells, and then click a button to apply one of the formats shown in Table 2.2.

NOTE   The Formatting toolbar is the toolbar displayed on the right side of the Personal toolbar. To see all the buttons on the Formatting toolbar, choose View ➢ Toolbars ➢ Customize. Click the Options tab and clear the Standard And Formatting Toolbars Share One Row checkbox.

T A B L E 2.2:   Numeric Formatting from the Formatting Toolbar

Button	Style	Example
$	Currency	Displays and lines up dollar signs, comma separators, and decimal points: 75.3 as $75.30
%	Percent	Displays number as a percentage: 0.45 as 45%
,	Comma	Same as Currency, but without dollar signs: 12345.6 as 12,345.60
+.0 .00	Increase decimal	Displays one more place after the decimal: .45 as .450
.00 +.0	Decrease decimal	Displays one less place after the decimal: 0.450 as 0.45

▶ Objective XL2000.3.5

If decreasing the number of digits eliminates a nonzero digit, the displayed number is rounded. For example, if the number 9.45 is displayed with only one decimal place, it is rounded to 9.5. If you display 9.75 with no digits following the decimal, Excel will display 10.

Formatting affects only the display of a cell, not the cell's contents. To view the contents of a cell, click the cell and look at the formula bar. The number entered in the cell appears in the formula bar exactly as entered regardless of the format that has been applied to the cell.

Applying Numeric Formats from the Formatting Toolbar

1. Select the cells to be formatted.

2. Click a button on the Formatting toolbar to apply a format to the selected cells.

Using the Format Cells Dialog Box

Objective XL2000E.4.1

Excel has more number formats that you can select from the Format Cells dialog box. To apply a different format, select the cells you want to format. Then open the dialog box; either choose Format ➤ Cells from the menu bar or right-click to open the shortcut menu and choose Format Cells. The Format Cells dialog box has separate pages for Number, Alignment, Font, Border, Patterns, and Protection. The Number page of the Format Cells dialog box is shown in Figure 2.2. If the Number page is not active, click the Number tab.

F I G U R E   2.2: The Number page of the Format Cells dialog box

The Number page includes a list of format categories and controls for the number of decimal places, thousands separator, and treatment of negative numbers. Table 2.3 shows the most commonly used categories. To apply a format, first choose a category, and then fill in the other options.

T A B L E   2.3:   Numeric Formatting in the Format Cells Dialog Box

Category	Description
General	This is the default format.
Number	This category is like General, but you can set decimal places, use a thousands separator, and include negative numbers.
Currency	Numbers are preceded with a dollar sign immediately before the first digit. Zero values are displayed.
Accounting	Dollar signs and decimal points line up. Zero values are shown as dashes.
Percentage	This category is the same as the Percent toolbar button.
Scientific	This category displays numbers in scientific notation: for example, $1.01E+03$.

NOTE   If you point to the button on the Formatting toolbar with the dollar symbol, the ScreenTip indicates it is the Currency Style button. However, when you apply this button's format, Excel applies the Accounting format, with dashes for zeros and the dollar signs lined up. Go figure!

Applying Other Formats

Objectives XL2000.1.3 and 3.2

When you click in a cell and type a date, Excel may reformat the date when you press Enter or click away from the date cell. For instance, you type **July 4, 1999** and when you press Enter, Excel converts it to "4-July-99." That's because dates (and numbers) have default formats. If you enter a text string that Excel recognizes as a date, Excel automatically formats it to match the default for dates.

Changing the date format is simple. Select the cell(s) with date(s) and click Format ➤ Cells on the menu to open the Format Cells dialog box. Select the Date category and then select the format you want from the scrollable list box.

In addition to Date and those listed in Table 2.3, the Format Cells dialog box includes five other specialized formatting categories. Date formats are used for dates and times. Use the Time format if you just want to display times without dates. The Fraction category allows you to choose from formats based on either the number of digits to display in the divisor (1, 2, or 3) or the fractional unit (halves, quarters, tenths, and so on). Special and Text both convert a number to text.

Special includes formats for kinds of numbers that aren't really mathematical values: Zip Code, Zip Code + 4, Phone Number, and Social Security Number. You wouldn't want to add or multiply any of these numbers; they are informational labels just like a last name.

Text changes a number to text, so it is no longer a number and can't be used in calculations. This is fine if the number is really a label. For example, you might need to include employee numbers in a worksheet: 8712, 0913, 7639. But how do you get Excel to leave the 0 in employee number 0913? All the regular numeric formats strip off leading zeros. To keep the leading zero in 0913, format the cell for text *before* entering the number. You won't be able to include the employee numbers in a calculation, but you wouldn't want to anyway, so it's no loss.

WARNING   Unlike the other formatting categories, Special and Text *change the underlying value of the number*. If you format a number with Special or Text, you will no longer be able to use the number in mathematical operations—unless you first reformat the cells with some other format. If you only have a few numbers that need to be treated as text, you can enter them manually. Simply type an apostrophe (') before the number, and Excel treats the number as text.

Custom allows you to select from or make an addition to a list of formats for numbers, dates, and times. (You'll learn more about the Custom category in Chapter 3.)

Using the Format Cells Dialog Box

1. Select the cells to be formatted.

2. Choose Format ➤ Cells, or right-click and choose Format Cells.

3. Click the Number tab.

4. From the Category list, choose the appropriate formatting category.

5. Set other available options, such as the color of text and the background of cells.

6. Click the OK button to apply the format and to close the dialog box.

Hands On

Objectives XL2000.1.1, 1.2, 1.3, 1.4, 1.10, 3.2, 3.5, 6.1, 6.2, 6.3, 6.5, and E.4.1

1. Open the workbook that contains the Cyclops Proposal worksheet. If you prefer to use your own worksheet or create one from scratch, you may do so.

   a) Edit any cells where you may have made data entry errors.

   b) Intentionally make a mistake and click Undo to correct it. Enter text in a cell where no text is needed. Select that cell and clear its contents.

   c) In the Price columns on the Cyclops worksheets, format the numbers using the Accounting style. Format them for Currency and notice the difference in placement of the dollar ($) sign.

   d) Format these same numbers Comma style. What's different about how they're displayed? Increase, then decrease, the number of decimal places being displayed.

   e) Experiment with the Percentage format. Why wouldn't you want these prices formatted as percentages?

   f) Select and reformat the prices as either Currency or Accounting.

   g) Make sure you're on Sheet 1 of the Cyclops workbook (or using similar data) and enter the text **Total Cost** in D4. In D5, enter a formula to calculate Quantity by Price. Fill the formula to the cells below and repeat this step on Sheet 2.

    h) Switch to edit mode and examine the formula you entered in the previous step to make sure it is calculating the correct values.

    i) Double-click one of the formula cells to view the Range Finder, then click away to turn it off. Save the workbook before closing it.

2. Create or open a worksheet that contains dates and numbers (like the Tickets worksheet in Figure 2.1).

    a) Edit the contents of B4, C4, and D4 so they display specific dates rather than just the months. (Example: Edit B4 to display January 5, 2000 rather than just January.)

    b) Experiment with different date formats in cells B4, C4, and D4.

    c) Use AutoSum to total the columns and rows as shown in Figure 2.1. Resave the worksheet before closing it.

Changing Worksheet Layout

As you have seen, the way you initially enter data in a worksheet doesn't necessarily produce the most attractive or useful presentation. You'll almost always want to make adjustments to the layout.

Adjusting Column Width and Row Height

Objective XL2000.3.3

By default, Excel columns are slightly more than eight characters wide. If the data in a worksheet is wider or much narrower than the column, you'll want to adjust the column width so it is wide enough to contain the data, but not so wide that data seems lost. You can adjust column width manually or use AutoFit to fit the column width to the existing data.

To adjust the width of a column manually, begin by pointing to the border at the right side of the column header. The mouse pointer will change to an adjustment tool, shaped like a double-headed arrow. Drag the edge of the column header to the desired width, and then release the button. If you double-click the column header border instead of dragging the border, Excel will AutoFit the column, making the column slightly larger than the widest entry in the column.

You can select several columns and size them all at the same time. By dragging the header border of any selected column, all columns are sized to the same width. Double-clicking the header border of any of the selected columns will size each column individually to fit the data in the column. You can also select the column(s) you want to adjust and select AutoFit from the menu (choose Format ➤ Column ➤ AutoFit Selection).

WARNING   The second very-important-Excel-rule: *Never* leave blank columns between columns in a worksheet. Blank columns create problems with charts, sorting, and many other advanced features. Instead, adjust column widths to provide adequate space for and between entries.

You can adjust row height the same way you adjust column width. If you move the pointer to the lower edge of a row heading, the pointer will change to an adjustment tool. Double-click to adjust the row height to fit the font size; drag to manually increase or decrease size.

Adjusting Column Widths

1. Select the column(s) you want to adjust.

2. Position the mouse pointer at the right edge of one of the selected columns' headings. The pointer changes shape to a double-headed arrow.

3. Double-click to have Excel adjust the width(s) of the selected columns to fit the contents of the column.

4. Click anywhere in the worksheet to turn off the selection.

5. To adjust column widths manually, drag the right border of a column's heading to make the column wider or narrower.

Inserting and Deleting Rows and Columns

Objective XL2000.5.1

To insert a column between the current columns A and B, begin by selecting column B. Right-click and select Insert from the shortcut menu, or choose Insert ➤ Columns from the menu bar to insert a column.

To insert multiple columns simultaneously, select more than one column before inserting. For example, you can insert three columns by first selecting B, C, and D. You can insert rows in the same fashion.

TIP To quickly insert a single row or column, select the row or column heading by right-clicking. As soon as the row or column is selected, Excel immediately opens the shortcut menu.

Deleting rows and columns is much like inserting. Begin by selecting one or more rows or columns. To clear the contents but leave the emptied row in place, press the Delete key on your keyboard. To delete the contents *and* remove the row or column, choose Edit ➢ Delete from the menu bar or right-click the row or column heading and choose Delete. When you delete a row or column, all information is deleted, including cells that may not be in the part of the worksheet you can see.

TIP You can use some nifty keystroke combinations to see if there is more data in a row or column. Select an occupied cell, hold Ctrl, and, using the arrow keys, press →. The cell pointer moves to the last occupied cell to the right of the original cell. If you press Ctrl+→ again, the cell pointer stops to the left of the first occupied cell. Ctrl+↑, Ctrl+↓, and Ctrl+← work the same way. Ctrl+End moves you to the outer limit of the used portion of the worksheet: a cell in the last used row and column.

Inserting and Deleting Rows and Columns

1. Select the row or column where you want the new inserted column to appear.

2. Right-click and choose Insert (or choose Insert ➢ Rows from the menu bar) to insert a row. To insert a column from the menu bar, choose Insert ➢ Columns.

3. To delete a column or row, first select it. Then right-click and choose Delete, or choose Edit ➢ Delete from the menu bar.

Inserting and Deleting Cells

Objective XL2000.1.6

Sometimes you'll need to add or delete cells in part of a worksheet without inserting or deleting entire rows or columns. For example, Figure 2.3 shows a section of a worksheet for a network switchover project. Tasks are listed in columns A–D, and project components (like software) are in column E.

F I G U R E 2.3: Network switchover worksheet

	A	B	C	D	E
1	Cyclops Software Division				
2	Windows NT Network Conversion Project				
4	Date	Task	Days	Resource	Project Components
5	10-Mar	Install NT Server 1	1.0	Ken	Windows NT Server
6	10-Mar	Install NT Server 2	1.0	Jody	Windows NT Client - 25
7	11-Mar	Switch sales printers	0.5	Ken	Innoculan Server
8	11-Mar	Switch service printers	0.5	Ken	Carbon Copy
9	12-Mar	Backup CS Sales files	0.3	Jody	
10	12-Mar	Backup CS Service files	0.5	Jody	

If you needed to add some tasks for March 10, you can't insert rows, because it would leave blanks in the components list in column E. Instead, you can insert cells in columns A–D. Select the range where new cells should be inserted, and then right-click and choose Insert. If you would like to delete cells, you can right-click and choose Delete from the shortcut menu.

When you insert or delete rows and columns, Excel automatically moves the surrounding rows and columns to fill the gap. If you insert or delete cells, Excel needs more instruction to know how to move the surrounding cells, so, depending on which option you choose, the Insert or Delete dialog box opens:

If you choose Shift Cells Down, the cells in the selection and all cells below them in the same columns are shifted down. If you choose Shift Cells

Right, cells in the same row(s) are moved to the right. Notice that you can also use this dialog box to insert entire rows or columns.

NOTE If you choose Delete from the shortcut menu, the Delete dialog box opens with the same four choices.

Moving and Copying Cell Contents

Objective XL2000.1.7

Basic move and copy techniques in Excel are discussed in Chapter 1. However, there are a few additional tips that make moving and copying in Excel even easier:

- If you paste cells on top of existing data, the existing data will be overwritten, so make sure that there are enough blank cells to accommodate the selection you want to paste. For example, if you want to move the contents of column E to the right of column A without overwriting column B, begin by inserting a blank column between A and B.

- *Cut and paste* and *copy and paste* operate differently in Excel than in other Office 2000 applications. Unless you open the Clipboard toolbar (View ➤ Toolbars ➤ Clipboard; see Chapter 1 for more about the Clipboard toolbar), you can't copy now, do a few other things, and then paste later. You must paste the data immediately; if you don't, the cut (or copy) operation is canceled.

- When you cut a cell in Excel, it is copied to the Clipboard but is not removed from the worksheet until you paste it in its new location by pressing Enter, by clicking the Paste button, or by pressing Ctrl+V.

- When you get ready to paste, just click the first cell, row, or column where you want pasted cells, rows, or columns to appear. If you select more than one cell to paste into, the selected range must be exactly the same size as the range you want to paste, or an error will occur.

- When you cut a selection, you can only paste it once, so you can't use cut to make multiple copies. However, you can *copy* and paste repeatedly. When you press Enter at the end of a paste operation,

Excel empties the Clipboard, so use the Paste button to paste the first, second, and so on copies that you want. Press Enter to place the final pasted copy.

- If you want to move or copy data from one worksheet to another, cut or copy the selection, and then click the sheet tab for the sheet that you want to paste into. Click in the appropriate cell, and then press Enter to paste.

- If you want to move or copy data from one workbook to another, both workbooks must be open. Select and cut or copy the data, and then choose Window from the menu bar and select the destination workbook from the list of open workbooks. Click in the destination cell and press Enter.

Moving and Copying Cells with Cut/Copy and Paste

1. If there is data below or to the right of the paste area, begin by inserting enough blank cells, rows, or columns for the data you want to move or copy.

2. Select the data you want to move or copy. To move, click the Cut button, choose Edit ➤ Cut, press Ctrl+X, or right-click and select Cut from the shortcut menu. To copy, click the Copy button, choose Edit ➤ Copy, press Ctrl+C, or right-click and select Copy from the shortcut menu.

3. Select the first cell, row, or column where you want to place the moved or copied data.

4. Press Enter to move or copy the data to its new location.

Using Drag-and-Drop

When you're moving or copying cells between worksheets or workbooks, it's easiest to cut or copy and paste. Another method, called *drag–and–drop*, works well when you can see the cells to be copied and their destination on one screen. After you select the cells, move the mouse so that it points to any part of the cell pointer except the fill handle (the mouse pointer will change to an arrow). Hold down the *right* mouse button and drag the cells to their new location. When you release the mouse button, a shortcut menu opens that lets you select whether you want to move or copy the cells:

You can also move cells by copying them with the *left* mouse button. To do so, hold the Ctrl key down, drag and drop the selected cells, then release the Ctrl key.

Moving and Copying Cells with Drag-and-Drop

1. Select the cells, rows, or columns to be moved or copied.

2. Point to any part of the cell pointer. The mouse pointer will change to an arrow shape.

3. To move the selection, drag and drop it in its new location. To copy a selection, hold the Ctrl key while dropping the selection.

Naming a Worksheet

▶ *Objective XL2000.5.7*

Because a workbook contains multiple worksheets, it is not always easy to remember which sheet contains what data. Excel allows you to give each worksheet a descriptive name so that you can locate it instantly within the workbook.

Naming a Worksheet

1. Double-click the sheet tab to select it.

2. Type a new name for the worksheet and press Enter.

Selecting Worksheets

You can move, copy, delete, and enter data in selected worksheets. To select one worksheet, click the sheet tab. To select more than one worksheet, hold the Ctrl key while selecting each worksheet. To select all worksheets in a workbook, right-click any tab and choose Select All Sheets from the shortcut menu.

Using Grouped Worksheets

When more than one worksheet is selected, the worksheets are *grouped*. Data entered into one sheet is entered into all sheets in the group, making it easy to enter the same title on five sheets in the same workbook. However, this also means that you need to remember to immediately *ungroup* worksheets when you are finished entering, moving, or copying common data. Otherwise, entries you make on one worksheet will be made on all worksheets, overwriting the existing entries on the other sheets in the group.

Ungrouping Worksheets

To ungroup worksheets, right-click any grouped worksheet tab and choose Ungroup Sheets from the shortcut menu. Alternatively, click any worksheet in the workbook that is not included in the group.

Grouping and Ungrouping Worksheets

1. To select one worksheet, click the sheet tab.

2. To select more than one worksheet, hold the Ctrl key while selecting each worksheet.

3. To select all worksheets in a workbook, right-click any tab and choose Select All Sheets from the shortcut menu.

4. To ungroup worksheets, right-click any grouped worksheet tab and choose Ungroup Sheets from the shortcut menu.

Copying and Moving Worksheets

▶ *Objective XL2000.5.9*

You can copy or move one or more selected worksheets within and between workbooks. You can copy or move a worksheet to a new workbook or to an existing workbook.

To move worksheets within the same workbook, drag the sheet's sheet tab to the new location (marked by a small triangle just above the tab) and drop it:

To copy a worksheet in the same workbook, hold the Ctrl key while dragging. The copy will have the same name as the original sheet, followed by the copy number:

Copying and Moving Worksheets

1. To move a worksheet within the same workbook, drag the sheet's sheet tab to the new location (marked by the triangle) and drop it. Hold down the Ctrl key while dragging to copy the worksheet.

2. To move or copy between workbooks, select the worksheet you want to copy, then either choose Edit ➤ Move or Copy Sheet from the menu bar. Select the name of the workbook you want to copy the sheet to. Click Create A Copy to copy it, and then click OK.

Inserting and Deleting Worksheets

Objective XL2000.5.8

When you insert a new worksheet into a workbook, it appears to the left of the selected sheet. You can save yourself the trouble of moving it later if you first select the sheet you want to be to the right of the inserted sheet. To insert a new worksheet, choose Insert ➤ Worksheet from the menu bar.

Delete one or more selected sheets by choosing Edit ➤ Delete Sheet from the menu bar, or right-click the sheet(s) and choose Delete from the shortcut menu. When you delete a worksheet, a dialog box will open, asking you to confirm the deletion.

TIP Excel includes three worksheets in every new workbook. If you frequently find yourself adding sheets to workbooks, you might want to increase the default number of sheets in a new book. To do so, select Tools ➤ Options from the menu bar, and change the Sheets In New Workbook setting on the General page of the Options dialog box.

Hiding and Unhiding Rows and Columns

Objective XL2000.5.2

You may find there are times when you want to hide certain rows or columns that contain data you don't want to be visible. For example, you may have a worksheet that you use to enter data into a new column each day. Rather than scrolling over to the column you need for today, you could hide the preceding day's columns and make today's column easily accessible.

To hide rows or columns, select the ones you want to hide and choose Format ➤ Columns/Row ➤ Hide. You know that rows or columns are missing because the row or column headings are not in sequence, as shown here:

	A	D	E	F
23	Beginning Database Design	Advanced Excel Databases		
24	Beginning Access	Beginning Database Design		
25	Advanced Database Design - Client Server Design	Beginning Access		
26	Advanced Access	Advanced Database Design - Client Server		
27	Project Management	Outlook – Workgroup Information Management		
28	Reporting Tools			
29	Access Reports and Queries	Intermediate Excel		
30	Beginning Crystal Reports	Beginning Excel or Beginning Impromptu		
31	Advanced Crystal Reports	Beginning Crystal Reports		
32	Beginning Impromptu	Beginning Excel or Beginning Crystal Reports		

TIP You can also hide rows and columns by dragging the column or row headings using the two-headed arrow pointer.

Freezing and Unfreezing Rows and Columns

Objective XL2000.5.3

When you have a large worksheet, it's difficult to navigate around when you can no longer see the row and column labels at the top and left of the worksheet. Excel can help by freezing row and column labels so they stay put while you scroll to see the rest of the data. In this example, notice how column F is next to column A, and row 33 is next to row 1:

	A	F	G	H	I
	Vendors	May-99	Jun-99	Jul-99	Aug-99
1					
33	Browning, Karla	1,340	1,984	1,119	3,840
34	Carol A. Fallis, P.C.	-	-	-	-
35	Charlotte Cowtan	-	-	-	-
36	Courter, Gini (Expenses)	2,233	-	-	1,000
37	Creative Printing and Graphics	421	-	-	200
38	Database Advisor	-	-	-	-
39	Federal Express	-	-	-	50
40	Flint Area Chamber of Commerce	-	-	-	-
41	Flint Journal	59	-	-	-

To freeze rows and columns, click in the first cell of the worksheet you do not want frozen. For example, if you clicked in B3, column A and rows 1 and 2 would be frozen. Choose Window ➤ Freeze Panes. To test to see if it works, scroll to see if the columns or rows you wanted to freeze stay in position.

To unfreeze the panes, choose Windows ➤ Unfreeze Panes.

NOTE Freezing panes does not affect what rows and columns of a worksheet print. However, hidden rows or columns do not print.

Hands On

Objectives XL2000.1.6, 1.7, 3.3, 5.1, 5.3, 5.7, 5.8, and 5.9

1. Practice naming worksheets in your workbooks. Open an existing workbook and rename each of the worksheets.

2. Open an existing workbook that contains a list of names or, if you don't have one, enter five last names in column 1 of a blank worksheet. Use cut and paste to alphabetize a list within a worksheet.

3. In an existing workbook:

a) Adjust column widths where needed.

b) Insert blank rows between column labels and data.

c) Practice moving cells, columns, and rows using cut and paste, copy and paste, and drag-and-drop techniques.

d) Name all used worksheets.

e) Move worksheets so they are ordered by sheet name.

f) Hide columns B and C and row 2. View the worksheet in Print Preview. Close Print Preview and unhide the columns and rows.

g) Freeze column and row labels and scroll to see that the frozen columns and rows stay in position.

4. In a new workbook, group all three sheets. Enter and format a title and some data; then ungroup the sheets and enter data on one sheet only.

5. Open a new workbook:

a) Name each of the sheets in the workbook by clicking each sheet tab and entering a name; then press Enter.

b) Hold Ctrl and select the first two sheets by clicking their sheet tabs.

c) Move to cell A1 in the first sheet and enter your name.

d) Click the second sheet and notice that your name has also been entered in A1.

e) Right-click either grouped sheet and choose Ungroup Sheets to turn off grouping.

f) Delete the extra sheet in the workbook, then reinsert it.

Other Formatting Options

There are additional ways in which you can enhance the appearance of a worksheet. You can call attention to certain cells by the way text is aligned in them—you can even rotate text!—and you can add borders, fill color, and font colors.

Aligning Text

Objective XL2000.3.4

By default, Excel left-aligns text and right-aligns numbers.

You can use the buttons on the Formatting toolbar to override the defaults and align text and numbers at the left, at the center, or at the right within cells:

Left		
	Center	
		Right

Excel has a fourth alignment called Merge And Center, which *merges* selected cells into one cell and centers the contents of the top-left selected cell across the new merged cell. Worksheet titles are often merged and centered.

 To merge and center a title, select the cell containing the title and the cells in the same row for all the used columns in the worksheet; then click the Merge And Center button. Excel only centers the text in the top-left cell of the selection, so if your worksheet's title is in more than one row, merge and center each title row separately.

There are other alignment options that aren't accessible from the toolbar but are set in the Alignment page of the Format Cells dialog box. Some of the more unique alignments, including text rotation, are illustrated in Figure 2.4. The Alignment page of the Format Cells dialog box is shown in Figure 2.5, and its options are discussed in the following four sections.

F I G U R E 2.4: Text alignments

	A	B	C	D	E
1	V E R T I C A L	*Text Rotated 45°*		The text in this cell is justified horizontally and vertically.	
2	M E R	Text centered vertically and horizontally	The text in this cell is wrapped.		
3	G	Left, 0 indent		Merged and centered	
4	E	Left, 1 indent			
5	D	Left, 2 indent		Shrunk to fit in this cell	

FIGURE 2.5: Alignment page of the Format Cells dialog box

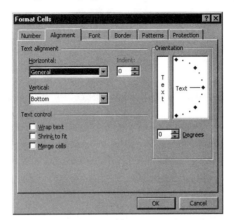

Horizontal Alignment and Indenting

There are seven types of Horizontal alignment:

General is the default alignment: text to the left and numbers to the right.

Left (Indent) aligns the contents of the cell at the cell's left edge, just like the Formatting toolbar button. However, if you choose Left in the dialog box, you can also specify a number of characters to indent in the Indent box.

Center and **Right** are identical to the Formatting toolbar buttons.

Fill "fills" the cell with the current contents by repeating the contents for the width of the cell. If, for example, "-" is the contents of the cell and you choose Fill for the alignment, "--------" will appear in the cell.

Justify wraps the text within the cell and adjusts the spacing within each line so that all lines are as wide as the cell, providing a smooth right edge, like text in a newspaper column.

Center Across Selection is applied to a range of cells. The contents of the leftmost cell are centered across all the cells selected. This is similar to Merge And Center, but it does not merge the cells.

Vertical Alignment

The default Vertical alignment (in the Text Alignment section of the Format Cells dialog box) is Bottom. Top and Center are used to float the contents nearer to the top or middle of the cell. Justify adds space between the lines in a wrapped cell.

Rotating Text

Objective XL2000.3.10

Use the rotation tools to orient text vertically or to rotate text to a specific orientation. Rotating text lets you create a splashy column or row label. Vertically orient and merge text (see below) to label a group of row labels.

To orient text vertically, in the Orientation section of the Format Cells dialog box, click the box with the vertical word Text in it. To rotate text to another orientation, either use the Degrees spin box or drag the Text indicator in the rotation tool.

Merge, Shrink to Fit, and Wrap Text

Objective XL2000.3.9

If you want a vertical title to cross several rows (such as the label "Vertical Merged" in column A of Figure 2.4), select the title and several additional cells below the title. In the Text Control section of the Format Cells dialog box, check the Merge Cells checkbox to merge the cells.

Also in the Text Control section, Shrink To Fit reduces the size of the type within selected cells so the contents fit. Wrap Text wraps the contents of a cell if it would exceed the cells' boundaries. Both Shrink To Fit and Wrap

Text use the current column widths. If you narrow or widen a column after you shrink or wrap a label, you'll need to reshrink or rewrap.

Aligning Text

1. Select the range of cells to be formatted.

2. Choose Format ➤ Cells from the menu bar or right-click and choose Format from the shortcut menu.

3. Click the Alignment page tab.

4. Choose horizontal, vertical, rotation, merge, and wrap options, and then click OK.

Borders and Color

Objective XL2000.3.8

Effective use of fonts, discussed in Chapter 1, can help make worksheets easier to understand. Borders and color provide further ways to highlight information in a worksheet. A *border* is a line drawn around a cell or group of cells. *Fill color* is used to highlight the background of part of a worksheet; *font color* is applied to text. Even if you don't have access to a color printer, you might still want to use color in worksheets that you or others use frequently. Color distinguishes between similar looking worksheets; for example, the sales department's budget could have a blue title, and Production's title could be burgundy.

The Borders, Fill Color, and Font Color buttons are found on the Formatting toolbar. All three buttons are combination buttons that include a menu opened by clicking the drop-down arrow attached to the button.

For example, this is the Borders menu:

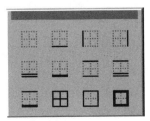

Borders can completely surround a group of cells, surround each cell individually, provide an underline, or double-underline the selected range. Selecting a border from the menu assigns it to the button and applies it to the selected cells. After you assign a border to the button, the next time you click the Border button, the same border style will be applied to your currently active cell or range of cells.

The Fill Color and Font Color buttons also have attached menus and are used the same way.

If you have a lot of borders, colors, or font colors to apply, you can open any or all of the menus as separate windows that float on your worksheet. Open the menu, and then point to the dark gray bar at the top of the menu. The bar will turn the same color as your program title bar; if you hover for a moment, a ScreenTip saying "Drag to make this menu float" will appear. Drag the menu into the worksheet and release the mouse button. Close the menu with its Close button.

Adding Borders, Colors, and Font Colors

1. To apply a font color or fill color, select the cells to be formatted. Click the Color button's drop-down arrow and select a color from the menu.

2. To add a border, select the cells to be formatted. Click the Borders button's drop-down arrow and select a border from the menu.

TIP If you need to apply several formatting changes to a group of cells, you may find it easier to use the Format Cells dialog box. Click the page tabs to move from page to page and set the desired formats for the selected cells. When you are finished, click OK to apply all the chosen formats to the selection.

Clearing Cell Formats

Objective XL2000.1.9

If you remove the contents of a cell by selecting it and pressing Delete or Backspace, Excel removes the cell contents but does not remove formatting. That means when you delete the contents of a cell that displays a number as a percentage, the next time you type a number in that cell, it will be formatted as a percentage.

To clear formatting from a cell, select it and click Edit ➤ Clear ➤ Formats.

Hands On

Objectives XL2000.1.9, 3.4, 3.8, and 3.9

1. Create an "alignment sampler" similar to Figure 2.4.

2. Use alignments, fonts, borders, and colors to format at least two different worksheets.

3. In an existing worksheet, use borders to separate numeric data from totals.

4. Select a cell or range of cells and clear the formatting.

Printing in Excel

Objective XL2000.4.1

Print Preview, Print, Page Setup, and Page Break Preview are interrelated features:

- Print Preview lets you see how each page of the workbook will appear when it is printed.

- Print prints the specified number of copies of selected worksheets or workbooks.

- Page Setup is used to change the margins, print quality, print area, and print features.

- Page Break Preview displays the current page breaks and allows you to adjust them.

Print Preview

Excel 2000 allows you to preview a spreadsheet before printing it. Click the Print Preview button on the Standard toolbar to open the preview window. The preview window displays the current worksheet as it will appear when it is printed, as shown in Figure 2.6.

F I G U R E 2.6: Excel's Print Preview window

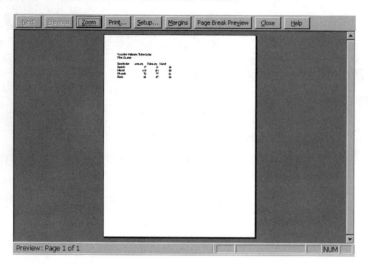

If the worksheet is wider or longer than one page, the Previous and Next buttons let you move between pages. (If the worksheet fits on one page, these two buttons are disabled.) The preview window's Zoom button toggles between full-page view and a magnified view of the worksheet. The full-page view lets you see the general layout of the page. Use the magnified view to look at specific details.

Adjusting Margins in Print Preview

The Print Preview Margins button displays the current margin settings. Point to any of the margin lines, and the pointer will change to an adjustment tool, as shown in Figure 2.7. Press the mouse button, and the status bar will indicate the name and current setting for the margin. Drag a margin to adjust it.

F I G U R E 2.7: Adjusting margins in Print Preview

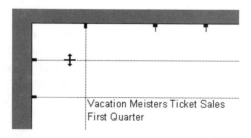

Excel's default margins are 3/4 of an inch on each side and 1 inch on the top and bottom, with a half-inch header and footer margin. Headers and footers print in the half-inch of space between the header/footer margin and the regular margin. The top and bottom margins define the limits of the printed worksheet, and the header and footer margins define the areas where the header and footer will print. If you use headers and footers, the top and bottom margins need to be inside the header and footer margins, or part of the worksheet will print on top of the header and footer.

Adjusting Margins in Print Preview

1. Click Print Preview to open the preview window.

2. Click the Margins button to display page margins.

3. Drag the margin you wish to change to its new location.

Printing a Document

 To immediately send a document to the printer using the default print options (and without opening a dialog box), click the Print button on the Standard toolbar. This is convenient if you want to print one copy of the active sheet to the default printer.

Changing Print Settings

To choose a printer, to specify what to print, and to set the number of copies, you must use the Print dialog box (see Figure 2.8).

F I G U R E 2.8: Excel's Print dialog box

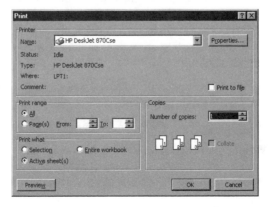

Click the Name drop-down list to select a different printer from the default. Click the Properties button to view or change the printer's settings.

Use the Print Range controls to print some, but not all, of the pages of a multi-page print job and the spin boxes to specify a starting and ending page to print. You cannot specify noncontiguous pages in Excel, so if you want to print pages 1–4 and 6–8, for example, you either have to print twice or choose the cells on those pages and specify them as your print area.

Objective XL2000.4.3

In the Print What section of the Print dialog box, specify which part of the worksheet or workbook you want to print. The Selection option provides another way to override the default print area: Select the cells you want to print, and then print the selection. Choose Workbook to print all used worksheets in the active workbook. To print some but not all worksheets in a workbook, select the sheets before opening the Print dialog box, and then choose Active Sheets.

Use the Number Of Copies spin box to print more than one copy of the selection, worksheet, or workbook. If you are printing multiple copies of more than one page, use the Collate control to print the pages in order. For example, two copies of a three-page worksheet will print 1–2–3, then 1–2–3. With Collate turned off, the same print request will print 1–1, 2–2, and 3–3.

Changing Print Settings

1. Choose File ➤ Print to open the Print dialog box.

2. Select a printer from the Printer Name drop-down menu.

3. Select what you wish to print: a selection, active worksheets, or the current workbook.

4. Set the number of copies using the Copies spin box, and turn Collate on or off for multi-page print jobs.

5. Specify a page range or leave the default as All.

6. Click OK to print and return to the worksheet.

Printing and Previewing Multiple Worksheets

Objective XL2000E.5.1

To print multiple worksheets from a workbook at one time, hold the Ctrl key while clicking the sheet tabs of the worksheet you want to print. The sheet tabs turn white, indicating that multiple sheets are grouped. When you choose File ➤ Print Preview, click the Next and Previous buttons to view each sheet. Click Print to print all of the selected sheets.

To ungroup the sheets, click the sheet tab of another sheet in the workbook.

Hands On

Objectives XL2000.4.1, 4.3, and E.5.1

1. Create a new workbook or open an existing workbook.
   a) View the spreadsheet in Print Preview.
   b) Use your mouse to zoom in on a section, then zoom back out.
   c) Print one copy of the spreadsheet on your default printer.
   d) Close Print Preview and return to Excel.
2. Select a portion of your worksheet.
   a) Print just the selected cells to your default printer.
3. Select more than one sheet in a workbook, and then preview and print them all.

Changing Page Setup

Objectives XL2000.4.4 and 4.5

To change page setup, choose File ➤ Page Setup from the menu bar to open the Page Setup dialog box. (If you're already in Print Preview, click the Setup button; from Page Break Preview, right-click and choose Page Setup from the shortcut menu.) The Page Setup dialog box splits page layout into four tabbed pages that contain Page, Margins, Header/Footer, and Sheet settings.

Page Settings

Use the Page options of the Page Setup dialog box, shown in Figure 2.9, to set orientation, scaling, paper size, and print quality.

F I G U R E 2.9: Page settings in the Page Setup dialog box

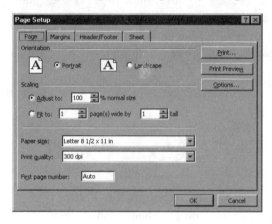

Orientation is the direction of print in relation to the paper it is printed on. Portrait, the default setting, places the short edge of the paper at the top and bottom. If your worksheet is wider than it is long, consider using landscape orientation.

Scaling is used to reduce or enlarge the print. If you simply need to make the print larger, use the Adjust To control and choose a size greater than 100 percent. The Fit To control instructs Excel to reduce a worksheet that exceeds a specific number of pages so it will fit.

Paper Size should be adjusted if you are using a paper size other than the default (for example, legal paper).

Print Quality is measured in dpi, dots per inch. Higher dpi means higher print quality, but there is a trade-off: It takes longer to print at higher dpi.

First Page Number is used to set an initial page number other than 1.

NOTE The Options button appears on every page of the Page Setup dialog box. Clicking it opens the Windows property sheet (or the manufacturer's property sheet, if there is one) for the printer that's currently selected.

Changing Page Settings

1. Open the Page Setup dialog box by choosing File ➤ Page Setup or by clicking the Setup button in the Print Preview window. Click the Page tab.

2. Change settings for Orientation, Scaling, Paper Size, Print Quality, and/or First Page Number.

3. Click OK to apply the settings.

Setting Margins in the Page Setup Dialog Box

Objective XL2000.4.5

The preview in the Margins page of the Page Setup dialog box (see Figure 2.10) displays the margins as dotted lines. You can change the margins here using the spin box controls for each margin. As you change settings on the Margins page, the preview will change to reflect the new margin settings.

F I G U R E 2.10: The Margins page of the Page Setup dialog box

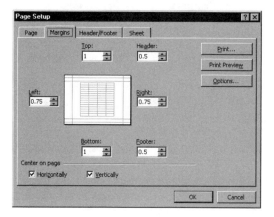

Use the Center On Page controls to center the printed worksheet horizontally between the side margins or vertically between the top and bottom margins.

Changing Margins in Page Setup

1. In the Page Setup dialog box, select the Margins page.

2. Using the spin box controls, set the top, bottom, left, and right margins.

3. If you are using a header or footer, use the Header and Footer spin boxes to set the distance for the header and footer margins.

4. Use the Center On Page checkboxes to center the printed worksheet.

Headers and Footers

Objective XL2000.4.8

A header appears at the top of each page of a document. Footers are printed at the bottom of the page. Excel's default setting is no header or footer. If you want a header or footer, choose or create it in the Header/ Footer page in the Page Setup dialog box, shown in Figure 2.11.

F I G U R E 2.11: The Header/Footer page of the Page Setup dialog box

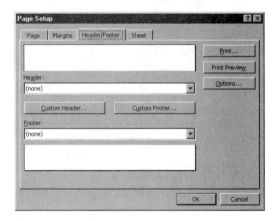

The currently selected header and footer are displayed in the two preview panes. To choose a different pre-designed header, click the Header drop-down list. Choose a footer the same way, using the Footer drop-down list. When you select a different header (or footer), the preview pane will reflect the change.

Creating New Headers and Footers To create a new header, click the Custom Header button to open the Header dialog box, shown in Figure 2.12. The header is separated into three sections: left, center, and right. Click in any section to place information in that portion of the header. You can enter text (such as your name) or insert a placeholder from Table 2.4.

F I G U R E 2.12: Header dialog box

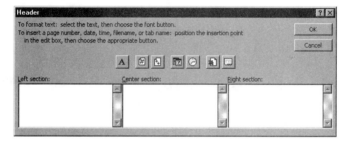

T A B L E 2.4: Header and Footer Placeholders

Button	Button Name	Placeholder
	Page Number	Current page number
	Total Pages	Total number of pages printed
	Date	Date worksheet was printed
	Time	Time worksheet was printed
	Filename	Name of workbook
	Tab	Name of worksheet

When the file is printed, Excel will replace each placeholder with the actual page number, date, time, workbook, or worksheet name.

Formatting Header and Footer Text To format header text, including placeholders, select the text and click the Font button to open the Font dialog box. Change the Font, Font Style, Size, Underline, and Effects that you want applied to the text. Click OK to save the font settings and return to the Header dialog box.

When you are finished creating the header, click OK to return to the Header/Footer page of the Page Setup dialog box and add the new header to the drop-down list.

Selecting and Creating Headers and Footers

1. Choose File ➢ Page Setup from the menu bar.

2. In the Page Setup dialog box, select the Header/Footer page.

3. Click the Header drop-down list and select a header, or click Custom Header to create a header. Click the Footer drop-down list and select a footer, or click Custom Footer to create a footer.

4. Press Enter to return to the Page Setup dialog box.

NOTE You can open the Header And Footer dialog box directly, rather than going through Page Setup, by selecting View ➢ Header And Footer.

Changing Sheet Settings

The Sheet page (see Figure 2.13) contains settings that relate to the sheet features that will appear in the printed copy, including the print area, repeating rows and columns, and gridlines.

NOTE The Print Area, Rows To Repeat, and Columns To Repeat controls are only enabled when you open the Page Setup dialog box from the menu (choose File ➢ Page Setup or View ➢ Header And Footer). If you go to Page Setup from Print Preview or the Print dialog box, you won't be able to change these three settings.

F I G U R E 2.13: Sheet settings

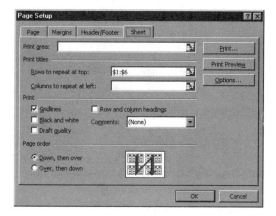

Objectives XL2000.4.7 and 4.9

Print Area   By default, Excel prints from the home cell (**A1**) to the last occupied cell in a worksheet. To specify a different range, type the range in the Print Area text box, or select the print area with the mouse. If the Print Area includes noncontiguous cells, each contiguous range will print on a separate page.

TIP   The easiest way to set the Print Area is from the menu bar. Select the cells to be printed, and then choose File ➢ Print Area ➢ Set Print Area from the menu bar. When you want to print the entire worksheet again, choose File ➢ Print Area ➢ Clear Print Area.

Print Titles   The options in this section allow you to print column and row labels on each page of the printout. Specify these rows or columns in the Rows To Repeat At Top and Columns To Repeat At Left text boxes. (Excel requires a *range* with a colon for these entries, even if it's only one row or column.)

Gridlines   This box determines whether gridlines will be printed but does not affect their display in the worksheet. Turning off the gridlines by clearing the checkbox gives your printed worksheet a cleaner appearance and can make it easier to read. Turn on the gridlines by checking the checkbox.

TIP To turn off screen gridlines, choose Tools ➤ Options and clear the checkbox in the Gridlines option on the View page of the Options dialog box.

Black And White If you used colors in the worksheet but won't be printing on a color printer, click this control to speed up the print process.

Draft Quality Checking this box chooses draft mode to print the worksheet without gridlines or graphics.

Row And Column Headings If this box is checked, the row numbers and column letters will be included in the printout. This is a useful feature when you are editing or trying to locate an error in a worksheet.

Page Order This section establishes the order in which multi-page worksheets are printed.

 If you find it difficult to select cells with the Page Setup dialog box in the way, click the Collapse Dialog button to minimize the dialog box while you select cells.

 Click the Expand Dialog button to return to the Print Setup dialog box.

Changing Sheet Settings

1. To open the Page Setup dialog box, choose File ➤ Page Setup. Click the Sheet tab.

2. Specify ranges for a print area and rows and columns to be repeated as titles on each printed page by entering them from the keyboard or by using the mouse.

3. Enter option settings in the Print and Page Order sections.

4. Click OK.

TIP   You can set Page Setup options for multiple worksheets by group-
ing (selecting) the worksheets before opening the Page Setup dialog box.
Remember to ungroup the worksheets after you've changed the Page
Setup.

Using Page Break Preview

Objective XL2000.4.6

Page Break Preview, shown in Figure 2.14, is a view of the worksheet window that shows you what will be printed and the order in which the pages
will be printed. To turn on Page Break Preview, click the Page Break Preview button in Print Preview , or choose View ➤ Page Break Preview from
the menu bar.

F I G U R E 2.14: Page Break Preview

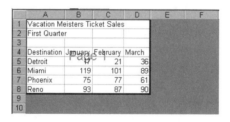

In Page Break Preview, areas that will be printed are white; cells that won't
be printed are gray. Each printed page is numbered. You can quickly
change the range to be printed by dragging the edge of the page break with
your mouse to include or exclude cells.

If a worksheet prints on multiple pages, you can adjust the breaks by dragging the page break. To add a manual page break, select the first column
or row you want to appear in the page after the break. Right-click and
choose Insert Page Break from the shortcut menu:

To remove a manual page break, right-click in the row below the horizontal page break or in the column to the right of the vertical page break, and choose Remove Page Break from the shortcut menu. To remove all manual page breaks, right-click any cell and choose Reset All Page Breaks from the shortcut menu. In Page Break Preview, you can also remove a page break by dragging it outside the print area.

To return to Normal view, choose View ➤ Normal from the menu bar. Note that you can also go directly from the worksheet to Page Break Preview from the View menu.

Previewing and Adjusting Page Breaks

1. From the Print Preview window, click the Page Break Preview button.

   or

   From the worksheet window, choose View ➤ Page Break Preview.

2. Using the mouse, drag the page break to extend or limit the range of cells to be printed.

3. Choose View ➤ Normal to close Page Break Preview.

Hands On

Objectives XL2000.4.4, 4.5, 4.6, 4.7, 4.8, and 4.9

Open the Cyclops Proposal workbook or another workbook of your choice.

1. In the first worksheet:

   a) Preview the worksheet.

   b) Center the worksheet horizontally and vertically on the page.

   c) Create a header that includes your name, and then create a footer with the current date and time left-justified and the sheet name right-justified.

   d) Preview and print the worksheet.

2. In the second worksheet:

   a) Use Page Break Preview to extend the print area to include two blank columns and one blank row.

   b) Reset the print area to include the entire worksheet.

   c) Change the paper orientation to Landscape.

   d) Change the top margin to 1.5 inches so the worksheet can be placed in a notebook.

   e) Add a horizontal page break so the worksheet prints on at least two pages.

   f) Print the worksheet title and column labels on each page.

   g) Preview and print the worksheet.

CHAPTER

3

Beyond Excel Basics

Once you've mastered the basics of Excel, it's only a matter of time before you need more advanced skills. You'll want to look at ways to graphically display data using Excel charts. Exploring financial and statistical functions might appeal to you, or perhaps you'll seek ways to sort and filter data for more focused reporting. In this chapter, you'll learn how to move beyond simple data entry and calculation into efficient use of Excel's more advanced features.

Working with Relative and Absolute Cell References

Objective XL2000.6.4

When you copy a formula from one cell to another, Excel automatically adjusts each cell reference in the formula. In the last chapter—and indeed, most of the time—this is exactly what you want Excel to do. However, there are exceptions. For example, Vacation Meisters would like to know the percentage of tickets sold for each destination city. To calculate a city's percentage, you would divide the city's total into the grand total for all cities.

To help visualize this process, take a look at Figure 3.1. We've entered a formula in cell G6 to divide the total Detroit tickets (74) into the grand total (866). The formula produces a reasonable answer for Detroit, but the same formula is obviously wrong when filled to the other cities.

F I G U R E 3.1: Calculating percentages

	A	B	C	D	E	F	G
1	Vacation Meisters Ticket Sales						
2	First Quarter						
3							
4	Destination	January	February	March	Total	Average	Percent of Total
5							
6	Detroit	17	21	36	74	25	9%
7	Miami	119	101	89	309	103	143%
8	Phoenix	75	77	61	213	71	288%
9	Reno	93	87	90	270	90	87%
10							
11	Total for Month	304	286	276	866		
12	Average for Month	76	72	69	217		
13	Minimum for Month	17	21	36	74		
14	Maximum for Month	119	101	90	309		

So what happened? The formula in G6 was =E6/E11. When it was filled from G6 to G7, Excel changed each cell reference, just as it did with the totals you filled earlier. You can see which cells were referenced in a formula by double-clicking the formula. The formula in G7 was changed to =E7/E12, and the change from E11 to E12 created the problem. Rather than dividing Miami's total into the total for all destinations, it divided it into the average in cell E12. The formulas for Phoenix and Reno have a similar problem.

When you fill this formula, you want E6 to change to E7 (*relative* to the formula's new location), but you don't want E11 to change at all. The reference to E11 should be *absolute*—not changeable. You instruct Excel to not change the reference to E11 by making it an *absolute cell reference*. Absolute cell references are preceded with dollar signs, such as E11. The dollar signs "lock in" the cell reference so Excel doesn't change it if you fill or copy the formula to another cell. The dollar sign in front of the E instructs Excel not to change the column; the dollar sign in front of the 11 locks in the row. As you fill the formula =E6/E11 to the other cities, E6 will change to E7, E8, and E9, but E11 will always be E11.

You create an absolute cell reference in the original formula. If you never intend to fill or copy a formula, you don't need to use absolutes, and absolutes won't fix a formula that doesn't work correctly to begin with. Remember, the original formula in G6 worked just fine. If you are typing the formula, just precede the column and row addresses with a $. You can also create an absolute cell reference using the F4 key, as you will see in the steps below.

Creating an Absolute Cell Reference

1. Place the cell pointer where you want the results of the formula to appear.

2. Begin entering the formula. After you enter the address of the cell that contains the absolute value, press the F4 key once to add dollar ($) signs to the row and column of the cell reference.

3. When the formula is complete, press Enter or click the green check mark.

4. Fill the formula to the appropriate cells.

You can also create a *mixed reference*, making a cell address part absolute and part relative, by locking in *either* the column *or* the row. Use mixed references when you want to copy a formula down *and* across and to have a reference change relatively in one direction but not in the other. For example, E$5 will remain E$5 when copied down, because the row reference is absolute, but it can change to F$5, G$5, and so on when copied across, because the column reference is relative.

TIP   The Absolute key (F4) is a four-way toggle. The first time you press it, it locks both the column and row: E11. Press it again, and only the row is locked: E$11. The third time you press F4, the column is locked: $E11. Press it a fourth time, and both row and column are relative again: E11.

Working with Ranges

Rather than using cell addresses as references, you can define a *name* to refer to a cell or a range of cells. Names provide multiple benefits:

- Names are more descriptive and easier to remember than cell addresses.

- When a cell moves, the name moves with it.

- You can use a name in place of a cell or range address in a formula or function argument, just like a row or column label.

- When you copy a formula that uses a named cell, the effect is the same as using an absolute cell reference.

Naming Ranges

Objective XL2000E.6.1

Names can be a maximum of 255 characters and can include letters, numbers, underscores, and periods. The name must begin with either a letter or the underscore character (_), and you cannot use spaces, commas, exclamation points, or other special characters. Names cannot be valid cell addresses; for example, FY1998 cannot be used as a name, because there's a cell with that address in every Excel worksheet. Names are not case-sensitive; INTEREST RATE and interest rate are the same name. The traditional naming practice is to exclude spaces and begin each word within the name with an uppercase letter: InterestRate. A name can't be repeated within a workbook, so you can't use the same name on two different sheets.

You can name a range in three ways. The easiest is to select the range (which can include noncontiguous cells) and then click in the Name box at the left end of the formula bar. (Click the box, not the drop-down arrow.) Type the name for the range, and then press Enter.

You can also name ranges and change or delete existing range names using the Define Name dialog box, shown in Figure 3.2. The dialog box displays a list of the names already used in the workbook.

F I G U R E 3.2: Excel's Define Name dialog box

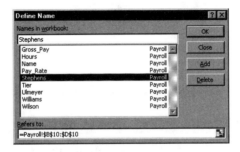

Defining, Changing, and Deleting Range Names

1. To define a name, select the range of cells you want to name.

2. Choose Insert ➤ Name ➤ Define from the menu bar.

3. In the Names In Workbook text box, type a valid range name, and then click Add.

4. To change a name, select the name from the Names In Workbook list. Select the name in the Names In Workbook text box, overtype the old name with the new name, and then click Add.

5. To delete a name, select the name from the Names In Workbook list, and then click the Delete button.

6. When you are finished, click OK.

Excel allows you to use a worksheet's row and column labels in formulas (choose Tools ➤ Options and enable Accept Labels In Formulas on the Calculation tab to enable this feature). Use the Create Names dialog box (see Figure 3.3) to *assign* a name to one cell from text in another cell, even if the text is not a row or column label.

F I G U R E   3.3: The Create Names dialog box

Excel edits labels as needed to make them valid names. If the label for a column or row contains spaces, Excel will replace the space with an underscore: Interest_Rate. If the cell contents begin with a number, like 8-Mar or 4 bags, Excel adds an underscore to the beginning of the name: _8-Mar or _4_bags. However, Excel does not create a name from a cell that contains *only* a number (like 1998, 78, or 1254.50). Excel will let you go through the motions, but it won't create the name.

Creating Names from a Row or Column of Text

1. Select the range to be named. Include the cells you want to use as names as either the top or bottom row, or the first or last column selected.

2. Choose Insert ➣ Name ➣ Create from the menu bar to open the Create Names dialog box.

3. In the Create Names In text box, select the row (Top or Bottom) and/or column (Left or Right) that contain the labels you want to use to name the selected range.

4. Click OK to apply the names and close the dialog box.

Using Names

▶ Objective XL2000E.6.2

You can enter a name anywhere a regular cell reference is valid. For example, you can type in the name of a range as an argument for a function: =SUM(Hours). Names also serve a valuable navigation function, particularly in large workbooks and worksheets. To move to and select a named range anywhere in the workbook, click the down arrow in the Name box and select the name from the list.

Hands On

Objectives XL2000.6.4, E.6.1, and E.6.2

1. Using the Cyclops Proposal Software worksheet or another worksheet:

   a) Practice naming ranges using both Name ➤ Create and Name ➤ Define.

   b) Move to a named range.

   c) Delete one of the named ranges.

2. Create a mileage worksheet to calculate mileage reimbursement for business travel. In column A, list the destinations. In column B, record the number of miles from your office to the destination. In column C, record the number of miles of the return from the destination to your office.

   a) Use Name ➤ Define to name the cells in column B; give a different name to the cells in column C.

   b) Create a formula in column D to add columns B and C using the named ranges. Name column D "TotalMiles."

3. Using the Cyclops Proposal Software worksheet or another worksheet, use absolute cell references to calculate the Percentage column (percentage of total).

4. In the mileage worksheet you created in Exercise 2,

   a) Enter $.31 in a cell at the top of the worksheet. Name it "Rate."

   b) Use absolute cell references and named ranges to create a new column that calculates Rate * TotalMiles.

Understanding Functions

Functions are pre-defined, structured programs that calculate a specific result: a total, an average, the amount of a monthly loan payment, or the geometric mean of a group of numbers, for example. Each function has a specific order, or *syntax*, that must be used for the function to work properly. Functions are formulas, so all functions begin with the = sign.

After the = is the *function name,* followed by one or more *arguments* separated by commas and enclosed in parentheses.

$$=\text{SUM(D6:D11)}$$

In Chapter 2, when you clicked the AutoSum button, you used the SUM function to total numbers. Excel includes hundreds of other functions that you can use to calculate results used in statistics, finance, engineering, math, and other fields. These functions are grouped into 10 categories, as listed in Table 3.1.

T A B L E 3.1: Excel Functions

Category	Examples
Financial	Calculates interest rates, loan payments, depreciation amounts
Date & Time	Returns the current hour, day of week or year, time, or date
Math & Trig	Calculates absolute values, cosines, logarithms
Statistical	Performs common functions used for totals, averages, and high and low numbers in a range; advanced functions for t-tests, Chi tests, deviation
Lookup & Reference	Searches for and returns values from a range; creates hyperlinks to network or Internet documents
Database	Calculates values in an Excel database table
Text	Converts text to uppercase or lowercase, trims characters from the right or left end of a text string, concatenates text strings
Logical	Evaluates an expression and returns a value of True or False, used to trigger other actions or formatting
Information	Returns information from Excel or Windows about the current status of a cell, an object, or the environment
Engineering	Included with Office 2000, but must be installed separately from the Analysis Toolpack

You don't have to learn all of Excel's functions, but you should know the common ones and have enough knowledge about others so that you can find them as you need them.

NOTE SUM is the only individual function included on the Standard tool-bar. You can access all the functions (including SUM) using the Formula Palette.

Entering Functions

Objective XL2000.6.8

Before entering a function, make sure the cell where you want the results to be displayed is activated. Click Edit Formula (the equal sign) in the formula bar to open the Formula Palette. The Name box (to the left of the formula bar) changes to a Function box, displaying the name of the last function that was used (SUM), as shown in Figure 3.4.

F I G U R E 3.4: Excel's Formula Palette and Function box

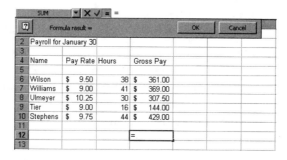

Click the Function drop-down list to choose from recently used functions:

If the function you want is on the list, select it to move the function to the formula bar and the Formula Palette. The Formula Palette includes a description of the function and one or more text boxes for the function's arguments, as shown in Figure 3.5.

F I G U R E 3.5: The Formula Palette (AVERAGE function)

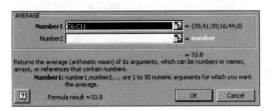

For common functions that use a single range of cells as an argument, Excel "guesses" which numbers you might want to sum or average and places the range in the argument text box. Required arguments are bold, like Number1 in Figure 3.5. Required arguments must be filled in to successfully use the function.

In Figure 3.5, you can't tell whether the range in the Number1 text box is correct, because the Formula Palette covers the cells. Click the Collapse Dialog button to shrink the Formula Palette.

Confirm that the correct cells are selected or use the mouse to select the correct cells before expanding the palette with the Expand Dialog button. After you have selected all the required arguments, click OK to finish the entry and to close the Formula Palette. As with any formula, the results of the function are displayed in the active cell; the function itself is displayed in the formula bar when the cell is active.

If the function you want is not listed in the Function box, choose More Functions at the bottom of the list to open the Paste Function dialog box, shown in Figure 3.6.

F I G U R E 3.6: The Paste Function dialog box

Objective XL2000.6.6

 If you're using a function that you rarely use, you can open the Paste Function dialog box directly by clicking the Paste Function button on the Standard toolbar.

Select a function category from the left pane of the dialog box, and then scroll the right pane and select a function. If you need more information, clicking the Office Assistant button opens the Assistant, which offers help on the selected function. Click the OK button to choose the selected function and to return to the Formula Palette.

Using Functions

1. Activate the cell where you want the result of the function to appear.

2. Click the Edit Formula button on the formula bar.

3. Choose a function from the Function Box drop-down list.

   or

   If the function does not appear on the list, choose More Functions to open the Paste Function dialog box. Choose a category in the left pane and a function from the right pane. Click OK.

4. In the Formula Palette, select the text box for the first argument. Click the Collapse Dialog button to move the dialog box, and then select the cells you want to include in the argument. Click the Expand Dialog button to return to the Formula Palette.

5. Click the OK button to complete the entry.

Hands On

Objectives XL2000.6.6 and 6.8

1. In a new or existing worksheet, use the Formula Palette to enter an AVERAGE function for a range of numbers:

   a) Enter a column of numbers.

   b) Click in the cell where you want the average.

   c) Click the = sign on the Formula Palette and choose Average from the list of available functions.

   d) In the Number1 box, enter or select the cells you want to average.

   e) Click OK.

2. Use the Paste Function button on the Standard toolbar to create an average for a range of numbers.

Financial Functions

Excel has more than 50 built-in financial functions, and you don't have to be an accountant to find ways to use them. You can use the financial functions to determine how much your monthly car payments will be, how long you'll be paying off your student loan, or how much you can afford to finance on a new home. If you have a small business, the financial functions give you five ways to calculate depreciation and several tools to manage the profit you invest in various stocks and bonds.

To work with the financial functions, it's helpful if you're familiar with the common arguments you encounter. These are the most common:

- FV (future value): What a loan or investment will be worth at a future time when all payments have been made

- NPER (number of periods): The number of months, years, days, or other periods for an investment or loan

- PMT (payment): The amount you periodically receive from an investment or are paid on a loan

- PV (present value): The initial value of an investment or loan

- RATE: The interest rate on a loan; the discount or interest rate on an investment

The amount of a periodic payment, present value, interest rate, and the total number of payments have a fixed relationship to each other. If you know any three of these, you can use one of the Excel financial functions to calculate the fourth:

- NPER: Calculates the number of periods
- PMT: Calculates the payment amount
- PV: Returns the present value for the amount loaned or invested
- RATE: Returns the interest rate

With these four functions, you can determine how much interest you paid on a loan or how much income you would receive from an annuity. The worksheet in Figure 3.7 uses the PMT function to calculate a monthly payment for various present values at an interest rate entered by the user.

F I G U R E 3.7: Loan Payment Calculator worksheet

	A	B	C	D	E	F
1	LOAN PAYMENT CALCULATOR					
2						
3	Enter an interest rate here:		12%			
4						
5	Loan Life (in years)	$5,000.00	$10,000.00	$15,000.00	$20,000.00	$25,000.00
6						
7	1	$444.24	$888.49	$1,332.73	$1,776.98	$2,221.22
8	2	$235.37	$470.73	$706.10	$941.47	$1,176.84
9	3	$166.07	$332.14	$498.21	$664.29	$830.36
10	4	$131.67	$263.34	$395.01	$526.68	$658.35
11	5	$111.22	$222.44	$333.67	$444.89	$556.11
12	6	$97.75	$195.50	$293.25	$391.00	$488.75
13	7	$88.26	$176.53	$264.79	$353.05	$441.32
14	8	$81.26	$162.53	$243.79	$325.06	$406.32
15	9	$75.92	$151.84	$227.76	$303.68	$379.61
16	10	$71.74	$143.47	$215.21	$286.94	$358.68
17						

When you work with financial functions, you need to make sure that all the arguments in a function are based on the same period: a day, a month, or a year. For example, in Figure 3.7 the payments are monthly payments, but the number of periods and the user-entered interest rate are based on years. In the PMT function arguments, then, NPER has to be multiplied by 12 and Rate divided by 12 so that all the arguments are based on a period of one month, as shown in Figure 3.8. (Pasting the PMT function in a cell opens this dialog box.)

FIGURE 3.8: When using the PMT function, make sure the payments, number of periods, and the interest rate are based on the same time period.

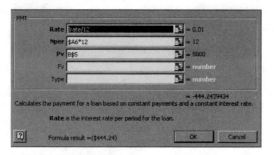

Calculating Payment (PMT) and Future Value (FV)

Objective XL2000.6.10

The Payment (PMT) function calculates the payments on a loan given constant payments and a constant interest rate. For example, if you want to buy a new truck, PMT can tell you how much your monthly payments would be based on the amount of the loan (the price of the truck minus the down payment or trade-in) and the amount of the interest rate charged by the lender.

To use the PMT function:

1. Click the Paste Function button and choose Financial as the category. Select PMT, and click OK.

2. In the Rate box, enter the interest rate of the loan divided by the number of payments in a year (e.g., /12 for monthly payments).

3. In the Nper box, enter the number of payments you plan to make on the loan (e.g., 3 years = 36, 4 years = 48, and so on).

4. In the Pv box, enter the amount of the loan.

5. Click OK to paste the result, which will be negative because it's a cash outflow.

TIP If you enter the interest rate, number of payments, and amount of the loan in the worksheet *before* using the PMT function, click the Collapse Dialog buttons on the Paste Function dialog box to select the cells from the worksheet.

The Future Value (FV) function calculates the future value of an investment based on period, constant payments, and a constant interest rate. Let's say you just paid off the truck you bought four years ago. Rather than buy another truck right away, you decide to save your truck payments and use the money you save as a down payment on a new truck in two years. If your truck payments are $353 per month and you save for 24 months at 3.5 percent interest, FV shows you how much money you'll have to buy your new truck.

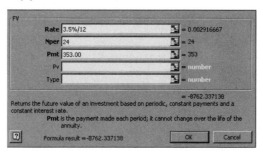

Working with Statistical Tables

Although you may never have a need for many of Excel's statistics functions, it is in this category where you find everyday statistics functions such as AVERAGE. Other common statistics functions include:

- COUNT: Returns the number of numbers in a selected range
- MEDIAN: Another kind of average; used to calculate the value in the middle of a range
- MODE: Returns the value that occurs most frequently
- MIN: Returns the lowest value in a range
- MAX: Returns the highest value in a range

If you don't have a statistics background, don't worry. All five of these functions are useful and easy to understand.

Using COUNT, MEDIAN, MODE, MIN, and MAX

Objective XL2000.6.7

The COUNT function tells you how many numbers are in a selected range. If you have a small worksheet, it's a breeze to glance down column C and say, "Looks like four numbers to me." It's a bit harder with larger worksheets, and the problem is compounded when some cells in a column are blank.

Entering a COUNT, MIN, or MAX function is as simple as following the same steps you used when practicing the AVERAGE function in the "Hands On" section earlier in the chapter:

1. Select the cell where you want the answer to go, then click the Paste Function button.

2. Choose COUNT (or MIN or MAX) from the Statistical category in the Paste Function dialog box.

3. Click OK to open the Formula Palette, and enter the range(s) you want Excel to examine.

4. Click OK to close the palette and apply your formula.

AVERAGE returns a value called the *arithmetic mean*—the total of all the values in a range divided by the number of values in the range. But there are two other types of averages: MEDIAN and MODE. MEDIAN tells you which value is the middle value in a range, and MODE tells you which value occurs most frequently, as shown in Figure 3.9. (We used COUNT to calculate the Number of Responses.)

FIGURE 3.9: Functions that return averages

Question 14: How much would you be willing to pay for this product?	
Survey Number	**Response**
109871	30
109874	30
109880	40
109881	150
109889	40
109899	30
110001	40
110051	30
110060	33
Number of Responses	9
Mean Average	47
Median	33
Mode	30

The Marketing department's survey question number 14 is "How much are you willing to pay for this product?" The AVERAGE answer is $47, but is it fair to say, "The average person is willing to pay $47 for our product."? No—only one person is willing to pay that much: the person who'll pay up to $150. If the Marketing department uses the average, they'll price the product so high that most customers won't buy it.

That's where MEDIAN and MODE come in. The response in the middle (the MEDIAN) is $33. There are as many people willing to pay less than $33 as there are people willing to pay more than $33, so this might be a good price. You can routinely use MEDIAN to test the AVERAGE. If MEDIAN and AVERAGE values are close to each other, there aren't too many bizarre values (such as the $150 answer) in the range. MODE tells us that more people are willing to pay $30 than any other price—more useful information for the Marketing department to know.

NOTE   Enter arguments for the financial and statistical functions as you would any other function.

Date and Logical Functions

Objective XL2000.6.9

The DATE function provides another way to insert a date in a cell. Enter arguments for year, month, and day (values, formulas, or cell references), and Excel inserts the corresponding date into the selected cell.

Using the NOW function to insert the system date and time is even easier, because it doesn't require any arguments. Choose the NOW function from the Paste Function dialog box, and then click OK when the Formula Palette opens. The current date and time are inserted into the selected cell. Be aware, however, that a cell with a NOW function doesn't update automatically. Press F9 to update all cells that use the NOW function.

Using the IF Function

Objective XL2000.6.11

Use IF to evaluate whether a value meets a certain condition and to display results depending on whether or not the condition is met. For example, a teacher who keeps her gradebook in Excel maintains a minimum passing score of 65 percent. An IF statement can be set up so that the cell adjacent to each student's score reads *Pass* or *Fail*, depending on whether that student's score is at or above 65 percent. Figure 3.10 shows an example of what this gradebook might look like.

FIGURE 3.10: Gradebook with IF statement

	A	B	C	D	E	F	G	H	I	J	K	L
1				TEAM PROJECTS			TESTS					
2												
3	POSSIBLE POINTS		10	10	5	15	30	40	110			
4												
5	Last Nam	First Nam	Project 1	Project 2	Project 3	Project 4	Midterm	Final	TOTAL POINTS	% GRADE		
6	Adams	Abby	10	9	5	15	29	39	107	100%	Pass	
7	Adams	Adam	5	3	5	7	17	20	57	53%	Fail	
8	Barney	Bill	0	10	4	10	22	33	79	74%	Pass	
9	Charles	Chuckie	10	10	5	15	26	35	101	94%	Pass	
10	Dawson	Denise	9	9	0	13	26	32	89	83%	Pass	
11	Ellis	Eileen	10	10	5	12	28	40	105	98%	Pass	
12	Friendly	Fritz	6	8	5	15	29	40	103	96%	Pass	
13	Gomez	Glen	9	10	5	15	28	40	107	100%	Pass	
14	Hill	Hector	6	8	5	15	25	32	91	85%	Pass	
15	Hill	Helen	10	7	4	13	20	29	83	78%	Pass	
16												
17	Class Averages		7.50	8.40	4.30	13.00	25.00	34.00	92.20	86%		
18												

You'll enter three arguments for an IF statement:

- Logical test: Any value or expression that can be considered True or False. For example, J6<65% is a logical expression; if the value in cell J60 is less than 65 percent, the expression is True. Otherwise, the expression evaluates to False.

- Value if true: The value that is displayed if logical test is True. Using the teacher's example, if the value in J6 is less than 65 percent, we want the word "Fail" to display, so we would type the word **Fail** in the Value if true argument.

- Value if false: Displays if logical test is False. In our case, we would type the word **Pass** to see the results in Figure 3.10.

Using an IF Function

1. Click in the cell where you want your first value displayed.

2. Click the Paste Function button and choose IF from the Logical category.

3. Enter the expression you want to use as a logical test.

4. Enter values for when the expression evaluates to True and False.

5. Click OK to close the Formula Palette.

6. Fill the formula to other cells as needed.

Using Lookup Functions

Objective XL2000E.6.3

Excel's *lookup functions* are used to look up information within an array. An *array* is an Excel database with one column or row that contains unique values. The VLOOKUP function searches vertically through the first column of an array until it finds a value. It then looks in a specified column of the value's row and returns the value in that column. VLOOKUP has one optional and three required arguments:

- Range lookup: This optional field can either be True or False.

- Lookup value: The value Excel searches for in the first column of the array. The lookup value can be a number, text, or a cell reference.

- Table array: The range of cells that contains the array. This can be a named range.

- Column index number: The column number in the array that contains the value that should be returned. The leftmost (first) column is column 1.

Range lookup requires a bit of explanation. If this argument is False, the array doesn't have to be sorted by the values in the first column, but VLOOKUP will only find exact matches for the lookup value. If you don't enter **False**, this value is assumed to be True; the array must be sorted on the first column in ascending order, and Excel will use the closest match in the column. If the lookup value is larger than the last item in the array, Excel returns the last item. If it is smaller than the first item in the array, Excel returns an error.

Figure 3.11 shows a portion of an inventory worksheet that we'll use as an example. If you're creating an order form for the items in the inventory, you don't have to enter the item's description, cost, or price—you can look these items up in the array. Let's say, for example, that a user will enter an item number in cell F15. You can enter a formula in G15 to look up the description. The formula =VLOOKUP(F15,A2:F5,2,FALSE) looks in the array A2:F5 to find a match for the value in cell F15 (the lookup value). The range lookup is False, so it will only be satisfied by an exact match, which is the behavior we'd like. If the wrong item number is entered, we don't want Excel to return a "close match." When it finds a match, it looks in the second column of the array (column index number = 2) and returns the value: the description of the item.

F I G U R E 3.11: Use VLOOKUP to find values in an array like this one.

	A	B	C	D	E	F
1	Part	Desc	Cost	Quantity	Markup	Price
2	23612	Raceway 7 ft section	17.89	5	19%	21.29
3	35781	10BT SOHO 5 port hub	35.22	7	17%	41.21
4	42351	CAT5 Patch Cable 5 ft	3.18	22	17%	3.72
5	98431	Bulk CAT5 PVC	0.18	1200	19%	0.21

TIP You can use the logical and lookup functions together to check first in the Quantity column, then return either the price or notification that an item's quantity is 0: =IF(VLOOKUP(F15,A2:F5,4,FALSE)>0, VLOOKUP (F15,A2:F5,6,FALSE),"OUT OF STOCK").

The HLOOKUP function searches the first row of an array, and has similar arguments: lookup value, table array, row index number, and range lookup. Figure 3.12 shows a portion of a worksheet that includes a ticket cost calculator and a ticket price array. There are three different types of ticket prices: Corporate (C), Educational (E), and Individual (I). This formula in cell C3 looks up the ticket price based on the lookup value (C, E, or I); the row index number is the number of tickets entered in C4 plus 1: =HLOOKUP(C1,B6:D12,C2+1,FALSE).

F I G U R E 3.12: HLOOKUP searches a row and then returns a value in the same column.

	A	B	C	D	E
1		Ticket Type:	E		
2		Quantity:	2		
3		Price Per Ticket:	=HLOOKUP(C1,B6:D12,C2+1,FALSE)		
4		Total Cost:	45.00		
5					
6			C	E	I
7		1	20.00	22.50	22.50
8		2	20.00	22.50	22.50
9		3	20.00	15.00	22.50
10		4	20.00	15.00	22.50
11		5	17.00	15.00	22.50
12		6	17.00	13.50	20.00

TIP You can use Excel's horizontal and vertical lookup functions to search for information in any database where the contents of one field are unique, so look for opportunities to use the HLOOKUP and VLOOKUP functions whenever you know one value in an Excel database and have to return other information from the same "record."

Hands On

Objectives XL2000.6.7, 6.9, 6.10, 6.11, and E.6.3

1. In this exercise, you'll create and modify the Loan Payment Calculator worksheet shown in Figure 3.7.

   a) Enter the titles and labels shown in Figure 3.7. Apply formatting as indicated in the figure.

   b) Name cell C3 "Irate."

   c) In B7, click the = button to open the Formula Palette. Click the Function drop-down list and choose More Functions. Select the PMT financial function and enter the required arguments, as shown in Figure 3.8. Notice that Rate uses an absolute reference, while NPER and PV are mixed references. NPER should change when filled down rows but remain unchanged when filled across columns; the opposite is true for PV.

   d) Enter a monthly interest rate in C3 to test the function. The monthly payment amounts will all be negative (because you're sending, not receiving, these payments). Edit the formula to begin =-PMT so that the payment value is positive. Fill the formula in B7 to the other monthly payment cells.

   e) Test the worksheet by entering different interest rates and amounts. Notice the changes in the monthly payments.

   f) For more practice with the PMT function, rebuild the worksheet so that the periods in column A are months rather than years.

2. Create the worksheet shown in Figure 3.9.

3. Open any worksheet that includes an average.

   a) Calculate the mode, median, min, max, and count for the same range as the average.

b) Practice using the DATE and NOW functions.

c) Incorporate an IF function into the worksheet.

4. Create the worksheet shown in Figure 3.12 or a similar worksheet using the HLOOKUP function.

5. Create the worksheet shown in Figure 3.11. In another worksheet in the same workbook, create part of an order form that includes space for at least five items. Add lookups to return the description of each item. Use IF and a lookup function to create formulas for each item that return the price if the quantity in stock is greater than or equal to the quantity ordered. If the quantity ordered is more than the quantity in stock, return the text string "INSUFFICIENT STOCK."

Charting Your Data

Charts are graphical representations of numeric data. Because charts make it easier for users to compare and understand numbers, they have become a popular way to present numeric data. Every chart tells a story. Stories can be simple—"See how our sales have increased"—or complex—"This is how our overhead costs relate to the price of our product." Either way, the story should be readily understandable. If you can't immediately understand what a chart means, it isn't a good chart.

Charts are constructed with *data points*—individual numbers in a worksheet—and *data series*—groups of related data points within a column or row. In the Vacation Meisters Tickets worksheet (see Figure 3.1), each of the numbers is a data point, and each column or row of numbers is a series. There are many possible sets of data series in this worksheet. One set includes four data series—one for each city's row. Another set includes a data series for each month's column.

The most commonly used charts fall into one of two categories: pie charts and series charts. *Pie charts* show the relationship between pieces of an entity. The implication is that the pie includes *all* of something: all the tickets sold in a month or all the tickets sold in the first quarter (see Figure 3.13). The pie chart isn't appropriate for illustrating *some* of anything, so if there's not an obvious "all" in the data you're charting, don't use a pie chart.

F I G U R E   3.13: Pie chart from the Tickets worksheet

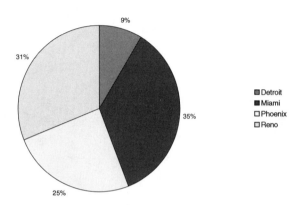

First Quarter Ticket Sales

Series Charts

Series charts allow you to chart more than one data series. This lets you compare the data points in the series, such as January versus February, Reno versus Phoenix, and so on. Series charts are open-ended; there is no requirement that the data shown is all the data for a month or year. There are several types of series charts: line, area, bar, and column. You can give the same set of data a very different look by simply changing the chart type.

Line and Area Charts

Line charts and *area charts* are typically used to show one or more variables (sales, income, price) changing over time. An area chart is simply a line chart with the area below the line filled.

Line and area charts share a common layout. The horizontal line is called the x-axis, and the vertical line is the y-axis (the same x- and y-axes you may have learned about in algebra or geometry class when plotting data points). Line and area charts are available in 2-D versions (as shown in Figure 3.14) or in 3-D versions. (The 3-D version of a line chart is sometimes called a *ribbon chart*.) The series chart in Figure 3.14 is a line chart showing the relationship between ticket sales and each city during the first quarter. Each data series is a city.

F I G U R E 3.14: A 2-D line chart

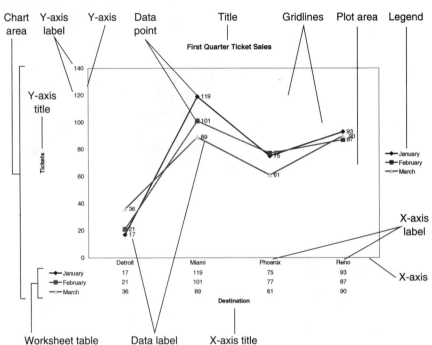

Bar and Column Charts

Figure 3.15 shows the same information as the line chart in Figure 3.14, but it is presented as a *bar chart*. Unlike area and line charts, a bar chart's axes are turned 90 degrees, so the x-axis is on the left side. Further, the bars give added substance to the chart. In a line chart, the reader notices the trend up or down in each line and the gaps between the lines. A bar chart makes all ticket sales seem more substantial, but it also makes the difference between destinations even clearer—like why doesn't anyone vacation in Detroit?

Column charts are the same as bar charts, but with the x-axis at the bottom. The chart shown in Figure 3.15 is a 3-D bar chart; you can also create 2-D bar and column charts. Cylinders, cones, and pyramids are variations of a column chart.

F I G U R E 3.15: A bar chart

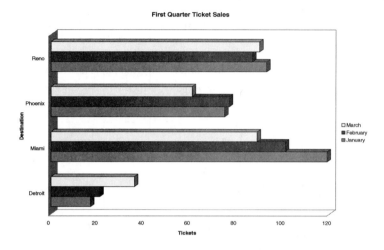

Excel also offers another style of bar and column chart—the *stacked chart*.
In a stacked chart, parallel data points in each data series are stacked on top
of or to the right of each other. Stacking adds another dimension to the
chart, since it allows the user to compare sales between as well as within
time periods—like providing a column chart and a pie chart for each time
period. Figure 3.16 shows a stacked 3-D column chart, using the same data
as Figures 3.14 and 3.15.

F I G U R E 3.16: A stacked 3-D column chart

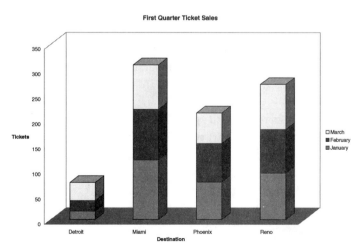

The 3-D charts have three axes. In a 3-D column chart, the x-axis is on the bottom; the vertical axis is the z-axis; the y-axis goes from front to back, providing the "three-dimensional" depth in the chart.

NOTE   Don't worry about memorizing which axis is which in each chart type; there are ways to know which is which when you're creating or editing the chart.

Creating Easy-to-Use Charts

▶ *Objective XL2000.7.2*

The easiest way to create a chart is by using the Chart Wizard. Begin the charting process by selecting the data to be used in the chart. With the exception of the chart's title, everything that appears in the chart will be selected from entries in the worksheet. Make sure that the ranges you select are symmetrical: If you select four labels in rows 9–12 of column A, select data points from the other columns in rows 9–12. If you select labels in columns A–D of row 5, the data series you select should also be in columns A–D.

TIP   If you include blank rows or extra empty columns in your selection, you'll have empty spaces in your chart. Remember that you can hold the Ctrl key to select noncontiguous ranges of data. If you select some cells you don't want to include, press Esc and start again.

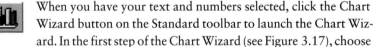 When you have your text and numbers selected, click the Chart Wizard button on the Standard toolbar to launch the Chart Wizard. In the first step of the Chart Wizard (see Figure 3.17), choose a chart type in the Chart Type list box. If the type of chart you want isn't listed, check out the chart types on the Custom Types tab.

F I G U R E   3.17: Step 1 of the Chart Wizard

 For more information about a chart type, select the chart type, click the Chart Wizard's Office Assistant button, and choose Help With This Feature. The Assistant will offer to provide a sample of the selected chart.

After choosing a chart type in the left pane, choose a subtype in the right pane. To see a rough sample of the type and subtype using your data, click the Press And Hold To View Sample button in the Chart Wizard. When you've selected a type and a subtype, click Next to continue.

In the second step of the Chart Wizard, shown in Figure 3.18, you have an opportunity to make sure the range you selected is correct. (If it isn't, click the Collapse Dialog button on the right side of the Data Range text box and re-select the proper range before continuing.) Choose how you would like your data to be laid out by selecting Rows or Columns in the Series In option group. The preview will change to reflect the range and series arrangement you specify. Click Next.

F I G U R E 3.18: Step 2 of the Chart Wizard

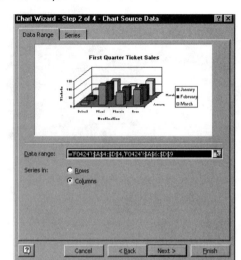

In the Chart Wizard's third step, use the tabs to change options for various aspects of the chart:

Titles   Enter titles for the chart and axes.

Axes   Display or hide axes.

Gridlines   Display gridlines and display or hide the third dimension of a 3-D chart.

Legend   Display and place a legend.

Data Labels   Display text or values as data labels.

Data Table   Show the selected range from the worksheet as part of the chart.

As you change options, the chart preview will reflect your changes. When you've finished setting options, click Next to continue.

TIP   Every chart needs a title. The title provides information that is not already included in the graphical portion of the chart. The chart's picture, legend, and title taken together should answer any questions about the timing, location, or contents of the chart.

In the last step of the Chart Wizard, you can place the chart on the current worksheet or on a new, blank sheet in the same workbook. If the chart is placed on its own sheet, it will print as a full-size, single-page chart whenever it is printed. If you add it to the current worksheet as an object, it will print as part of the worksheet, but it can also be printed separately. Enter a new sheet name, or choose As Object In, and click Finish to create and place the chart.

TIP Don't spend a lot of time deciding whether to place the chart in the current worksheet or in its own worksheet. You can easily move it later.

Moving and Sizing Chart Objects

If you place a chart as an object in the current worksheet, you might find that you'd like to move or resize the chart—especially if the chart is too small or if it covers part of the worksheet data. If you need to, moving a chart in Excel is a snap!

TIP You can always move a chart object to its own worksheet or make a chart an object in another worksheet. Select the chart or chart object, right-click, and choose Location from the shortcut menu to open the Chart Location dialog box.

When the chart is placed in the worksheet, it is selected; it has square *handles* on the corners and sides. If the chart isn't selected, clicking once on the chart selects it. To deselect the chart and return to the worksheet, click once on part of the worksheet that isn't covered by the chart.

TIP You might want to turn on Page Break Preview when sizing and moving charts to make sure they remain within the boundaries of a page. Page Break Preview isn't an option while a chart is selected, so click anywhere in the worksheet to deselect the chart, and then choose View ➤ Page Break Preview.

Moving and Sizing Charts

1. If the chart isn't selected, click once on the chart to select it.

2. To move the selected chart, point to the chart object's border. Hold down the mouse button and drag the chart's border to its new location. Release the mouse button to drop the border and move the chart.

3. To size the chart, move the mouse pointer to one of the handles. Hold down the mouse button and drag the handle to change the size of the chart.

Printing Chart Objects

▶ *Objective XL2000.7.1*

Even if you placed your chart as an object in the current worksheet, you can still print it separately. If the chart is selected when you print, it will print by itself on a full page. If the worksheet is selected, the worksheet prints, including the chart object.

Printing Chart Objects

1. To print a worksheet, including a chart object, activate any worksheet cell before printing.

2. To print a chart object as a full-page chart, select the chart before printing.

Hands On

▶ *Objectives XL2000.7.1 and 7.2*

1. Create any or all of the charts shown in this section. Place at least one chart as an object in the current worksheet.

2. Create a pie chart to illustrate the Cyclops Proposal Software worksheet. Place the chart on the same page as the worksheet. Move and size the chart appropriately, and then print the entire worksheet.

3. Create a series chart to illustrate the payroll information shown in Figure 3.4. Include a data table. Place the chart in a separate worksheet. Print the chart.

4. Select the row and column labels and all the regular numbers (not the formulas) in the Tickets worksheet. Open the Chart Wizard and choose each of the chart types in turn to see how it would chart your data.

Editing and Formatting Charts

Creating a chart in Excel is really easy, and often you can use one of Excel's preformatted charts right "out of the box." But you can also customize charts so that they reflect exactly the emphasis and information that you want to convey.

Adding a Data Series

Excel's charting tools allow you to modify charts quickly and easily. You can, for example, create a simple series chart and then add another data series using drag-and-drop. (You can't add individual data points, just data series.)

Adding Data Series to a Chart

1. In the worksheet, select the data series to be added (be sure to select the same number of columns or rows represented in previous data series).

2. Drag the series and drop it in the chart.

Deleting a Data Series

A chart is a collection of graphic objects. To access the objects, select the chart, and then click the object you want to select. The selected object (data point, data series, title, and so on) will have handles. When an object is selected, you can delete or format the object.

Deleting a Data Series from a Chart

1. In the chart, select the data series or any data point in the series.

2. Press the Delete key on the keyboard.

Modifying and Formatting Charts

▶ Objective XL2000.7.3

The *chart area* is a rectangular area within the chart window bounded by the chart border (refer back to Figure 3.14 for an example). Changing the size of the chart window changes the size of the chart area. All objects in a chart must be within the chart area.

The *plot area* is bounded by the axes and contains the columns, lines, wedges, or other objects used to represent the data points. Objects within the plot area have fixed locations and cannot be moved or individually sized. For example, the x-axis labels must be located near the x-axis. You can, however, resize all the objects in the plot area by increasing or decreasing the plot area itself. (There's an exception to this rule; see "Exploding Pies" later in this section.)

Objects outside the plot area and axes can be sized or moved to other locations in the chart area. The title and legend can be placed above, below, or in the plot area.

Any object in a chart can be selected and then formatted or deleted, with the exception of individual data points. Data points can be formatted, but only data *series* can be added or deleted. To select a data point, first select the data series, and then click once on the data point.

Using the Chart Toolbar

Common formatting options are available on the Chart toolbar, as indicated in Table 3.2. To display the Chart toolbar, right-click any toolbar and click Chart. Select the chart object you want to format from the Chart Objects drop-down list, and then use the toolbar buttons to format the object or the entire chart.

T A B L E 3.2: Chart Toolbar Buttons

Button	Button Name	Function
	Format Object	Opens the Format dialog box for the selected object.

TABLE 3.2: Chart Toolbar Buttons *(continued)*

Button	Button Name	Function
	Chart Type	The drop-down menu lists chart types; clicking the button applies the type indicated on the button face.
	Legend	Displays or hides the legend.
	Data Table	Displays or hides the data table.
	By Row	Uses the selected worksheet rows as a data series.
	By Column	Uses the selected worksheet columns as data series.
	Angle Text Downward	Angles selected text downward.
	Angle Text Upward	Angles selected text upward.

Double-click an object to open the formatting dialog box for the object. For example, double-clicking any column in a data series opens the Format Data Series dialog box, shown in Figure 3.19.

FIGURE 3.19: Format Data Series dialog box

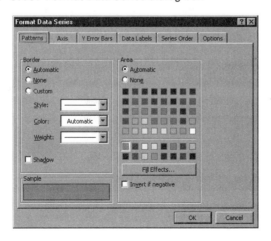

There are five or six pages in this dialog box, and each contains a group of settings for the selected data series. Depending on the chart type, the dialog box may or may not include Shape, Axis, or Y Error Bars tabs.

Patterns   These options are used to set the color and pattern for the series.

Shape   This option is only available with 3-D charts when you can choose from a variety of shapes to display the data series.

Axis   If the chart has more than one series, this tab allows you to add a second vertical axis at the right end of the plot area scaled to this data series.

Y Error Bars   This option adds a graphic display of the standard error; it is used to approximate sampling error when the data in a chart is a statistical sample being applied to a larger population.

Data Labels   Use this tab to add a descriptive label or the numeric value for each data point in the series.

Series Order   This tab allows you to reorder the series in a chart; this is especially helpful with 3-D charts, in which the selected range is charted in reverse order.

Options   This tab offers settings for the bar or column overlap, gap, and color variation.

TIP   For more information on a specific control within the Data Series dialog box, click the dialog box Help button (?), and then click the control.

Similar options are available when you double-click a selected data point, the plot area, chart area, or other chart object.

TIP   You can select any object or series: right-click, then select Format from the shortcut menu. Chart Type is always a shortcut menu option, giving you access to all the types and subtypes. If the entire chart is selected, Chart Options appears on the menu.

Inserting and Formatting Titles

If you decide to insert a title, select the chart, right-click, and open the Chart Options dialog box from the shortcut menu to open the Titles page of the dialog box. You can edit or format existing titles (including place-holders) in a selected chart without having to use the Chart Options from the shortcut menu. To change the text in a title, click once to select the title, and then click again to edit the selected text.

TIP   To separate a title into multiple lines, place the insertion point where you want the second line to begin, hold the Ctrl key and press Enter.

To format a title, double-click a title (or select the title, right-click, and choose Format Title from the shortcut menu) to open the Format Chart Title dialog box. Use the controls in the Patterns, Font, and Alignment pages to format the title as you would format other text.

TIP   To change all the fonts used in a chart, double-click in the chart area and change fonts in the Format Chart Area dialog box.

Exploding Pies

If you want to emphasize specific data points in a pie chart, you can *explode* the pie chart by moving one or more pieces of the pie farther from the center (see Figure 3.20). Usually, you'll move one or two individual slices to emphasize specific data points in the chart.

F I G U R E   3.20: Exploded pie chart

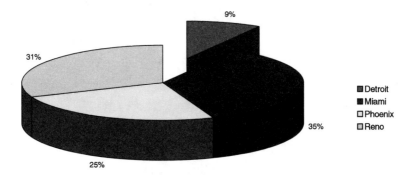

First Quarter Ticket Sales

9%

31%

35%

25%

■ Detroit
■ Miami
□ Phoenix
□ Reno

In Figure 3.20, the Detroit slice has been exploded. Although you can select an exploded pie in the Chart Wizard, the Wizard explodes all slices of the pie or the first slice, depending on which explosion sample you choose. It's easiest to create an unexploded pie of the type you wish and then edit the chart to explode specific slices.

If you want to explode all the slices in an existing chart, select the chart, and then select the pie in the plot area. Excel will put handles on the outside edge of each slice of the pie. Drag any slice away from the center to explode all the pie slices.

To explode a single pie slice, first select the chart, and then click the pie to select the data series. With the series selected, click to select the slice you want to explode and drag the slice away from the center.

When you explode all slices in a pie, each slice gets smaller as you increase the space between the slices. If you explode slices individually, the other slices remain centered in the plot area, and the slices don't get smaller.

Hands On

Objective XL2000.7.3

1. Create or open a 2-D pie chart. Change the chart to a 3-D pie. Explode one slice, and change the color and pattern of all the slices.

2. Create or open a series chart object. Move the chart to its own worksheet. Format each series. Edit the text and then format the chart's title (insert a title if the chart doesn't have one).

Using Custom and Special Formats

You already know how to apply cell formats from the toolbar and the Format Cells dialog box. In this section, you'll kick your skills up a few notches with four tools for specialized formatting: AutoFormat, styles, conditional formatting, and custom formats.

AutoFormatting

Objective XL2000.3.7

Excel's AutoFormat feature includes a number of canned worksheet designs, including formal business, list, and 3-D formats. If you're in a hurry, the predesigned formats allow you to quickly apply a standard format to all or part of a worksheet.

Before you AutoFormat, select the cells to be formatted. This will usually include all the text and numbers in your worksheet, but you might want to apply an AutoFormat to titles or data only. Choose Format ➤ Auto-Format from the menu bar to open the AutoFormat dialog box. Click the Options button to expand the dialog box to display the formatting elements you can apply, as shown in Figure 3.21. For example, you might choose not to apply column widths if you've already adjusted column widths and don't want them changed. As you select formats and turn the Formats To Apply options on and off, the selected preview will change to reflect your choices.

F I G U R E 3.21: AutoFormat dialog box

Working with Styles

Objective XL2000.3.11

AutoFormats are composed of *styles*, specifications about one or more formatting options. Most AutoFormats include several styles: Arial 14-point teal bold for the title; Arial 12-point, accounting format, for the numbers; Arial 12-point bold with a top border for totals.

Creating Your Own Styles

Although you can't create your own AutoFormats, you can create individual styles and apply them to ranges in a worksheet. You can create a style in two ways: from existing formatted entries or by specifying formatting options as you create the style. If the formatting you want to save as a style already exists in the worksheet, select a range that includes the formatting; if not, select a cell that's close to what you want so you'll have less formatting to modify. Choose Format ➤ Style from the menu bar to open the Style dialog box shown in Figure 3.22.

F I G U R E 3.22: Style dialog box

Don't begin creating a style by clicking options. First, enter a descriptive name for the new style in the Style Name text box. As soon as you begin entering the name, previously disabled options will be enabled. Use the check boxes to exclude format settings from the style, or click the Modify button to open the familiar Format Cells dialog box and set other formatting attributes before clicking OK. When you return to the Style dialog box, the Style will include the options you selected in the Format Cells dialog box. Click the Add button to create the style.

Creating a Style

1. Select cells that are the same as, or similar to, the style you want to create.

2. Choose Format ➤ Style from the menu bar to open the Style dialog box shown in Figure 3.22.

3. Enter a new name for the style.

4. Use the check boxes to disable formatting features that should not be included in the style.

Creating a Style *(continued)*

5. Click the Modify button and change any format options you wish in the Format Cells dialog box. Click OK to close the dialog box.

6. Click the Add button to add the new style. Click Close to close the dialog box, or click OK to apply the style to the current selection and close the Style dialog box.

Using Existing Styles

Applying a style that already exists in a workbook is simple:

1. Select the range you want to format.

2. Choose Format ≻ Style to open the Style dialog box.

3. Choose the style you want from the Style Name drop-down list.

4. Click OK.

If the style you want to apply is in a different workbook, you can merge the style into the current workbook and then apply it:

1. Open the workbook that contains the style.

2. Choose Format ≻ Style to open the Style dialog box.

3. Click the Merge button to open the Merge Styles dialog box:

4. Choose the open workbook that contains the styles you want to add to the existing workbook, and then click OK.

5. Choose the merged style from the Style Name drop-down list.

Notice that you don't get to select which styles to merge; you get them all. If you have a style in both workbooks with the same name, Excel will open a dialog box asking if you want to merge these styles, too. If you choose Yes, the styles from the selected workbook will replace styles with the same name in the current workbook. If you choose No, the current styles remain.

> **TIP**   Possible conflicts in style names is a good reason to give styles descriptive rather than functional names.

Deleting and Editing Styles

Styles hang around forever unless you delete them. To delete a style, open the Style dialog box, select the style from the Style Name drop-down list, and click the Delete button.

To change an existing style, choose the style from the Style Name drop-down list. Change any formatting options you wish, and then click the Add button to add the changes to the style.

Conditional Formatting

▶ *Objectives XL2000E.4.3 and E.10.1*

With *conditional formatting*, you can apply formats to selected cells based on a *condition*. A condition is an expression that, when evaluated, is either true or false. Examples of conditions are: Hourly Rate greater than $10.00, State equal to CA, and Cost between 2000 and 3000.

For any given cell, each of the conditions will either be true or false: the value in the cell either is or is not greater than $10.00, equal to CA, or between 2000 and 3000. You can apply font attributes, borders, or patterns to cells based on whether the condition is true or false. In Figure 3.23, for example, all values greater than 200 are bold and have a border.

F I G U R E 3.23: Loan Payment worksheet with conditional formatting

Interest Rate					
10%					
	Amount Borrowed				
Loan Life (Years)	$5,000.00	$10,000.00	$15,000.00	$20,000.00	$25,000.00
					M
1	$420.14	$840.28	$1,260.42	$1,680.56	$2,100.69	O
2	$210.94	$421.88	$632.82	$843.76	$1,054.71	N
3	$141.21	$282.42	$423.63	$564.84	$706.05	T
4	$106.35	$212.69	$319.04	$425.38	$531.73	H
5	$85.43	$170.86	$256.28	$341.71	$427.14	L
6	$71.48	$142.97	$214.45	$285.94	$357.42	Y
7	$61.52	$123.05	$184.57	$246.10	$307.62	
8	$54.06	$108.11	$162.17	$216.22	$270.28	P
9	$48.25	$96.49	$144.74	$192.99	$241.23	M
10	$43.60	$87.20	$130.80	$174.40	$218.00	T

To apply conditional formatting to selected cells, choose Format ➤ Conditional Formatting from the menu bar. The Conditional Formatting dialog box opens (see Figure 3.24).

F I G U R E 3.24: Conditional Formatting dialog box

From the first drop-down list, choose either Cell Value Is to base the formatting on the value in the cell or Formula Is to base the formatting on a formula that returns a value of True or False. Don't let this confuse you; it doesn't matter whether the cell contains a typed-in value or a formula. If you want the format to be applied based on the number or text that appears in a cell, use Cell Value Is. You'll only use Formula Is with specialized functions such as the Date and Logical functions.

In the second drop-down list, choose one of the conditional operators: Between, Not Between, Equal To, Not Equal To, Greater Than, Less Than, Greater Than Or Equal To, or Less Than Or Equal To. In the condition text box, either type in a constant (such as **200**), select a cell in the worksheet, or enter a formula. (There's more about the second and third options in the "Using Cell References in Conditions" section below.)

Now click the Format button to open an abbreviated version of the Format Cells dialog box. Some of the formats are disabled (such as font type and size), so you know you can't use them for conditional formatting. You can, however, pile on borders, shading, and different colors to make cells jump off the page. Choose the format options you want to apply when the condition is true, and then click OK to return to the Conditional Formatting dialog box. Click OK to close the dialog box, and the formats will be applied to the appropriate cells.

What if you want more than one alternate format? For example, you might want to show last month's sales increases in blue and decreases in red. In this case, you need two conditions. Create the first condition in the Conditional Formatting dialog box, and then click the Add button to add another condition.

Using Cell References in Conditions

Objective XL2000.6.4

You can compare the value in a cell to the value in another cell in the worksheet. For example, you might select a cell that shows an average and apply a conditional format to all the numbers that are above average. In this case, each cell you conditionally format will refer to the cell that contains the average, so you'll use an absolute cell reference. Simply click the cell with the average to place the absolute reference in the condition text box.

Using relative references in conditional formats is just as easy. In the section of the Tickets worksheet shown below, February sales that were greater than January sales are bold and shaded:

	A	B	C
1	**Vacation Meisters Ticket Sales**		
2	First Quarter		
3			
4	Destination	January	February
5			
6	Detroit	17	**21**
7	Miami	119	101
8	Phoenix	75	**77**
9	Reno	93	87

To decide what kind of reference to create, think about how you would create a formula for each cell in column C to compare it to the value in column B. Each cell needs its own formula relative to column B, so to create this condition, make sure that you use relative cell references. In this example:

1. Select the cells.

2. Open the Conditional Formatting dialog box and choose Cell Value Is and Greater Than.

3. Click in the conditions text box, then click cell B6. B6 is added as an absolute cell reference: B6.

4. Use the F4 key to change the reference to a relative reference.

Extending Conditional Formatting   You don't have to apply conditional formatting to all the cells in a range at once. You can create conditional formats for one cell and tweak them until they're exactly what you want. Then select the entire range you want to format, including the formatted cell. Choose Format ➤ Conditional Formatting, and the dialog box will open, displaying the format you created. Just click OK, and the format will be adjusted and applied to the other selected cells.

Using Formulas as Conditions

Now add one more flourish: You can compare a cell to a formula. For example, you only want to bold and shade a cell in column C if the value is at least 3 greater than the value in column B. If sales didn't go up by at least three tickets, it's not a substantial enough increase to warrant special formatting. So instead of using the condition greater than B6, create the condition greater than B6+3. Use formulas like this to format the sales that went up more than 20 percent or individual items that represent more than 5 percent of the total budget.

Conditionally Formatting Cells

1. Select the cells you want to format.

2. Choose Format ➢ Conditional Formatting from the menu bar to open the Conditional Formatting dialog box.

3. Choose Cell Value Is (most of the time) or Formula Is.

4. Select a conditional operator.

5. In the condition text box, enter a value, cell reference, or formula.

6. Click the Format button. Set up a format for this condition and click OK.

7. If you have additional conditions or formats, click the Add button and repeat steps 3–6 for each condition.

8. Click OK to close the dialog box and apply conditional formatting.

Using Formatting Codes

Excel includes a huge number of formats, but you might need a particular format that isn't part of the package. You can use codes to create *custom formats* to handle specialized formatting needs. A common use of custom formats is creating formats that include a text string: 10 mpg, $1.75/sq ft, or $3.00/dozen. You create custom formats in the Format Cells dialog box. But before you open the dialog box, let's look at the codes you'll use to create custom formats.

Codes for Numbers

▶ Objective XL2000E.4.2

Each of the codes shown in Table 3.3 is a placeholder for a digit or a character. You string together a number of placeholders to create a format. If a number has more digits to the right of the decimal than there are placeholders, the number will be rounded so it fits in the number of placeholders. For example, if the format has two placeholders to the right of the decimal, 5.988 will be rounded to 5.99.

NOTE Excel differentiates between significant digits and insignificant digits. A *significant digit* is part of a number's "real value." In the value 3.70, the 3 and the 7 are significant; the zero is an *insignificant digit*, because removing it doesn't change the real value of the number. Only zeros can be insignificant. Insignificant zeros after the decimal are called trailing zeros. Different placeholders display or hide insignificant zeros.

TABLE 3.3: Number Format Codes

Code	Use	Example
#	Displays significant digits.	###.## formats 3.50 as 3.5 and 3.977 as 3.98
0	Displays all digits; placeholders to the right of the decimal are filled with trailing zeros, if required.	##0.00 formats 3.5 as 3.50 and .7 as 0.70
?	Displays significant digits and aligns decimal or slash placeholders.	???.?? aligns decimals and displays 3.50 as 3.5, 57.10 as 57.1, and 3.977 as 3.98
/	Displays a number as a fraction.	# ??/?? displays 7.5 as 7 1/2
,	Thousands separator; this code is also used to format numbers as if they were divided by a thousand or a million.	##,### displays 99999 as 99,999; ##, displays 9,000 as 9; ##,, displays 9,000,000 as 9

T A B L E 3.3: Number Format Codes *(continued)*

Code	Use	Example
( )	Formats negative numbers.	(##,###) formats -99999 as (99,999)
–	Places a hyphen in a number.	000-000 formats 123456 as 123-456
" "	Indicates a text string.	###"/per hour" formats 100 as 100/per hour

You can add color to a format. Simply type the name of the color in brackets at the beginning of the format: [BLUE], [GREEN], [RED].

There are a couple of approaches to conditional formatting within a custom format. If you include two formats, separated by a semicolon, Excel uses the first format for positive numbers and the second for negative numbers. For example, the format ##,###; [RED]##,### will format negative numbers in red. If you have three sections of format, the third format is used for zero. The format [BLUE]##; [RED]##; [WHITE]## will display blue positive numbers, red negative numbers, and white zeros. On a white background, this makes zeros disappear. A fourth section can be used for text that appears in the cell (see "Codes for Text" below).

You can enter a condition in brackets, followed by the two formats to be used based on whether the condition is true or false. A common use for a conditional custom format is formatting zip codes when some have nine digits and others have five. The condition [>99999] will be true for nine-digit zip codes, so the format [>99999]00000-0000;00000 will format both nine-digit and five-digit zip codes correctly, including leading zeros.

Codes for Dates and Times

Use the format codes shown in Table 3.4 to create date and time formats. The m code is used for both months and minutes. Excel treats the m as a month code unless it appears directly after a code for hours or before a code for seconds.

If you don't include one of the versions of am/pm, Excel bases time on the 24-hour clock.

T A B L E 3.4: Date and Time Format Codes

Code	Use	Examples
m	Months as ##	Formats January as 1 and December as 12
mm	Months as 00	Formats January as 01 and December as 12
mmm	Months as three-letter abbreviation	Formats January as Jan
mmmm	Month's name spelled out	Formats Jan as January
mmmmm	Month's first letter	Formats January as J and December as D
d	Days as ##	Formats 1 as 1 and 31 as 31
dd	Days as 00	Formats 1 as 01 and 31 as 31
ddd	Days as weekday abbreviation	Formats 1/1/99 as Fri
dddd	Days as weekday	Formats 1/1/99 as Friday
yy	Years as 00	Formats 1999 as 99
yyyy	Years as 0000	Formats 1/1/99 as 1999
h, m, s	Hours, minutes, and seconds as ##	Formats 3 as 3
hh, mm, ss	Hours, minutes, and seconds as 00	Formats 3 as 03
AM/PM	12-hour clock, uppercase	h AM/PM formats 3 as 3 AM
am/pm	12-hour clock, lowercase	hh am/pm formats 3 as 03 am
a/p	12-hour clock, short form	hh:mm a/p formats 3 as 3:00 a

NOTE According to Microsoft, Excel 2000 is fully Y2K compliant. Additional date formats for displaying four-digit years have been added. Choose Format ➤ Cells, click the Number tab, and then scroll through the Type list to see them. For more information, go to www.microsoft.com/technet/topics/year2k/default.htm.

Codes for Text

If you want to include text along with a number in a cell, put quotes around the text string or precede the text with a backslash (\ ). For example, ##"mph" formats 10 as 10mph. If you want to include a format for text entered in a cell, make it the final section in your format. The @ symbol stands for any text typed in the cell, so [BLUE]@ will format text in the cell in blue. (If you just type the format [BLUE], the text won't appear at all, but it would be blue if it did appear!)

If you don't include a text format, text entered in the cell is formatted according to the defaults or the formatting applied with the toolbar and Format Cells dialog box.

Spacing Codes

You'll use spacing codes for two reasons: alignment and filling. In some formats, negative numbers are surrounded by parentheses. If you use parentheses in a custom format, you need to add a space to the end of the positive format that will line up with the right parenthesis in a negative value. (This keeps the decimal points lined up.) To create a one-character space in a format, include an underscore: ##,##0.00_.

You can fill any empty space in a cell by entering an asterisk (*) and then a fill character in the number format. For example, the accounting format begins with an underscore and a dollar sign, followed by an asterisk and a space before the digit placeholders: _$* #,##0.00. This ensures that the dollar sign is one space from the left edge of the cell, and that all the room between the dollar sign and digits is filled with spaces.

Creating a Custom Format

To create a custom format, select the cells to be formatted and open the Format Cells dialog box. When you've decided which format you want to create, you can enter the custom format in the Format Cells dialog box. On the Number page, choose Custom from the Format Type list. The Type list already includes formats. Scroll the list and choose a format similar to the custom format you want to create, and then edit the format, adding or deleting placeholders. Alternatively, you can select the format in the Type text box and begin typing a format from scratch. As you enter a format, the sample will reflect your changes. Click OK to create the format.

To delete a custom format, select it from the Type list, and then click the Delete button in the Format Cells dialog box.

Creating a Custom Format

1. Select the cells to be formatted. Choose Format ➤ Cells from the menu bar or right-click and choose Format Cells from the shortcut menu.

2. On the Number page of the Format Cells dialog box, choose Custom from the category list.

3. Enter a format in the Type text box.

4. Click OK to apply the custom format.

Hands On

Objectives XL2000.3.7, 3.11, 6.4, E.4.2, E.4.3, and E.10.1

1. Use AutoFormat to format an existing worksheet.

2. Create conditional formats in an existing worksheet. Create at least one format that includes two or more conditions.

3. In an existing worksheet, create:

   a) A custom format that includes a text string.

   b) A custom format that includes different colors for positive and negative numbers.

   c) A custom format that prints the word "Zero" if the value in a cell is 0.

4. Create a style suitable for header rows or columns. Select some cells in your worksheet and apply the new style.

Tracking Data with Excel

You've worked with Excel's spreadsheet and charting features. In the next two sections, you'll use Excel's database capabilities to create and manage lists. A *database* is a list with a specific structure defined by its *fields*, the categories of information it contains. A telephone directory, for example, is a printout of a computer database whose fields include last name, first name, middle initial, address, and telephone number. An individual listing in the phone book is a *record* in the database, containing a single set of the fields: one phone user's last name, first name, middle initial, address, and telephone number. Each field must have a unique *field name*: Last-Name, last name, LASTNAME, and LastNameforListing are all possible field names for a field containing last names. In Excel, fields are columns, and each record is an individual row.

The Traverse Tree Sales worksheet (shown in Figure 3.25) is an Excel database. Each field is a separate column. Field names (Month, County, Type, Quantity, and Bundles) are used as column labels. Each individual row is a record.

F I G U R E 3.25: The Traverse Tree database

	A	B	C	D	E	F
1	TRAVERSE TREE SALES					
2	County Cooperative Tree Orders					
3	Deliver for Distribution 15th of Month					
4						
5	Month	County	Type	Quantity	Bundles	
6	Apr-98	Genesee	White Pine	37000	74	
7	Apr-98	Oakland	Blue Spruce	22500	45	
8	Apr-98	Oakland	White Pine	15500	31	
9	Apr-98	Oakland	Concolor Fir	13500	27	
10	Apr-98	Genesee	Blue Spruce	12500	25	
11	Apr-98	Oakland	Scotch Pine	11000	22	
12	Apr-98	Genesee	Frazier Fir	6500	13	
13	May-98	Lake	Blue Spruce	42500	85	
14	May-98	Lake	White Pine	32000	64	
15	May-98	Lake	Frazier Fir	14500	29	
16	May-98	Kalkaska	Blue Spruce	13500	27	
17	May-98	Lake	Concolor Fir	12000	24	
18	May-98	Kalkaska	Concolor Fir	10000	20	
19	May-98	Kalkaska	Frazier Fir	7500	15	
20	Sep-98	Lake	Blue Spruce	31000	62	
21	Sep-98	Lake	White Pine	26500	53	

Microsoft Access is designed specifically to create databases and allows you to create and manage incredibly large numbers of records. Excel databases are limited to the number of rows in a worksheet: 65,536. Despite these and other limitations, Excel's list management features are powerful tools for creating small databases and manipulating smaller sets of records from larger databases.

Creating a database is as simple as creating any other worksheet, but there are two additional rules for worksheets that you intend to use as databases:

Blank rows   Signal the end of a database. *Don't* leave a blank row between column headings and data records. *Do* leave a blank row after all records and before totals, averages, or other summary rows.

Field names   At the top of columns. Field names must be in a single cell and unique within a worksheet. Be consistent: label every column.

NOTE   Any worksheet you've already created can be used as a database, but you might have to delete or add rows or edit column labels to meet these requirements.

Sorting a Database

Objective XL2000E.10.2

Database software must allow you to do two distinct things with data: organize, or *sort*, the data in a specific order (for example, alphabetized by state), and separate, or *filter*, the data to find specific information (for example, all your customers who live in Oregon).

To sort the data in a database, first select any cell in the database (do *not* select more than one cell). Then choose Data ➤ Sort from the menu bar to have Excel select the records in the database and open the Sort dialog box, shown in Figure 3.26.

Excel will select all cells above, below, to the right, and to the left of the cell you selected until it encounters a blank column and row. Excel will examine the top row of the database and assign it as a record by including it in the selection, or deselect it, assuming it is a row of column headings. The last section of the Sort dialog box lets you correct an incorrect selection by specifying whether you have a header row.

F I G U R E   3.26: Excel's Sort dialog box

NOTE   If you didn't select a cell within the database before choosing Data ➤ Sort, Excel will open a message box and warn you that there was no list to select. Click the OK button in the message box, select a cell in the database, and choose Data ➤ Sort again.

In a telephone book, records are sorted initially by last name. This is called a *primary sort*. What if there is a tie: for example, all the people whose last name is Smith? If you know that lots of your records will have the same entry in the primary sort field, you can do a *secondary sort* on another field, such as first name. And if you have two David Smiths, you can use middle initial as a *tertiary sort*. Note that the secondary and tertiary sorts occur only in case of a tie at a higher level of sorting.

You can sort a maximum of three levels using the Sort dialog box. Records can be sorted in *ascending order* (i.e., A–Z or 1–100) or *descending order* (i.e., Z–A or 100–1).

1. In the Sort By text box, enter or use the drop-down menu to select the field name you want to sort by.

2. Choose a sort order.

3. If some of the records have the same value in the Sort By field, use the first of the two Then By text boxes to select the field you want to sort by when there is a tie in the primary sort field. For databases with many similar records (like the family reunion mailing list), you might want to add a tertiary sort.

4. When you have made all the sort selections, click the OK button to sort the database according to the specifications you entered.

TIP You can sort a database that includes no column headings—just records. However, the drop-down lists in all the database dialog boxes contain the words "Column A," "Column B," and so on rather than the field names.

Sorting Data Using the Menu

1. Select any cell within the database.

2. From the menu bar, choose Data ➢ Sort.

3. Select the field you want to sort by from the Sort By drop-down list.

4. Use the Then By drop-down lists to select secondary and tertiary sort fields.

5. Click the OK button to sort the database.

You can also sort a database using the sort buttons on the Standard toolbar. Select a single cell within the *column* you want to sort by. Click the Ascending Sort or Descending Sort button to sort the database. This is an easy way to sort, but it has one major drawback: Excel doesn't allow you to verify that the correct cells have been selected as the database. It's best to sort each database once using the Sort dialog box and ensure that the correct rows and columns have been selected before using the toolbar.

WARNING When sorting, it is vital that all the *columns* of a database are selected. If some columns are not selected, the selected columns will be sorted, but the unselected columns will not be, thus ruining the integrity of the data by mixing up the records. (Another reason why you never include empty columns in a worksheet.) Always check to be sure that all columns were included before sorting. Click Undo immediately if some columns were omitted in a sort.

Once you know how Excel sorts, you can use the sort buttons to do secondary and tertiary sorts. When Excel sorts the records in a database, it only rearranges records when necessary. If a list is already sorted by city, sorting it by state will create a list sorted first by state, then by city within each state, because the existing city sort will only be rearranged to put the states in order. If you need to sort by more than the three fields allowed in the Sort dialog box, sort the least important field first and work backward through the sort fields to the primary sort field.

Sorting Using the Toolbar

1. Select any cell within the database in the column you want to sort by.

2. Click the Ascending or Descending Sort button.

3. For secondary, tertiary, and other sorts, use the Ascending and Descending Sort buttons to work through the sorts in reverse order.

Filtering a Database

Objective XL2000E.10.6

Many times you'll want to work with a database *subset*, a group of records in the database. For example, you might want to print all sales records for one salesperson, all the orders from one client, or all the customers who haven't made a purchase this year. A *filter* is used to select records that meet a specific criterion (which you enter to set the filter) and temporarily hide all the other records.

To set up an AutoFilter, select any cell in the database and choose Data ➢ Filter ➢ AutoFilter. Excel reads every record in the database and creates a filter criteria list for each field:

NOTE If you have occupied rows above the header row in a database, insert a blank row above the header row or select the entire database before turning on AutoFilter.

Click the drop-down arrow that appears next to each field name (see Figure 3.27) to access the field's criteria list:

All   The default criteria setting in each field, meaning that the contents of the field are not being used to limit the records displayed.

Top 10   Used in numeric fields to display the top or bottom ten, five, or any other number or percentage of values.

Custom   Prompts you to create a custom filter (see "Creating a Custom Filter" below) for choices that don't appear on the list.

F I G U R E   3.27: Database with an AutoFilter

	A	B	C	D	E	F
1	TRAVERSE TREE SALES					
2	County Cooperative Tree Orders					
3	Deliver for Distribution 15th of Month					
4						
5	Month	County	Type	Quantity	Bundles	
6	Apr-98	Genesee	White Pine	37000	74	
7	Apr-98	Oakland	Blue Spruce	22500	45	
8	Apr-98	Oakland	White Pine	15500	31	
9	Apr-98	Oakland	Concolor Fir	13500	27	
10	Apr-98	Genesee	Blue Spruce	12500	25	
11	Apr-98	Oakland	Scotch Pine	11000	22	
12	Apr-98	Genesee	Frazier Fir	6500	13	
13	May-98	Lake	Blue Spruce	42500	85	
14	May-98	Lake	White Pine	32000	64	
15	May-98	Lake	Frazier Fir	14500	29	
16	May-98	Kalkaska	Blue Spruce	13500	27	
17	May-98	Lake	Concolor Fir	12000	24	
18	May-98	Kalkaska	Concolor Fir	10000	20	
19	May-98	Kalkaska	Frazier Fir	7500	15	
20	Sep-98	Lake	Blue Spruce	31000	62	
21	Sep-98	Lake	White Pine	26500	53	
22						

When you apply a filter, all the records not included in the subset are hidden, as shown in Figure 3.28, where the records are being filtered on Lake County. The number of records found and the total number of records in the database are displayed in the status bar. Each record retains its original row number; the row numbers of filtered records appear in blue. The field criteria drop-down arrow for the filtered field turns blue, to show that it is being actively used to filter the database.

Filter on more than one field to select, for example, all the Scotch Pine sales in Oakland County. Set the criteria using each field's drop-down list. Only records that meet all the criteria you selected will be included in the filtered subset. To redisplay the entire database, change the filter criteria for all filtered fields back to All, or simply choose Data ➤ Filter ➤ Show All. You'll know at a glance that all filters are set to All because the drop-down arrows and the row headings will return to the default color.

F I G U R E 3.28: Filtering a database

	A	B	C	D	E	F
1	TRAVERSE TREE SALES					
2	County Cooperative Tree Orders					
3	Deliver for Distribution 15th of Month					
4						
5	Month ▼	County ▼	Type ▼	Quantity ▼	Bundles ▼	
13	May-98	Lake	Blue Spruce	42500	85	
14	May-98	Lake	White Pine	32000	64	
15	May-98	Lake	Frazier Fir	14500	29	
17	May-98	Lake	Concolor Fir	12000	24	
20	Sep-98	Lake	Blue Spruce	31000	62	
21	Sep-98	Lake	White Pine	26500	53	
22						
23						

TIP Sometimes the field criteria drop-down list has so many entries that it runs off the top or bottom of the screen. You can scroll down to see a list that runs off the bottom. If the list runs off the top, insert several blank rows above the column labels to force the filtered list down the screen.

Applying and Using the AutoFilter

1. Select any cell in the database.

2. Choose Data ➤ Filter ➤ AutoFilter to turn on the filter.

3. Click the drop-down arrow for the field you want to use to filter, and choose a filter from the criteria drop-down list.

4. To see all the records in the database, reset all filter criteria to All.

Using the Top 10 Filter

When you choose Top 10 as your filter criterion, the Top 10 AutoFilter dialog box opens:

In the first drop-down box, choose Top or Bottom, depending on whether you want to see the highest or lowest values in the database. In the spin box, enter a number larger than 0. In the last drop-down box, choose Items or Percent. To see the top 10 percent of the scores in a column of test scores, choose Top, enter **10**, then choose Percent. The Top 10 filter only works with numbers (including dates and times).

Creating a Custom Filter

When you filter using the drop-down criteria, you are always looking for records that exactly equal specific criteria or fall in a Top 10 criterion. Custom filters give you access to other ways to set criteria:

- All records with fields that are *not* equal to a criterion
- Records that are greater than or less than a criterion
- Records that meet one condition or another

To create a custom filter, choose Custom from the drop-down criteria list to open the Custom AutoFilter dialog box, shown in Figure 3.29.

F I G U R E 3.29: Custom AutoFilter dialog box

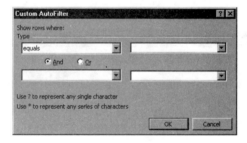

The first drop-down box under Show Rows Where opens a list of operators. The list includes regular logical operators such as Equals and Is Greater Than Or Equal To, but as you scroll the list, you'll notice other operators that allow you to look for entries that do or do not begin with, end with, or contain a string.

The right drop-down list displays the record entries in the field from the field criteria list. To find all records that are *not* in Lake County, choose Not Equal To as the operator and select Lake from the drop-down. You can also enter text in the criteria control. In the bottom of the dialog box, notice that you can use the * and ? wildcards to broaden the search string. To find all orders for Oakland and Ottawa counties, you could:

- Use the wildcard character and search for `Equals O*`
- Use the Begins With Type option and search for `Begins with O`

Using AND and OR   The AND and OR options are used when you want to filter by more than one criterion in a column. AND is used to establish the upper and lower ends of a range and is almost always used with numeric entries: "Quantity is greater than 100 AND Quantity is less than 201" leaves only the quantities between 100 and 201. OR is used to filter by two different criteria: "Lake County OR Oakland County."

If you use AND when you mean OR, you'll often get a *null set*—no records. (There are no records in Lake County AND Oakland County— it's one or the other.) If you use OR when you mean AND, you'll get all the records. (Every record is either less than 201 OR greater than 100.)

Creating a Custom Filter

1. If the AutoFilter is not turned on, turn it on (choose Data ➤ Filter ➤ AutoFilter). Choose Custom from the Filter Criteria drop-down list to open the Custom AutoFilter dialog box.

2. Set the operator (Type) for the first criterion.

3. Enter or select the first criterion from the drop-down list.

4. Set an operator, and enter or select the second criterion.

5. Set AND for a range; set OR to filter for more than one possible value.

6. Click OK to apply the custom filter.

The filter criteria drop-downs don't appear when you print a database, so there usually isn't a reason to turn the AutoFilter off until you are done working with a database. To turn the AutoFilter off, choose Data ➤ Filter ➤ AutoFilter again.

Working with Filtered Records

You can work with the filtered set of records in a number of ways. If you print the database while it is filtered, only the filtered records will print; this is a quick way to generate reports based on any portion of the information in the Excel database.

Filtering is also useful when you need to create charts using part of the data in the database. Filter the records you want to chart, and then select and chart the information as you would normally.

WARNING   When you create a chart based on a filter, you need to print the chart before changing the filter criteria. Changing the criteria changes the chart. If you need to create a permanent chart, create a new database with the subset you want to chart.

Creating a New Database from a Filtered Subset

1. Filter the active database to create a filtered subset.

2. Select the filtered database, including the column labels and any other titles you wish to copy.

3. Click the Copy button or choose Edit ➤ Copy.

4. Select the first cell where you want the new database to appear.

5. Press Enter (or click Paste) to paste the database.

Extracting a Subset

Objective XL2000E.10.7

If you prefer, you can create a subset by *extracting* the subset's records from the database using Excel's Advanced Filter. This requires you to establish a *criteria range* that includes the column labels from your database and one or more criteria that you enter directly below the labels.

The criteria range is the heart of advanced filtering. If the criteria range is incorrect, the extracted data will be wrong—so take your time with this. The column labels must be precisely the same as they are in the database, so begin by copying the column labels to another location in your workbook (a separate worksheet that you name Criteria is good).

Then, on this same worksheet, type the criteria you want to establish. For example, if you want to extract records where the Quantity is over 10000, enter >10000 in the cell just below the Quantity column label. If you have more than one criterion in a single column (for example, County = Genesee or County = Oakland), use one cell for each criterion:

Month	County	Type	Quantity	Bundles
	Genesee			
	Oakland			

There are two ways to filter for two criteria in separate columns, based on whether you want to use AND or OR. Enter criteria on the same row for an AND condition:

Month	County	Type	Quantity	Bundles
	Genesee		>20000	

Place criteria on separate rows for an OR condition:

Month	County	Type	Quantity	Bundles
	Genesee			
			>20000	

In this example, criteria are established to find quantities over 20,000 in Oakland County or over 10,000 in Lake County:

Month	County	Type	Quantity	Bundles
	Oakland		>20000	
	Lake		>10000	

You can't create this last criterion with an AutoFilter in one pass. You would need to find each county separately. A need to mix AND and OR conditions is one of the two reasons to use an Advanced Filter.

TIP   You'll need to refer to the criteria range in the Advanced Filter dialog box, so you might want to name it.

When the criteria range is set, click anywhere in the database and open the Advanced Filter dialog box (choose Data ➢ Filter ➢ Advanced Filter) to see the second reason to use an advanced filter: You can instruct Excel to return only unique records, as shown in Figure 3.30.

F I G U R E 3.30: Advanced Filter dialog box

Excel will automatically select your database for the List Range text box.
Select the Criteria Range text box and identify your criteria range, including the column labels. Choose whether you want to filter the records in
their current location (as AutoFilter does) or extract the records by copying them to another location. If you choose another location, the Copy To
text box will be enabled so that you can select the first cell of the range
where the filtered records should be copied.

NOTE   As with any copy operation, just select one cell; if you select a
range, it must match exactly the range required by the extracted data. Be
sure that there is room in the destination area for the extracted data.

You can enter a cell in any open workbook in the Copy To text box, so
you can put the filtered subset of your database in a different workbook
or a different worksheet than the original database. If you want to eliminate duplicate records from the filtered list, turn on the Unique Records
Only checkbox. Finally, click OK, and Excel will filter in place or extract
data as you have indicated.

TIP   You have a database with 10,000 records, many of them duplicate
records. Don't eliminate the duplicates manually. Set up a criteria range
without criteria and use the Unique Records Only option to extract a list
without duplicates.

When you use the Advanced Filter to filter in place, the filtered subset will
have blue row numbers, just as it does with AutoFilter. To turn the filter
off, choose Data ➢ Filter ➢ Show All.

Using the Advanced Filter

1. Copy the database column labels to another location.

2. Enter criteria in the cells directly under the column labels.

3. Select any cell in the database and choose Data ➢ Filter ➢ Advanced
Filter to open the Advanced Filter dialog box.

Using the Advanced Filter *(continued)*

4. Check to ensure Excel has accurately identified the database range. If not, adjust it in the List Range text box.

5. Enter the criteria range in the Criteria Range list box.

6. Choose the Filter In Place or Copy To option.

7. If you are extracting (copying) the filtered list to another location, enter the upper-left cell of that location in the Copy To text box.

8. Enable or disable the Unique Records Only checkbox.

9. Click OK to create the filter.

Creating Subtotals

Objective XL2000E.10.5

You can create subtotals based on any field in the database. A *subtotal* is not necessarily a sum; it can be an average, count, minimum, maximum, or other statistical calculation based on a group of records. Before subtotaling, you need to sort the database on the field you want to subtotal. For example, if you want to subtotal each month's orders, first sort by month. Then, select a cell anywhere in the database and choose Data ➤ Subtotals to open the Subtotal dialog box, shown in Figure 3.31.

F I G U R E 3.31: Subtotal dialog box

In the At Each Change In drop-down list, select the field the database is sorted on. The trigger for Excel to insert a subtotal is a change in this column. If you choose an unsorted field, you'll get a multitude of subtotals (interesting, but useless). Select a type of subtotal from the Use Function drop-down list. In the Add Subtotal To control, select each field you want to subtotal. You can subtotal more than one field at a time, but you have to use the same function: average three fields, sum three fields, and so on.

Enable the Replace Current Subtotals checkbox if you have subtotaled earlier and want to replace the former set with new subtotals. If you want both sets of subtotals to appear (for example, sums and averages), deselect this option.

If you are going to print the worksheet with subtotals and want each sub-totaled set of records to print on a separate page, check the Page Break Between Groups checkbox. Selecting Summary Below Data places a summary (grand total, grand average) row at the bottom of the database.

When you have entered the information for subtotals, click the OK button to add subtotals, as shown in Figure 3.32. To remove subtotals from a worksheet, open the Subtotal dialog box again and click the Remove All button.

F I G U R E 3.32: Traverse Tree Sales subtotals

	Month	County	Type	Quantity	Bundles
1	County Coorperative Tree Orders				
2	Deliver for Distribution 15th of Month				
3					
4	Month	County	Type	Quantity	Bundles
5	Apr-00	Genesee	White Pine	37000	75
6	Apr-00	Oakland	Blue Spruce	22500	45
7	Apr-00	Oakland	White Pine	15500	31
8	Apr-00	Oakland	Concolor Fir	13500	27
9	Apr-00	Genesee	Blue Spruce	12500	25
10	Apr-00	Oakland	Scotch Pine	11000	22
11	Apr-00	Genesee	Frazier Fir	6500	13
12	Apr-00 Total				238
13	May-00	Lake	Blue Spruce	42500	85
14	May-00	Lake	White Pine	32000	64
15	May-00	Lake	Concolor Fir	12000	24
16	May-00	Kalkaska	Concolor Fir	10000	20
17	May-00	Kalkaska	Frazier Fir	7500	15
18	May-00 Total				208
19	Sep-00	Lake	Blue Spruce	31000	62
20	Sep-00	Lake	White Pine	26500	53
21	Sep-00 Total				115
22	Grand Total				561

Creating Subtotals

1. In your database, sort the records on the field you want to trigger the subtotal.

2. Select any cell in the database.

3. Choose Data ➤ Subtotals from the menu bar.

4. Select the sorted field from the At Each Change In drop-down list.

5. Select a type of subtotal.

6. Select the numeric fields to be subtotaled when the value of the At Each Change In field changes.

7. If necessary, change the settings for Replace Current Subtotals, Page Break Between Groups, and Summary Below Data.

8. Click OK to generate subtotals.

9. To remove subtotals, choose Data ➤ Subtotals, and then click Remove All.

Querying a Database

Objective XL2000E.10.8

Combine Excel 2000's database features with the power of Microsoft Query, and you have an analysis and reporting tool for any ODBC-compliant database on your system. *ODBC* (Open Database Connectivity) is an industry standard for database access. ODBC was not developed by Microsoft, but is often thought of as a Microsoft standard, because Windows was the first operating system to support ODBC. Access and SQL Server are both ODBC-compliant, as are many other database programs. For example, you may want to retrieve information from an Oracle database and work with it in Excel 2000. To do this, you will use a combination of software:

- Microsoft Query to create a query

- Excel 2000 to open the query

- The ODBC Driver Manager, which is part of Windows

- The Oracle database
- A specific ODBC driver designed to allow Query to "talk to" the Oracle database

The combination of a database and the ODBC driver to connect to it is called a *data source*. Excel 2000 includes ODBC drivers for the following programs:

- dBASE
- Microsoft Access 2000
- Microsoft Excel
- Microsoft SQL Server
- Microsoft SQL Server OLAP Services
- Oracle
- Paradox
- Text database files (for example, comma-delimited files)

To query a database in Excel 2000, you select a data source, then specify the data you want to return to Excel.

Selecting a Data Source

From Excel, choose Data ➤ Get External Data ➤ New Database Query to launch Microsoft Query. Query will display the Choose Data Source dialog box, shown in Figure 3.33. The Databases page of the dialog box shows data sources that have already been created as well as available ODBC drivers you can use to connect to databases and create data sources. The Queries page has a list of saved queries. OLAP Cubes are multidimensional data sources.

F I G U R E 3.33: Select a data source for your query

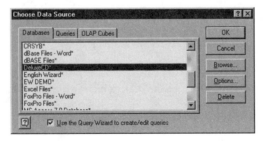

If you've created ODBC data sources to use with programs like Seagate Crystal Reports, Cognos Impromptu, or Access 2000, they'll be listed on the Databases page, and you can use them in Excel. If you don't have a data source and need to create one, visit this book's page on the Sybex Web site (www.sybex.com) for instructions on creating a data source. Select your data source, and then click OK to launch the Query Wizard.

Creating Queries with the Query Wizard

The Query Wizard opens with a list of the views (queries), tables, and columns (fields) in your data source. In Figure 3.34, the data source is the Deluxe CD database that is included with Windows 98 and Windows Plus.

F I G U R E 3.34: Select fields or entire tables to include in your query.

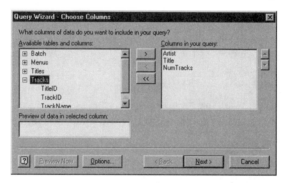

The left pane of the Query Wizard works like Windows Explorer. Tables and views have a plus sign; click the plus sign to display the table's fields. The right pane displays the columns included in your query. Select a view, table, or column, and use the pick buttons to move the selection to the right pane. To display data from the column for a quick reminder of its contents, select a column in the left pane and click the Preview Now button in the dialog box. You can select data from more than one related table or view.

When you have finished selecting columns, click the Next button. If you selected columns from more than one table, the Query Wizard will check to see if there are relationships between the tables before proceeding. If any of the tables from which you included columns is not related to the others in the data source, you'll be prompted to leave the Wizard and define the relationships in Microsoft Query. You can Cancel the message and remove some fields from the Query Wizard, or click OK and move into Query so you can indicate the appropriate relationships.

In the next step of the Query Wizard, if you want to restrict the results based on values in specific columns, use the drop-down lists and text boxes to specify filter criteria. Use the AND operator between criteria when all conditions must be met; use OR when any of the conditions should place a record in the query result set. After you've set any filters, click Next.

When setting sort columns, you can set up to three; then click Next. In the final step of the Query Wizard, you can save the query by clicking the Save Query button. (This saves the query so it can be used in another Excel workbook or another program. When you save the current Excel workbook, it will save a copy of the query.) Finally, choose Return The Data To Excel and click Finish. An Excel dialog box will open so you can specify the placement of the results.

Working with Query Results

In Excel, you can use the query result set as you would any Excel data. You can, for example, add formulas, create totals or averages, and chart the information.

When the query results open in Excel, the External Data toolbar also opens. If you want to change the query, click the Edit Query button to launch Microsoft Query and reopen the Query Wizard so you can add or delete tables and columns, or change filters or sort order.

To view the latest data from the data source, click the Refresh Data button on the Query toolbar to rerun your query. The Refresh All button reruns all queries in the current workbook.

Outlining Worksheets

Objective XL2000E.10.3

Outlining makes it easy to focus in on the data within a worksheet that contains multiple levels of detail. For instance, a budget worksheet might have a line item for "4th Quarter Revenue." That line item consists of data from each of the individual sales offices in the East Coast and West Coast regions, and all the detail rolls up into the main line item. Excel's outlining feature allows you to view as much or little of the detail as you want.

When you add subtotals, Excel's outlining feature automatically turns on. Use the level (1, 2, 3, and so on) buttons in the upper-left corner of the worksheet window (see Figure 3.32) to view different levels of the outline. Use the plus and minus buttons to expand or collapse sections of the outline. In Figure 3.32, all sections of the worksheet are expanded. Clicking any one of the minus buttons, such as the one next to April 00 Total, collapses that section of the worksheet.

You can outline any worksheet with formulas. Just choose Data ➤ Group And Outline ➤ AutoOutline to turn the outline on or off.

Using a Data Form

> *Objective XL2000E.10.4*

Data forms provide an easy way to enter or search for data yourself, and a bulletproof way to let a less accomplished user enter data. To open a data form, select any cell in a database and choose Data ➤ Form. The first record in the database will be displayed in the data form. A sample data form for Traverse Tree Sales is shown in Figure 3.35.

F I G U R E 3.35: Traverse Tree Sales data form

Because data forms have a portrait orientation, they're particularly helpful when the columns in your database exceed the width of the screen.

Using the form allows you to see all the database fields at once without scrolling horizontally—use the vertical scroll bar or the arrow keys to browse the records. Use the Tab key to move between fields in the form; pressing Enter moves to the next record.

You can change the contents of a field by editing the text box next to the field name. The contents of *calculated fields* (like the Bundles field in Figure 3.35) are displayed without a text box, because you can't edit them. However, if you change a value that a calculated field is based on, Excel will recalculate the field. To discard changes made to a record, click the Restore button before moving to another record.

Adding and Deleting Records

Clicking the New button or scrolling to the last record of the database opens the New Record form. Enter each field in the appropriate text box control. When you have entered information for the last field, press Enter or, if you want to keep entering new records, click the New button again. Press the up arrow or click the scroll bar to close the New dialog box.

To delete the record currently displayed in the data form, click the Delete button. A dialog box appears, warning that the record will be permanently deleted. Pay attention to the warning—clicking Undo will *not* bring the record back. Click the OK button to delete the record's row from the database.

Adding and Deleting Records with a Data Form

1. Select any cell in the database.

2. Choose Data ➤ Form from the menu bar to open the data form.

3. To add a record, click the New button or scroll to the end of the database. Enter the record using the data form text box controls. Tab between controls. Press Enter on the last field of a record to open another New Record form. Press the up arrow or scroll the database to close the New Record form.

4. To delete the record displayed in the form, click the Delete button. When prompted, click OK to delete the row that contains the record.

NOTE   It isn't always more convenient to use the data form. Excel's Auto-Complete feature (which fills in the remaining characters if the first few characters you type in a cell match an existing entry in that column) doesn't work with the data form, so you have to type each entry fully. However, when you close the data form, you'll notice that Excel has automatically filled calculated values.

Hands On

Objectives XL2000E.10.2, E.10.3, E.10.4, E.10.5, E.10.6, E.10.7, and E.10.8

1. Open any worksheet that can be used as a database, or create the Traverse Tree Sales worksheet in Figure 3.25. The values in Bundles are formulas (Qty/500). Sort the database:

   a) Using the Sort dialog box

   b) Using the toolbar buttons

   c) By one field

   d) By two fields (primary and secondary sort)

2. Open any worksheet that can be used as a database. Filter the database:

   a) By a value in a field

   b) Using a Top 10 filter in a numeric field

   c) Using a custom filter with the Begins With or Contains Type

   d) Using a custom filter and AND or OR

   e) Extract a subset of data based on criteria you set

3. Open any worksheet that can be used as a database.

   a) Create at least two types of subtotals.

   b) Use the outline buttons to show/hide different levels of the outline.

   c) Remove the subtotals.

4. Create a data form for the worksheet like the Traverse Tree Sales worksheet. Enter at least five records using the form.

5. Query a database created in an application other than Excel. Retrieve all the data from one table.

   a) Edit the query and remove one or more fields from the query.

   b) In Excel, add a calculation or formula that uses the query results. Refresh the query data.

CHAPTER

4

Taking Excel to the Max

Chapter 3 introduced you to several tools for working with data. In this chapter, you'll take Excel one step further with sophisticated analysis using pivot tables and data validation. You'll learn about features that separate casual users from Excel experts, proficiencies that make other users wonder, "How did they *do* that?" After pivot tables, we'll look at other nifty analysis and presentation tools including Goal Seek, Solver, custom views, and the Report Manager. Throughout the chapter, we'll use Excel practice worksheets to illustrate concepts, beginning with the Traverse Tree Sales example from Chapter 3.

Analyzing Data with Pivot Tables

Often when you work with Excel, you use it to support decision making: the data provide a means to an end. *Pivot tables* are the best tools for analyzing the endless rows and columns in a typical database. A pivot table summarizes the columns of information in a database in relationship to each other.

Creating Pivot Tables

Objectives XL2000E.11.3 and E.11.6

The Traverse Tree Sales database shown in Figure 4.1 is a small database, but it would still take time and effort to answer the following questions precisely:

- How many trees of each type were delivered each month?
- How many blue spruces were delivered each month?
- How many white pines were delivered in each county?
- What was the average number of each type of tree sold to Oakland County?

F I G U R E 4.1: Traverse Tree Sales database

	Traverse Tree Sales				
1	Traverse Tree Sales				
2	County Cooperative Tree Orders				
3					
4	Month	County	Type	Quantity	Bundles
5	January, 1999	Genesee	White Pine	37000	74
6	January, 1999	Oakland	Blue Spruce	22500	45
7	January, 1999	Oakland	White Pine	15500	31
8	January, 1999	Oakland	Concolor Fir	13500	27
9	January, 1999	Genesee	Blue Spruce	12500	25
10	February, 1999	Oakland	Scotch Pine	11000	22
11	February, 1999	Genesee	Frazier Fur	6500	13
12	February, 1999	Lake	Blue Spruce	42500	85
13	February, 1999	Lake	White Pine	32000	64
14	March, 1999	Lake	Frazier Fur	14500	29
15	March, 1999	Kalkaska	Blue Spruce	13500	27
16	March, 1999	Lake	Concolor Fir	12000	24
17	March, 1999	Kalkaska	Concolor Fir	10000	20
18	April, 1999	Kalkaska	Frazier Fur	7500	15
19	April, 1999	Lake	Blue Spruce	31000	62
20	April, 1999	Lake	White Pine	26500	53

You could sort the list and then add subtotals to answer any one of these questions. Then, to answer any other question, you would have to sort and subtotal again. A single pivot table helps you answer all the above questions and more, with much less effort than sorting and filtering.

NOTE If you have data that resides outside of Excel in an ODBC or OLE DB–compliant database such as Microsoft Access or Oracle, you can create a pivot table by retrieving the data through Microsoft Query. (See Chapter 3 for information on querying databases in Excel 2000.)

Using the PivotTable Wizard

You use a Wizard to create pivot tables in Excel 2000. To launch the PivotTable And PivotChart Wizard, select any cell in a database and choose Data ➤ PivotTable And PivotChart Report. In the first step of the Wizard, select a data source: data in a single Excel database, data from an external source such as Microsoft Access, data that you want to consolidate from several worksheets or sources, or an existing pivot table or pivot chart. You also specify whether you want to create a pivot table or a pivot chart with a pivot table.

In the Wizard's second step, verify the range of the database. A flashing line appears around a suggested range of cells. Use the scroll bars to verify that the entire database—including the field names—is selected. If there is no range selected, or if the range is incorrect, select the correct range before clicking the Next button.

TIP Excel identifies a database as a range of cells bounded by the edge of the worksheet or by an empty row or column. If Excel doesn't select the entire database, we encourage you to close the Wizard, insert/delete rows and columns to properly define your database area, and then start the Wizard again.

In the third step of the Wizard, select a location for the pivot table: a new worksheet or an existing one. If you want to place the pivot table in an existing worksheet, choose the Existing Worksheet option and then select a cell for the upper-left corner of the pivot table.

You'll be able to modify the arrangement of the pivot table's fields after the pivot table is created, but you can set the initial layout in the Wizard. Click the Layout button to open the dialog box shown in Figure 4.2.

F I G U R E 4.2: The Layout dialog box of the PivotTable And PivotChart Wizard

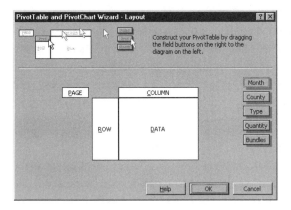

A pivot table contains four areas: the Page number, the Column labels, the Row labels, and the Data. Each area has a corresponding layout area in the Layout dialog box. At the right side of the dialog box is a group of *field buttons*, one for each field name in the database. You design the pivot table layout by dragging the field buttons into one of the four sections of the layout area. The Row, Column, and Data areas must have fields assigned to them; Page is an optional area.

Place fields you want to compare in the Row and Column areas. For example, you might want to compare sales regions by month or by types of trees sold by county. When the table is created, Excel will examine the fields you choose. Each unique entry in a field becomes a row or column heading in the pivot table.

The Page area works like a filter in the completed pivot table. If you'll need to create separate reports for values in one or more columns (such as a separate report for each department in a company or each county in our example), drag that field's button to the Page area.

Information in the Data area is summarized using the SUM, MIN, MAX, COUNT, or AVERAGE functions, so numeric fields are generally placed in the Data layout area. (With a non-numeric field you can only COUNT the number of entries.) For Traverse Tree Sales, we could place either Quantity, Bundles, or both in the Data area.

As you drop a field button in the Data area, Excel will indicate the type of summary that will be performed. SUM is the default for numeric fields. To change the type of summary, double-click the field button to open the PivotTable Field dialog box, then choose a summarization method from the list:

Click the Number button in the PivotTable Field dialog box to format the numbers for this field (the default is General), or wait and format the completed pivot table. Clicking the Options button extends the PivotTable Field dialog box so that you can perform custom calculations. Click OK to close the dialog box and return to the Layout dialog box. Click OK again to return to the PivotTable And PivotChart Wizard.

Click the Options button in the Wizard to open the PivotTable Options dialog box, shown in Figure 4.3. You can name the pivot table just as you name any other range of cells. If you don't name it, Excel will give it a riveting name such as PivotTable1. For more information about any other option, click the dialog box's Help (?) button, and then click the option. When you are finished setting options, click OK to return to the Pivot-Table And PivotChart Wizard.

FIGURE 4.3: Excel's PivotTable Options dialog box

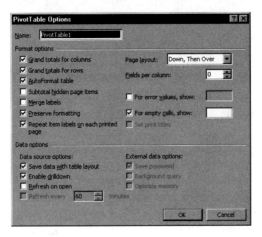

Click Finish to close the Wizard and create the PivotTable Report. The pivot table in Figure 4.4 shows the total trees sold by county and month. The PivotTable toolbar will also open.

FIGURE 4.4: PivotTable Report

Type	(All)				
Sum of Quantity	Month				
County	Jan-99	Feb-99	Mar-99	Apr-99	Grand Total
Genesee	49500	6500			56000
Kalkaska			23500	7500	31000
Lake		74500	26500	57500	158500
Oakland	51500	11000			62500
Grand Total	101000	92000	50000	65000	308000

Using the PivotTable Toolbar   If the PivotTable toolbar does not appear once your PivotTable Report has been created, turn it on by choosing View ➤ Toolbars ➤ PivotTable. The PivotTable toolbar lets you change the completed table's layout and options:

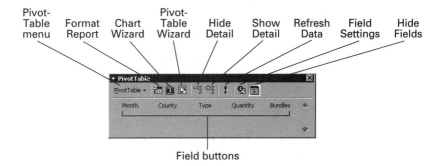

Field buttons

Objective XL2000E.11.1

Format Report displays a group of AutoFormats appropriate for pivot tables. To apply the AutoFormat, select a format sample and click OK.

Clicking the Chart Wizard button creates a PivotTable Chart. If you want to return to the Wizard, just click the PivotTable Wizard toolbar button.

To drill down in the pivot table and reveal the details underlying the data in a cell, select the cell and click the Show Detail button. Excel will extract the details records in another worksheet.

Perhaps the most amazing feature of Excel's implementation of pivot tables is the ability to quickly generate reports for any column of data in the original database. Simply move the field you want to create reports for to the Page area, and then either click the arrow on the PivotTable button and select Show Pages from the menu, or right-click anywhere in the pivot table and choose Show Pages from the shortcut menu. Excel will create a separate pivot table for each value in the field in the Pages area. Check it out—each pivot table appears on its own sheet, and Excel even names them all.

Filtering Pivot Tables   If you need to work with some but not all of the values in a field, use the PivotTable Filter feature:

1. Click the arrow attached to the field button in the Row or Column area.

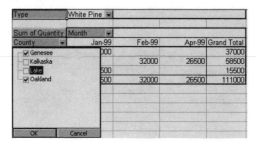

2. Turn values on or off until the values you want to see in the pivot table are enabled.

3. Click OK.

Changing Pivot Table Layout

There are a number of ways to summarize a database. Rather than create a new pivot table, you can change the layout of an existing one. The field buttons you placed in the Page, Column, and Row areas are in the pivot table; change the table by dragging a field button to another area, and Excel will update the table. For example, if you want to view the data in Figure 4.4 by county and date, you can drag the County button to the Column area and the Month button to the Row area. The pivot table will change to reflect the new layout.

Drag a field button from the PivotTable toolbar and drop it in the table to add a new field. To remove a field from the pivot table, in the Layout dialog box drag the field button out of the pivot table area.

Keeping the PivotTable Up-to-Date   A pivot table is dynamically linked to the database used to create the table. If you edit values within the database, simply choose Data ➤ Refresh Data, or click the Refresh Data button on the PivotTable toolbar; Excel will update the pivot table to reflect the database changes.

However, if you add rows or columns to the database, you *cannot* simply refresh the data. You must return to the PivotTable And PivotChart Wizard and identify the new range of records that should be included in the table. If you don't, the pivot table values won't include the added data.

To update the range being used by the pivot table, choose Data ➤ Pivot-Table And PivotChart Report from the menu bar, or click the PivotTable menu in the toolbar and choose Wizard. The PivotTable Wizard will open at step 3. Reselect the database, or hold Shift and extend the current selection. Click the Finish button to close the PivotTable And PivotChart Wizard and return to the updated pivot table.

Creating Pivot Charts

Objective XL2000E.11.3

Pivot charts can be created at the same time you generate a pivot table or later on after you have studied the pivot table. The default pivot chart type is a simple column chart, but you can change the chart to any of Excel's other chart types, except for the scatter, bubble, and stock charts.

You can rearrange the way the pivot table data fields are displayed on the chart, but the pivot chart will start out with the row fields in the table becoming the *category fields* (horizontal, or x-axis) in the chart. Similarly, the column fields in the table become the *series* (vertical, or y-axis) fields in the chart. Pivot charts also have *page fields*, which are optional.

To create a pivot chart, select any cell in a database then choose Data ➤ PivotTable And PivotChart Report. In the first step of the PivotChart Wizard, select PivotChart (With PivotTable) and click Next. In the second Wizard step, check that the data range selected is the right one. If not, select the correct range, and then click Next.

TIP   If you have already created a pivot table with the selected data range, Excel will ask whether you want to create a chart based on the existing pivot table. If more than one pivot table exists for the data, Excel will prompt you to pick the one you want to use. To quickly create a pivot chart from an existing pivot table, click the PivotChart button on the PivotTable toolbar.

The third and final step in the Wizard asks you where to put the pivot table, if you are creating one along with the chart. You can change the layout and other options here, as described in the "Using the PivotTable Wizard" section. Choose New Worksheet or Existing Worksheet and click Finish.

You will see the blank pivot chart and the PivotTable toolbar with fields from the pivot chart. Drag fields from the toolbar onto the labeled chart areas to create the chart. The fields you drag onto the chart become labels with list buttons. Click these labels to change the data displayed. You can select any of these data display options and click OK to redisplay the chart with your data choice. Use the Chart menu to modify the pivot chart in the same way you would modify a regular Excel chart.

TIP   See Chapter 6, *Internet Publishing with Excel 2000*, to learn how to create interactive pivot charts and pivot tables for the Web.

Creating a PivotChart

1. Open the workbook that contains the data you want to chart and choose Select Data ➢ PivotTable And PivotChart Report.

2. Select PivotChart (With PivotTable) and click Next.

3. Make sure the data range selected is the right one. If not, select the correct range.

4. Change the layout and other options, choose New Worksheet or Existing Worksheet, and click Finish.

5. Drag fields from the toolbar onto the labeled chart areas to create the chart.

6. Click the list buttons and make another selection to change data display options. Click OK.

Hands On

Objectives XL2000.11.1, E.11.3, and E.11.6

1. Open any worksheet that contains a database with text or dates in more than one column. (The Traverse Tree Sales worksheet shown in

Figure 4.1 works very well if you don't have a worksheet already.)
Practice using pivot table features by:

a) Creating a pivot table that uses the SUM function in the data area

b) Changing the SUM function to AVERAGE or COUNT

c) Altering the pivot table layout in the worksheet by moving columns and rows

d) Adding and deleting a column or row

e) Drilling down through a value

f) Making separate pivot tables based on a value in a column using Show Pages

g) Applying an AutoFormat

2. Add one or two new records to the database, then reset the range for the pivot table.

3. Edit a record in the database and note the changes in the pivot tables based on the database.

4. Create a PivotChart using this data or one of your own workbooks.

Error-Proofing Your Workbook

Excel makes numbers look believable—even when results are so incorrect that no one should believe them. You know how to use Excel to create flashy worksheets and reports, complete with pivot tables and charts. But part of creating a worksheet is checking the completed worksheet for errors before you or other people rely on the results for decision making.

You can make two kinds of errors when creating a worksheet: *data-entry errors* and *logical errors*. With Excel, you can minimize data-entry errors and use the auditing tools to resolve logical errors.

Minimizing Data-Entry Errors

You're entering payroll. You're in a hurry. Instead of entering Richard Steinhoff's 10 hours, you enter 100. When payday rolls around, Rich is a very happy person. You, on the other hand, are not.

A helpful tool called *data validation* allows you to build business rules into your workbook so that grossly incorrect entries result in error messages.

Business rules are the policies and procedures, formal and informal, that govern how a business operates. Examples of business rules include: no refunds after 30 days; no one ever works more than 80 hours; and all employees must be at least 16 years of age. Validation ensures that the data entered falls within the range allowed by the business rule.

Objective XL2000E.10.9

To create a validation rule, select the cell or range of cells that have the same business rule. Then choose Data ➤ Validation to open the Data Validation dialog box, shown in Figure 4.5. The dialog box has three pages: Settings, Input Message, and Error Alert. The business rule you want to enforce goes on the Settings page. On the Input Message page, you can enter a prompt that lets users know how to enter data in the cell. And on the Error Alert page, you can enter a message that a user will see when invalid data is entered.

F I G U R E 4.5: Excel's Data Validation dialog box

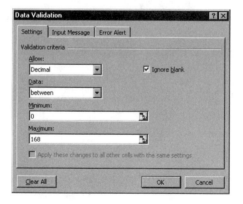

Setting Validation Rules

Let's use the error in entering payroll hours mentioned above as an example for setting validation rules. In the Settings page:

1. Select the type of value that's an acceptable entry for this cell from the Allow drop-down list. There are two possible choices: whole number and decimal. When you select either, additional text box controls open so you can enter values.

2. If the Ignore Blank checkbox is checked, the user can leave the cell blank. Uncheck the box if entries are required in all the selected cells.

3. In the Data drop-down list, choose the operator that you need. In Figure 4.5, we used the Between operator, because there is an upper and a lower limit that employees can work.

4. Enter values for the Minimum and Maximum values. No one can work fewer than 0 hours. If no maximum is established in the workplace, you could use 168. It's not possible to work more than 168 hours in a week—that's all there are. Notice that you can use the value in another cell as the minimum or maximum.

Displaying Input Messages

The Input Message page of the Data Validation dialog box lets you display a message (like a ScreenTip) to tell the user how to enter data in the cell. The message is displayed each time a user selects one of the cells in the range. This is a great help if you have a number of users working infrequently with this worksheet. However, if the same people use the worksheet over and over, input messages become cloying. If you add a title, it will appear in bold above the message.

Input messages are great additions to worksheets you build for other people to use, even if you don't want to validate the data they enter in a cell. On the Settings page, leave the default Any Value setting, and then enter your message on the Input Message page.

Adding Error Messages

Use the Error Alert page of the Data Validation dialog box to build an error dialog box like those used throughout Excel. Choose one of three styles—Information, Warning, or Stop—based on the severity of the error:

- The Information style is a casual notice.
- A Warning is a bit more severe than Information.
- Stop uses the same icon that users see when an application is about to shut down; it really catches people's attention.

Include an error message and a title if you wish.

You don't have to include an error message; you might prefer to enter data and then have Excel show you all the data that isn't valid. Whether you show error messages is a matter of practicality. If someone is entering data in the worksheet, you should probably let them know when the data is incorrect so they can find the correct data and enter it. Sometimes, however, the person entering data isn't in a position to correct it; in that case, you might want to dispense with the error message and handle the validation afterward (see "Using the Auditing Toolbar" later in this chapter).

Validating Data and Providing Input Messages

1. Select the cells you want to validate.

2. Choose Data ➢ Validation to open the Data Validation dialog box.

3. If you want to set validation rules, on the Settings page, set validation criteria for entries allowed, data, and minimum and/or maximum.

4. If you want to include an input message, enter a message and optional title on the Input Message page. Make sure the Show Input Message When Cell Is Selected checkbox is checked.

5. If you want to display an error message when invalid data is entered, choose a style and enter an error message and optional title on the Error Alert page. Make sure the Show Error Alert After Invalid Data Is Entered checkbox is checked.

6. Click OK.

7. Test the input message, validation, and error message by entering invalid data in one of the cells you selected.

Removing Validation or Input Messages

To remove data validation or input messages, select the cells, open the Validation dialog box, and click the Clear All button to clear all three pages of the dialog box.

Resolving Logical Errors

The other kind of error is a logical error: adding rather than subtracting, or multiplying the wrong numbers. Some logical errors violate Excel's rules about how formulas are constructed and result in an *error code* in the cell or an interruption from the Office Assistant. Those errors are the easy ones to catch and correct. But errors that don't violate Excel's internal logic are the really nasty ones, because nothing jumps out and says, "This is wrong!"

If you are familiar with the data, you can check the logic yourself to make sure the results make sense. If you are not conversant with the data, find someone who is and review the worksheet with them before relying on it for critical operations or reporting.

Working with Error Codes

Objective XL2000E.9.2

Excel has eight standard error codes that pop up in cells to let you know that a formula requires your attention. The codes, listed in Table 4.1, give you information about what caused the error. The first is the ###### error, which is telling you that the data is too wide for the column. This is easy to fix (hardly an error, but you get the idea).

T A B L E 4.1: Error Codes

Error Code/ Error Name	Cause
#####	1. Data is too wide for the cell, *or* 2. You subtracted one data from another, and the result is a negative number. Double-check your formula.
#DIV/0 (Division by Zero)	The number or cell reference you divided by is either zero or blank. If you see this in cells you just filled, you need an absolute cell reference in the original formula.
#N/A (Not Available)	1. You omitted a required argument in a function, *or* 2. The cell that contains the argument is blank or doesn't have the kind of entry the function requires.
#NAME	1. You misspelled the name of a range or function, *or* 2. You referred to a name that doesn't exist, *or* 3. You used text in a formula or format without putting it in quotes, *or* 4. You left out the colon in a range (B3:D7).
#NULL	You referred to an intersection that doesn't exist by using a space between two ranges in an argument.

T A B L E 4.1: Error Codes *(continued)*

Error Code/ Error Name	Cause
#NUM	1. You used text or a blank cell in an argument that requires a number, *or* 2. You entered a formula that creates a number too large or too small for Excel to handle.
#REF (Invalid Reference)	You deleted some cells that this formula requires, so the formula can't find the cell that it refers to. You may have deleted some cells by pasting other cells over them.
#VALUE	You entered text when a formula requires a number or a value such as True or False.

Resolving Circular Cell References

If you enter a formula that contains a *circular cell reference*, Excel doesn't just place an error code in the cell; it displays a message box and immediately offers help. A circular cell reference occurs when a formula refers to the cell that it is in. For example, when the formula =SUM(J15:J20) is in cell J20, Excel tries to add J20 to itself over and over again. This is called *iteration*. Excel will iterate 100 times; then it will give up and display an error message:

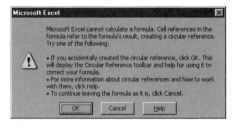

Click OK in the message box, and Help opens with information about circular references. (Help only opens the first time you create a circular reference in a session.) Excel places a blue dot next to the formula that created the circular reference and displays Circular and the reference for the offending cell in the status bar. If Help opened, clicking the cell with the circular reference opens the Circular Reference toolbar (or you can turn it on from the View menu).

Objectives XL2000E.9.3 and E.9.4

The drop-down list in the Circular Reference toolbar displays the current circular reference; clicking the drop-down list shows all the circular references in open workbooks.

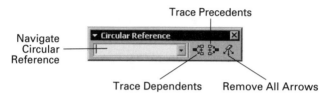

The first two buttons on the toolbar are used to trace dependents and precedents. *Dependents* are cells with formulas that rely on the cell in the drop-down list; *precedents* are the cells that are referred to in this cell's formula. Click the Trace Precedents button, and Excel will show you the precedent cells, as shown in Figure 4.6.

F I G U R E 4.6: Tracing precedents

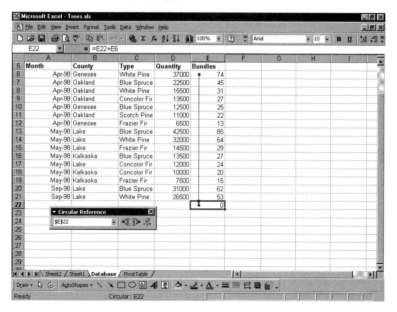

The arrow in the Bundles column shows that all the cells in the column, including cell E22, are included in the formula in E22.

Click the Remove All Arrows button, and Excel will turn the arrows off. Then move to the circular reference cell and fix the formula so that it does not include a reference to itself.

Indirect Circular References   In the example we used, the circular reference was easy to find, because the formula referred directly to the cell it was stored in. *Indirect circular references* are harder to find. For example, Excel reports a circular reference in J24. When you trace the precedents, the formula in J24 refers to cells E4:E11. So where is the problem? A formula in cells E4:11 refers to J24 or refers to another cell whose formula refers to J24. This is an indirect circular reference. Just continue clicking the Trace Precedents button, and you'll eventually find a formula that refers to the cell where the circular reference was reported.

Resolving a Circular Reference

1. If the Circular Reference Error dialog box is open, click OK to clear the dialog box and open the Circular Reference toolbar, or open the toolbar (choose View ➣ Toolbars) from the menu bar.

2. Choose the circular reference cell from the drop-down list on the toolbar.

3. Click the Trace Precedents button to see the cells that the formula refers to. Continue clicking Trace Precedents until an arrow points back to the cell with the reference.

4. Fix the formula in the original cell (or, if necessary, in a precedent cell) to remove the circular reference.

5. Click Remove All Arrows, and close the Circular Reference toolbar.

Using the Auditing Toolbar

Objective XL2000E.9.1

The Auditing toolbar is one-stop shopping for error checking in your worksheet. Turn on the toolbar from the Tools menu (not the View menu) by choosing Tools ➤ Auditing ➤ Show Auditing Toolbar.

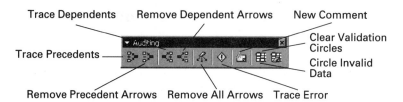

The Auditing toolbar includes tracing tools from the Circular Reference toolbar and a Trace Error tool to check the precedents for cells displaying error codes. Tracing works for DIV/0, but not for many other common errors. When the error is a missing reference or name, for example, the problem is that the formula doesn't have precedents, so there's nothing to trace.

The last three tools on the toolbar work in conjunction with validation rules. Use the Circle Invalid Data button to mark cells with contents that violate established validation rules. If you find invalid entries, insert comments using the New Comment button to note values that need to be corrected. Use the Clear Validation Circles button to hide the circles. (If the entry is corrected so that it's valid, Excel removes the validation circle.)

Hands On

Objectives XL2000E.9.1, E.9.2, E.9.3, E.9.4, and E.10.9

1. In any worksheet you're not too attached to, add a formula that includes a circular cell reference. Use the Circular Reference toolbar to view the precedents and resolve the error. Create a DIV/0 error by using a blank cell as the divisor in a formula. Open the Auditing toolbar and trace the error.

2. In any worksheet, add data validation, including input messages and error alerts. Test the validation, messages, and alerts by entering invalid data. When the error alert appears, continue and enter the

invalid data. Then use the Circle Invalid Data button on the Auditing toolbar to identify the invalid data.

3. In any worksheet, use the Data Validation dialog box to add several input messages without validating the entries in the cell. Add a comment to another cell. Edit the comment, then Delete it and clear the input messages.

Using and Constructing Templates

Templates are workbook models that you use to create other workbooks. Templates let you quickly construct workbooks that are identical in format, giving your work a consistent look. Excel includes some templates, and you can create others for your personal use or for novice users in your workplace. An Excel template can include text, numbers, formatting, formulas, and all the other features you already use.

NOTE   When you open a template, a copy is opened—the original template is not altered.

Working with Existing Templates

Objective XL2000E.2.1

Excel includes predesigned workbook templates that you can use or modify. To open a template:

1. Choose File ➤ New from the menu bar to open the New dialog box. (You can't simply click the New button on the Standard toolbar. The New button opens the default template—an empty workbook.)

2. Click the Spreadsheet Solutions tab to view the built-in Excel templates, such as Invoice and Village Software.

NOTE   Some templates are included in the Typical Excel installation; others have to be custom installed, but they can always be added later.

---

3. Select the template in the Spreadsheet Solutions window.

4. Click OK.

Entering Data

The Invoice template, shown in Figure 4.7, is a typical template. There are two worksheets in the template: Invoice and Customize Your Invoice. Each template includes a special toolbar. As you use each template, its toolbar is added to the list in the Toolbars dialog box. The Invoice toolbar initially appears as a palette in the worksheet window. You can move the toolbar if you wish.

FIGURE 4.7: Excel's Invoice template

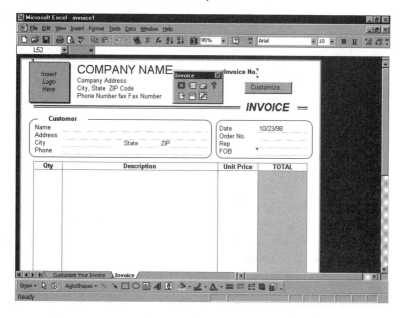

To view the entire worksheet template, click the Size To Screen button on the Invoice toolbar. Clicking the button again returns the worksheet to its original size.

Cells with a red triangle include comments (also called *CellTips* when they're used as a form of online help) to explain the information you should enter in the cell. To view a comment, move the mouse pointer over the cell. You can click the Hide Comments/Display Comments button on the Invoice toolbar to suppress or enable comment display.

Click the New Comment button to add your own comment to the template.

The canned templates include sample data that you can examine as a guide to enter your data. To view the sample data, click the Display Example/Remove Example button on the template's toolbar. To enter data in the template, turn off the example. Activate the cell, and then enter the information.

NOTE   Cells with a light-blue fill color contain formulas, so don't enter information in shaded cells.

Customizing the Template

Objective XL2000E.2.2

The Invoice sheet includes placeholders for generic title information: the company name, a place for a logo or picture, and so on. To add your personal information, click the Customize button in the Invoice worksheet to move to the Customize Your Invoice worksheet. At the top of the worksheet is a Lock/Save Sheet button. *Locking* a template prevents users from accidentally changing the customized information in this workbook, but it does not alter the template. You can always choose to customize again and unlock the template if you want to change it.

Alternatively, you can save a copy of the template that includes the custom information you entered. It's more convenient to permanently alter the template by saving. To lock or save template changes, click the Lock/Save Sheet button. A dialog box opens so that you can select locking or locking and saving:

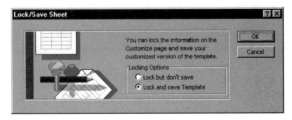

Customizing a Template

1. Activate the Customize worksheet.

2. Enter your custom information as indicated in the worksheet.

3. Click the Lock/Save Sheet button.

4. Choose Lock But Don't Save or Lock And Save Template; then click OK.

Creating a Template

Objective XL2000E.2.3

You can create a template for workbooks that you use frequently. For example, you might use Excel to complete a weekly payroll and put all the payroll worksheets for one month into a separate workbook. Rather than construct a new workbook each month, you can create a monthly payroll template; then, at the beginning of each month, you can create a new workbook from the template. Your template will differ from a regular workbook in three specific ways:

- The template will contain only the text, formulas, and formatting that remain the same each month.

- The template will include visual formatting clues and comments to assist users.

- The completed workbook will be saved as a template in the Office 2000 Templates folder or in a subfolder rather than as a regular Excel workbook.

Adding and Testing Formulas

You can create a template from scratch or base it on an existing workbook. If you're using an existing workbook, first make sure that all the formulas work and that numbers and text are formatted as you want them. Then remove the text and numbers that will be entered each time the template is used. Don't remove formulas—although the results of the formulas change, the formulas remain the same. If you're creating a template from scratch, you'll still need to enter test values, then remove them before saving the template.

Providing User Cues and CellTips

Now, use borders and shading to let users know where they should—and shouldn't—enter text or other information. The Invoice template is a good model.

Objective XL2000E.12.1

Add comments (choose Insert Comment from the shortcut menu) to provide CellTips where users might have questions about data entry. To edit or delete an existing comment, right-click the cell with the comment and choose Edit or Delete from the menu. If you're editing, simply select and overtype the old comment and then click away from it to exit edit mode.

Saving Your Template

Before you save your template, remove any blank worksheets from the workbook to improve its overall appearance. When you're finished formatting the worksheet, choose File ➢ Save As, and save the workbook as a Template type.

NOTE   Excel templates have the .xlt extension, but simply typing the extension does not save the workbook as a template.

When you choose Template as the Save As file type, Excel switches the Save In location to the Templates folder. You can create a folder within the Templates folder to hold your personal templates. Other than the General tab, tabs in the New dialog box represent subfolders of the Templates folder that contain Excel templates or workbooks. To automatically open a template every time Excel is launched, save the template in the XLStart folder or in the folder specified as the Alternate Startup File Location on the General tab of Excel's Options dialog box.

Opening and Editing Your Template

When you choose File ➢ New, your new template will be included on the General page or the specific folder you saved it in. Double-click the template's icon to open a workbook based on your template.

Saving a Template

1. Click the Save button or choose File ➤ Save As.

2. In the Save As Type control, choose Template from the drop-down list. The Save In control will change to the default Templates folder.

3. Use the New Folder button to create a new folder if you want to add a tab to the New dialog box. Enter a filename for the template.

4. Click the Save button.

When you or other users use your template to create new workbooks, the template itself will not be altered. To modify a template, open the template from the Templates folder with File ➤ Open rather than File ➤ New. When you are finished editing, save and close the template.

TIP   The location of the Templates folder depends on a number of installation options. Use the Find feature on the Start Menu and search for files with the .xlt extension if you're having trouble locating the folder.

Hands On

Objectives XL2000E.2.1, E.2.2, E.2.3, and E.12.1

1. Use another of the templates (such as Expenses) included with Excel 2000. Customize the template with your company's information. Save the customized template.

2. Create a template that calculates and totals gross pay, taxes, and net pay for 10 employees based on information entered by the user. Users should enter the following information for each employee: social security number, last name, first name, hourly rate, tax rate (as a percentage), and hours worked.

3. Modify the template in step 2 to allow for payroll deduction of employee contributions to National Public Radio. The deduction amount will be entered with the employee information and deducted from the pay after taxes are calculated. Total the contribution column. Resave the template.

Linking Information

A *link* is a reference to a cell or range in another workbook. Links are commonly used to avoid double-entering workbook information, or to obtain the most current data from a shared data source.

Linking Workbooks

> **Objective XL2000E.3.2**

Suppose that in your company, departments are responsible for their own budgets. As the time to finalize the coming year's budget approaches, each manager is working furiously on his or her budget. The vice president for finance has a master budget that is a roll-up of the department budgets. It's not practical to put all the department worksheets and the master budget in one large workbook, because many people would need to use the workbook at the same time, and only one user needs to work with all the data for the various departments.

What's the practical solution? By linking the workbooks, the changes made by the department managers can be immediately reflected in the vice president's master budget workbook.

Each link establishes a relationship between two workbooks. The vice president's workbook is called the *dependent workbook*, because the value that the v.p. sees depends on a value in departmental workbook. The department's workbook that contains that value is called the *source workbook*.

Creating a Link

You can create a link in two ways: by using an open workbook or by referring to a workbook on disk. The first method is much easier. It's the same as creating any other reference in a formula, but you need to switch to the source workbook before selecting the cell to reference in the formula.

To create a link to an open workbook:

1. Open the source workbook, then switch to the dependent workbook.

2. Begin entering the formula in the dependent workbook with an equal sign (=).

3. At the point in the formula where you want to include a cell reference from the source workbook, choose Window on the menu bar and select the source workbook.

4. In the source workbook, click the cell that you want to reference to include it in the formula as shown in Figure 4.8.

5. Switch back to the dependent worksheet by pressing Enter.

6. Double-click the cell with the formula and notice that the cell reference includes the workbook and worksheet names as well as the cell address.

FIGURE 4.8: Creating a link

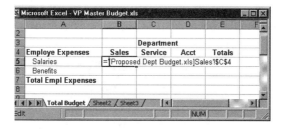

You may prefer to arrange the source and dependent workbooks so that you can see the results cell and the cell to be referenced at the same time. With both workbooks open, choose Window ➢ Arrange to open the Arrange Windows dialog box:

Choose how you want the open workbooks arranged, and then use each workbook window's sizing tool to further size and arrange the windows.

TIP You can also arrange copies of a single workbook so that you can work in two different areas of the workbook in separate windows. First, choose Window ➢ New Window, and then choose Windows ➢ Arrange to open a dialog box.

To link to a workbook that is not open, you must provide all the information that Excel needs to find the source workbook, including the full path. For example, if you want to refer to cell **D4** in the Sales sheet of the Proposed Dept Budget workbook, stored in the Sales Management folder on the C drive, the reference would be `'C:\Sales Management\[Proposed Dept Budget.xls]Sales'!D4`. There are many places to make a mistake when typing an entry like this. Try to create links with open source workbooks whenever possible.

Linking with Paste Link

If you simply want to refer to a cell in another workbook (as opposed to using it in a formula), create a link with Copy And Paste Link. To do so, open both workbooks, and then select and copy the cell(s) from the source workbook. Next, activate the destination workbook and choose Edit ➤ Paste Special from the menu bar to open the Paste Special dialog box:

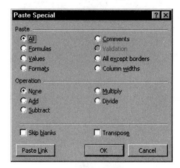

A normal paste simply pastes the formula(s) from the Clipboard, but here you can paste values, formula, formats, and other cell attributes or perform a math operation during the paste.

Once you've made your choices in the Paste Special dialog box, click the Paste Link button, select a destination for the pasted selection, and then press Enter to paste the link to the source workbook.

Updating Links

When you open a dependent workbook and its source workbook is not open, Excel will ask if you want to update the links. If both workbooks are open, changes in the source workbook are automatically updated in the dependent workbook.

If, however, the source workbook can be opened by other users, they could be making changes to the workbook while you are working with the dependent workbook. In this case, the links will not be updated automatically; you have to instruct Excel to update the links:

1. With the dependent workbook open, choose Edit ➢ Links to open the Links dialog box:

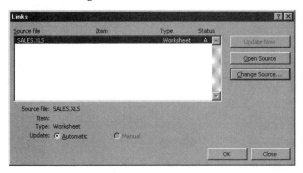

2. From the Source File list, choose the source workbook that you want to update from.

3. Click the Update Now button to update the dependent workbook with information from the latest saved version of the source workbook.

References That Span Worksheets

In Excel, you can reference ranges that occur in the same cell or group of cells on two or more worksheets. For example, Figure 4.9 shows the First-Quarter worksheet for reporting types of media sold at various locations.

F I G U R E 4.9: Media Types worksheet

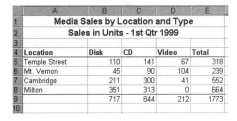

	A	B	C	D	E
1	Media Sales by Location and Type				
2	Sales in Units - 1st Qtr 1999				
3					
4	Location	Disk	CD	Video	Total
5	Temple Street	110	141	67	318
6	Mt. Vernon	45	90	104	239
7	Cambridge	211	300	41	552
8	Milton	351	313	0	664
9		717	844	212	1773
10					

▶ *Objective XL2000.5.10*

The January, February, and March worksheets have exactly the same layout, and the FirstQuarter worksheet summarizes the figures from the three monthly worksheets. You can total all worksheets at one time with a 3-D cell reference, which can be filled or copied like any other Excel formula.

Creating a 3-D Reference in a Formula

1. Arrange the workbook so the sheets you want to include as a 3-D reference are next to each other.

2. In the results cell, begin constructing the formula.

3. To include the 3-D reference, click the sheet tab of the first sheet of the 3-D range.

4. Hold Shift and select the last sheet you want to refer to.

5. Select the cell or range of cells to include in the formula.

6. Finish the formula and press Enter.

Using 3-D Names

You might want to use 3-D names if you're creating a lot of 3-D cell references. For example, if cell B10 in three worksheets is the value for April's Salaries, you could name all three cells SalaryApr or AprSalary.

Defining 3-D Range Names

1. Arrange the workbook so the sheets that include cells to be named are next to each other. Choose Insert ≻ Name ≻ Define from the menu bar.

2. In the Names In Workbook text box, type the name.

3. In the Refers To text box, delete the existing reference except for the equal sign (=).

4. Click the sheet tab of the first worksheet with a cell you want to include in the named range.

5. Hold Shift and select the sheet tab for the last worksheet to be included.

6. Release Shift and select the cell or range to be named in the last worksheet.

7. Click Add to add the name, and click OK to close the dialog box.

Using a Workspace

> ### Objective XL2000E.3.1

If you're frequently using a particular group of workbooks together, you can save time opening them by creating a *workspace file*. A workspace file saves information about all open workbooks: their on-screen positions, window sizes, and drive and folder location. When you open a saved workspace file, it opens all the workbooks in the workspace.

Creating a Workspace File

1. Open the workbooks you want to include in the workspace file.

2. Move and resize the workbook windows so they are in the exact position you want them to be when you open the workspace.

3. Click File ➢ Save Workspace.

4. Enter a name and location for the workspace file and click Save.

WARNING   Make sure you continue to save changes you make to the individual workbooks while working with the workspace file.

Hands On

> ### Objectives XL2000.5.10, E.3.1, and E.3.2

1. Create the worksheet shown below for the Sales department. Re-create or copy the Sales worksheet to two separate workbooks. Edit the worksheet for the Accounting and Service departments. Save all three workbooks.

	A	B	C	D
1	**Proposed Budget - 1999**			
2				
3	**Employee Expense**	**1998 Budget**	**1998 Actual**	**1999 Proposed**
4	Salaries	147,000	148,540	151,000
5	Benefits	39,690	38,790	40,770
6	**Total Employee Expense**	186,690	187,330	191,770

    a) In a new workbook, create the Budget Summary worksheet shown in Figure 4.8. Use links to refer to the figures in column D of the three departmental workbooks.

b) Close all four workbooks. Open the Accounting department workbook and change the proposed salaries and benefits for 1999. Close and save the Accounting department workbook.

c) Open the Budget Summary workbook. Do not update the links. Note the figures for Accounting. Update the links.

d) Open and arrange all four workbooks.

2. In a new workbook, create at least three periodic worksheets and one total worksheet. Use 3-D cell references to total the periodic worksheets on the total worksheet.

Working with Others in Excel

Excel 2000 was designed to allow multiple users to view and modify a single workbook simultaneously. If you want others to be able to use a workbook while you have it open, you need to share the workbook and ensure that it is stored on a network or shared drive that other users can access.

Sharing Workbooks

Objective XL2000E.12.6

To share a workbook, open the Share Workbook dialog box (choose Tools ➤ Share Workbook):

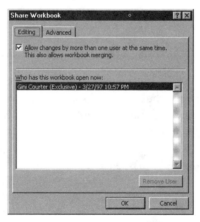

On the Editing page, enable the Allow Changes checkbox to make the file accessible to other users. Then click the Advanced tab to set options for tracking changes and resolving conflicts.

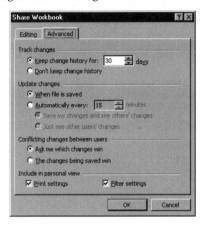

Tracking Changes

Tracking is only available in shared workbooks. If you choose to track changes in a *change history*, select the number of days changes should be kept. (If you intend to distribute copies of the workbook, see "Merging Workbook Changes" later in this chapter for more about this setting.) If you don't want to track changes, tell Excel not to keep a history.

Whether you track changes or not, you need to determine when changes are updated. The default only updates changes When File Is Saved. This means that each time you (or another user) save, Excel will save your changes and update your workbook with changes made by other users. Alternatively, you can choose to have your workbook updated Automatically Every set number of minutes; by choosing the Save My Changes And See Others' Changes option, your changes will be saved when the update occurs. (If you update changes Automatically, other users still won't see your changes until you save; however, they can also choose to see saved changes Automatically rather than waiting until they save.)

When two or more users try to save different changes in the same cell, it causes a conflict. Set the Conflicting Changes Between Users option to indicate how conflicts should be resolved. Excel can prompt you to resolve conflicts, or it can automatically accept your changes.

The Personal view section of the Advanced page contains your print and filter settings for the workbook. These settings do not affect other users' view of the workbook. Use the checkboxes to include or exclude these settings when the workbook is saved.

Sharing a Workbook

1. With the workbook open, choose Tools ➤ Share Workbook from the menu bar.

2. On the Editing page, enable Allow Changes By More Than One User.

3. On the Advanced page, set Track Changes, Update Changes, Conflicting Changes, and Personal View options.

4. Click OK to close the dialog box.

When you close the dialog box, Excel will save the workbook as a shared workbook; if you haven't previously saved, the Save As dialog box will open.

TIP Excel tracks workbook users by username. If the name listed in the Editing tab is incorrect, you can change it on the General page of the Options dialog box (choose Tools ➤ Options).

Working in a Shared Workbook

Objective XL2000E.12.5

When Tracking Changes is enabled, each change made is noted in a comment, and changed cells are flagged. For example, if you delete the value in a cell, a triangle appears in the upper-left corner of the cell. When you move the mouse pointer over the cell, a comment tells you who changed the cell, when they changed it, and what the former value in the cell was.

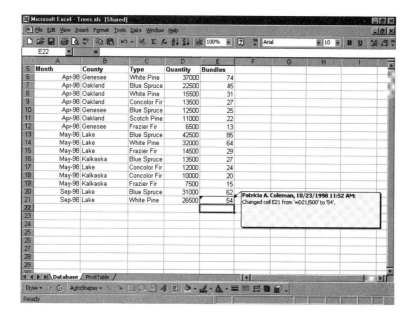

Excel assigns a different color for each user who modifies the workbook, so you can visually inspect the workbook to find all the changes made by one user. Reject a change by right-clicking that cell and choosing Reject Change from the shortcut menu.

When you save the workbook, you accept the changes, so the triangles and comments disappear.

Limitations of Shared Workbooks

Some Excel 2000 features aren't available in shared workbooks. For instance, while a workbook is shared, you can't:

- Delete worksheets

- Add or apply conditional formatting and data validation

- Insert or delete ranges of cells (you can still insert and delete individual cells, rows, and columns), charts, hyperlinks, or other objects (including those created with Draw)

Limitations of Shared Workbooks *(continued)*

- Group or outline data

- Write, change, view, record, or assign macros

Though not available when working in a shared workbook, you can use the features before you share a workbook, or you can temporarily unshare the workbook, make changes, and then turn sharing on again.

See Excel's Online Help for the complete list of limitations of shared workbooks.

Resolving Conflicts

If changes you are saving conflict with changes saved by another user, you'll be prompted to resolve the conflict (unless you changed the Conflicting Changes setting in the Advanced page of the Share Workbook dialog box). The Resolve Conflict dialog box will open automatically. You can review each change individually and accept your change or others' changes, or accept/reject changes in bulk.

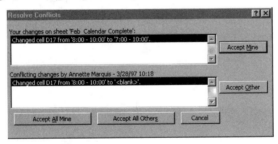

Viewing the Change History

If you have chosen to track changes in a change history, you can examine all the changes saved in a workbook since you turned on the change history.

Choose Tools ➤ Track Changes ➤ Highlight Changes to open the Highlight Changes dialog box:

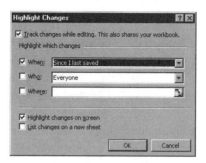

In the dialog box, select the time period for the changes you want to review, and specify the users whose changes you want to see. If you only want to see changes for a particular range or sheet, select the range you want to view. You can view the changes on screen or on a separate worksheet in the workbook.

Viewing the Change History

1. Choose Tools ➤ Track Changes ➤ Highlight Changes.

2. In the Highlight Changes dialog box, set the When, Who, and Where options.

3. Enable or disable viewing on screen or in a separate worksheet.

4. Click OK.

When you view the history on a separate worksheet, you can filter the changes to find changes made by different users or on specific dates, as you would with any set of data. When you remove a workbook from shared use, the change history is turned off and reset. If you want to keep the changes, select the information on the History worksheet and copy it to another worksheet before unsharing the workbook.

Merging Workbook Changes

Objective XL2000E.12.7

If you want users to be able to make changes independently and then review all changes at once, make and distribute copies of the shared workbook. To create the copies, use Save As and give each copy of the workbook a different name. Then you can merge the copies when users are done with their changes.

You can only merge workbooks that have the same change history, so it's important that none of the users turns off sharing while using the workbook. Also, the history must be complete when you merge the workbooks. If, for example, you set the number of days for the history at 30 days and users keep the workbooks for 32 days, you won't be able to merge the workbooks. Before you make copies of the shared workbook, make sure you set the history to allow enough time for changes and merging. If you're uncertain, set 600 days or an equally ridiculous length of time.

Merging Shared Workbooks

1. Open your copy of the shared workbook that you want to merge changes into.

2. Choose Tools ➤ Merge Workbooks. If you haven't saved your copy of the workbook, you'll be prompted to do so.

3. In the Select Files To Merge Into Current Document dialog box, choose the copy of the shared workbook that has the changes you wish to merge. (Use Ctrl or Shift to select multiple workbooks from one location.) Click OK.

Setting Passwords and Protection

Objective XL2000E.12.4

You can restrict who can view and modify the data in any workbook by setting passwords to open or modify the workbook. To do so:

1. Choose File ➤ Save As and click the Tools button in the Save As dialog box. Choose General Options to open the Save Options dialog box:

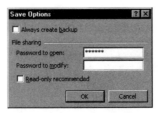

2. Enter passwords that users (including you) must enter to open or modify the workbooks.

3. Click OK to return to the Save As procedure.

Give anyone who should be able to open the file the Password To Open, which they will be prompted to enter when they try to open the file. Users who can supply the Open password are then prompted to enter a second password (the Modify password) or open the file as Read Only. If you forget a password, you won't be able to open/modify the file.

The two-password system lets you control who can change the file. If you want lots of users to be able to look at the file (or save a copy of the file), but reserve modification rights for yourself, use different passwords and only distribute the password that opens the file. If any user who can open the file should be able to modify it, use the same password for Open and Modify passwords.

Deleting or Changing Passwords

Delete a password from a file by changing the Password To Open or Password To Modify field in the Save Options dialog box. Select the asterisks that represent the current password and press Delete if you want to remove the password. If you want to change the password, select the asterisks and type a new password. Retype it, click OK, and then save the workbook. Any user who can modify the workbook can change both passwords.

Using Workbook and Worksheet Protection

Objective XL2000E.12.2

If you don't want to password-protect the workbook file, but you're still concerned about others' errors, consider using Workbook and/or Worksheet Protection. Protection prevents other users from changing or deleting data and other objects in your worksheet or changing the structure of the workbook. To enable Protection:

1. Click Tools ➤ Protection ➤ Protect Workbook or Tools ➤ Protection ➤ Protect Sheet.

2. Enable the items you want to protect.

3. Type a password if you want to limit users' ability to unprotect the workbook.

4. Click OK when you're finished.

Remove Protection by clicking Tools ➤ Protection ➤ Unprotect Workbook (or Sheet).

Changing Workbook Properties

Objective XL2000E.12.3

Workbook properties describe the workbook and make it easy to organize and locate specific workbooks. To access the properties for an open workbook, choose File ➤ Properties; the workbook's Properties page opens:

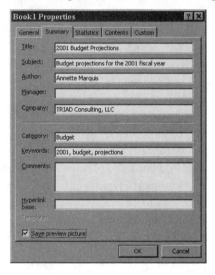

The workbook's Properties dialog box has five tabs:

- General displays type, location, size, MS-DOS name, and attributes of the file.

- Summary is an editable tab that includes such things as title, subject, author, company, category, and keywords.

- Statistics displays when the file was created, modified, accessed, printed, and last saved, its revision number, and total editing time.

- Contents displays the workbook name and the names of each sheet in the workbook.

- Custom includes options for entering values for 27 additional properties such as Date Completed, Editor, Owner, Project, Publisher, Purpose, and so on.

You can modify the properties on the Summary and Custom pages. On the Summary page, click in an open text box and enter property information. To add a value for a Custom property:

1. Switch to the Custom tab of the Workbook Properties dialog box.

2. Select the property from the list.

3. Indicate if the Type is Text, Date, Number, Yes, or No.

4. Enter the actual value for this property.

5. Click the Add button.

To delete a custom property, select it from the Properties list and click Delete.

Hands On

Objectives XL2000E.12.2, E.12.3, E.12.4, E.12.5, E.12.6, and E.12.7

1. Open one of the practice workbooks you've used in this chapter, or use another file with non-critical data.

   a) Set up the workbook for sharing.

   b) Apply Open and Modify passwords to the workbook, then resave and close it. Open the workbook and then remove both passwords.

   c) Turn on Track Changes and use Save As to save the file under a different name. Send the renamed workbook to a colleague and ask her/him to make several changes and send it back to you.

   d) In the original shared workbook, make your own changes.

   e) Open the workbook your colleague modified and review the changes s/he made. Accept or reject them as desired.

   f) Merge the two workbooks, resolving conflicts as necessary.

2. In the same or another workbook, apply Worksheet Protection against modifying cell contents. Test it to make sure it worked, then remove Worksheet Protection.

3. Open the workbook's Properties page and enter a title and subject for the workbook.

   a) Add a category and enter some comments.

   b) Add values for at least two custom properties.

Forecasting and Modeling

If you were going to fly across the country for a week of business meetings, chances are you would at least think about checking the weather forecast to find out what type of clothing to pack. And even though the forecast prompted you to pack a raincoat, you wouldn't be too surprised if the snow turned to rain or even sunshine. Regardless of the forecast, no one can personally alter the weather that actually "arrives." Following the forecast does, however, increase the possibility that you will be properly prepared.

Business forecasts—predictions of business factors like product demand, production costs, income, and expenses—are the "weather prediction" for a business unit's future. Like a weather forecast, the business forecast may be less than completely accurate. However, there is one important difference between a weather forecast and a business forecast: while you can't change the weather, managers can monitor the progress a business makes and alter business decisions so that actual performance is more closely related to the forecast.

Forecasts try to *simulate* or predict future behavior of variables like Gross Profit based on many types of information. A forecast may be based on:

- Historical information, such as last year's earnings

- Judgments or educated guesses by people in a position to help predict future performance, such as managers, clients, industry experts, and sales staff

- Information about indicators, such as the prices charged by competitors, the local employment level, or the current interest rate

The more sources of information you consider, the more accurate your forecast will be. You might be more likely to trust a weather person who looked at a radar display than one who simply looked out the window.

There are different ways to construct forecasts. In Excel, forecasting always involves creating a *model*, one or more worksheets that use formulas to show how different variables interrelate. Amortization schedules are an example of a forecasting model. If you enter different values for principal or interest, you can see how the payment amount or length of loan changes. Payroll worksheets are models of the relationships between hours worked, pay rate, gross pay, taxes, and net pay. Inventory worksheets model the interactions of quantity, cost, and total cost.

Forecasting is always based on assumptions. Each model has specific, built-in assumptions, but there are some assumptions common to most models. One general assumption is that the future will be much like the present: the world's financial markets won't fall apart during the life of a loan (pre- or post-Y2K), and you will need to make a loan payment this month, and every month in the future until the loan is paid off. There is also an assumption that a modeled forecast will not be perfect. There will always be some neglected piece of information that ends up being important (like the month that the payment is received late, resulting in a penalty).

Another assumption is that the distant future is more difficult to predict than the near future. (That's why it's difficult to get 50-year mortgages.) No one could have accurately predicted the last four years of stock market prices, or the growth of the Web over the past decade. As the time period involved in a forecast increases, the accuracy of the forecast decreases, even if the model was essentially accurate for a shorter time frame.

Building a Business Model

There are several steps involved in building a model and using it to forecast performance:

1. Decide what you need to know from the model.
2. Make explicit assumptions.
3. Define and collect information for the model.
4. Create the model in Excel.
5. Use the model to forecast the future value of variables.
6. Compare real performance to the model and adjust the model (or change actual performance) as necessary.

The amount of effort spent on each step should be based on the importance of the information you intend to obtain from the model. You don't want to spend hours researching and modeling a decision that will save two dollars. But you need to spend sufficient time when you are creating a model to support decision making that involves hundreds of thousands of dollars.

Let's use a fictitious company, the WellBilt Corporation, to look at business modeling. The WellBilt Manufacturing Corporation makes a variety of PC accessories. WellBilt's CD Division makes organizers for compact disks.

What You Need to Know

WellBilt needs to decide how many organizers the CD Division should make each month. You have been put in charge of collecting and modeling the information needed to decide how the CD Division can maximize monthly gross profit.

Model Assumptions

WellBilt assumes that they will be able to market the CD organizers to large computer stores and e-commerce sites as they have in the past. More assumptions will be added as information is collected.

Collecting Information

You will need to collect information on the income generated by organizer sales and the expenses involved in manufacturing the CD organizers. Some of the expenses are *fixed expenses*, expenses that, in the short run, are the same amount no matter how many CD organizers are manufactured. Other expenses (like labor and materials) are *variable expenses*.

You talked to the Accounting department and found that the CD Division's fixed expenses are not expected to change from current monthly costs ($80,000 for building mortgage, maintenance, and salaries) in the next year. There are several pieces of variable cost information: hourly employees make $6.00; overtime hours are paid at time and a half. During a month, the current workforce can build 48,000 organizers without working overtime. Each CD organizer takes an hour to make and uses $1.25 in raw materials.

You also spoke with the Marketing department. It has already created an Excel statistical model to determine sales at various prices for the CD Organizer. They have determined that the formula `Price=$20-(Quantity/5000)` expresses the price needed to sell a particular quantity. In other words, the most anyone will spend for a CD organizer is $20. At a price of $19, WellBilt would be able to sell only 5,000 units. For each additional 5,000 units sold, WellBilt has to drop the price $1. From the Production and Sales managers, you know that WellBilt manufactured and sold 45,000 units this past month.

Creating the Model

You now have enough information to create an Excel model of the basic factors that influence production of CD organizers. (You also have some new assumptions: that the information from Accounting and Marketing is accurate, and that the Marketing model is good for the next year.)

The Accounting department information contains an IF statement: if production is less than or equal to 48,000 units, then the cost of labor is $6 per hour. Hours in excess of 48,000 cost $9 per hour. Since this month's sales were 45,000, let's begin by modeling production of sales of 40,000, 45,000, and 50,000 units, as shown in Figure 4.10.

F I G U R E 4.10: CD Division model

	A	B	C	D
1	WellBilt Manufacturing			
2	CD ROM Disk Organizer Production			
3				
4	Income	High	Medium	Low
5	Units Produced & Sold	50,000	45,000	40,000
6	Unit Price	10.00	11.00	12.00
7	Total Income	500,000	495,000	480,000
8				
9	Expense			
10	Fixed Expense	80,000	80,000	80,000
11	Labor Expense	306,000	270,000	240,000
12	Material Expense	62,500	56,250	50,000
13	Total Expense	448,500	406,250	370,000
14				
15	Gross Profit	51,500	88,750	110,000

Cells B6, B11, and B12 use the following formulas, respectively:

- =20-(B5/5000)
- =IF(B5<48000,B5*6,(48000*6)+(B5-48000)*9)
- =1.25*B5

Total Income is, of course, Unit Price multiplied by Units Produced & Sold. Gross Profit is a subtraction formula: Total Income minus Total Expenses.

The model indicates that lower levels of production produce higher levels of gross profit. Since your model includes the current level of production, you have a way to check the accuracy of the model. Is gross profit currently $88,750 a month? If it is not, you know that there is information missing from the model that you need to identify and include. If current gross profit is close to the figure in the model, you can have more confidence in the model's ability to predict gross profit at other levels of production. Remember, though, that the model has a limitation: It's only valid for the three production figures that you included. You can't draw conclusions about the gross profit at other quantities produced and sold without expanding the model.

Using Excel's Forecasting Tools

Excel provides a number of good tools for numerical forecasting. You already know how to use many of these tools: the functions and formulas. For more advanced work, Excel includes specialized forecasting tools called What If tools, used in What If analysis. (Using What If tools is sometimes called *wiffing*, short for "What If"ing.)

Goal Seek

Objective XL2000E.11.2

Use Excel's Goal Seek tool when you need to find a specific solution to a formula. Goal Seek is used to calculate backwards—to determine the values necessary to reach a specific goal. Once you have created a worksheet model, you can use Goal Seek to get a specific answer. For example, one of the WellBilt managers wants to know how many units must be manufactured and sold to result in gross profits of exactly $100,000 per month. You know the goal, and Goal Seek will help you find the answer.

Goal Seek changes the value of an underlying number (the Quantity Produced & Sold) until the value in the goal cell (Gross Profit) is equal to the goal ($100,000). Excel will begin by trying an upper and lower value for the Quantity Produced. If the goal falls between the initial values, Goal Seek then narrows the value in small increments until the Gross Profit value is within 0.001 of the goal. If the goal value is outside the initial range, Goal Seek will try larger values. Each attempt to meet the goal is called an *iteration*. The default Calculation settings (Tools ➢ Options ➢ Calculation) instruct Excel to try 100 iterations before giving up.

Choose Tools ➤ Goal Seek to open the Goal Seek dialog box:

You must enter references or values in all three controls of the Goal Seek dialog box:

Set Cell   The cell (B15, gross profit) that will contain the goal result

To Value   The goal we're trying to reach (100,000)

By Changing Cell   The cell (B5) that contains the value that will be incrementally changed to try to reach the goal in the Set Cell control

You can type in the Set Cell and Changing Cell references, or use the mouse to enter the references. The contents of the To Value control must be a number. After you have entered all three pieces of information, click the OK button, and Goal Seek will begin testing different values in the changing cell.

There are two possible results of a Goal Seek operation: the goal can be reached within the number of iterations set in Excel's options, or it cannot. If Goal Seek finds a value that results in the target value you specified, it will let you know in the Goal Seek Status dialog box:

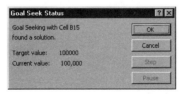

The dialog box indicates both the goal value and Goal Seek's progress in matching the value. In this case, the match is exact. Goal Seek was able to find a value for Quantity Produced & Sold that resulted in a gross profit of exactly $100,000. Clicking the OK button replaces the figures in B5 and B15 with the Goal Seek results. Clicking Cancel leaves the original figures in the two cells.

Some problems don't have a solution. Figure 4.11 shows the Goal Seek dialog box when a solution could not be found. The target value entered for Gross Profit was 250,000. Goal Seek has already tried 100 numbers.

The last number tried is displayed as the Current Value—a very large negative number. Goal Seek has already tried both positive and negative numbers as large as the Current Value shown in the dialog box.

F I G U R E 4.11: Goal Seek: No Solution

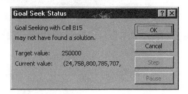

Even when Goal Seek can't find a solution, you know more than you did before: there is no solution. Given the current values for price, fixed expenses, and variable expenses, WellBilt cannot make $250,000 a month from the CD Division no matter how many CD organizers they manufacture. You can click Cancel to discard the value and close the dialog box.

Using Goal Seek

1. Open the workbook that has the figures you want to calculate from.

2. Choose Tools ➤ Goal Seek from the menu.

3. Select a Set Cell where you want the goal value to appear. The cell must contain a formula.

4. Enter the goal value in the To Value control.

5. Enter the value to change in the By Changing Cell control.

6. Click OK to start Goal Seek.

7. To accept the solution, click OK in the Goal Seek Status dialog box to enter the Goal Seek solution. To reject the solution, click Cancel.

Using Solver for Optimization

Objective XL2000E.11.5

Another Excel forecasting tool, Solver, is used to find the best or optimal solution. Optimization has many business applications. Solver can be used to find the least expensive solution to a problem, or a solution that maximizes income. Remember that our original assignment was to maximize gross profit. This is a job for Solver. Choose Tools ➤ Solver to open the Solver Parameters dialog box, shown in Figure 4.12.

F I G U R E 4.12: The Solver dialog box

NOTE Solver is an add-in and may not have been installed on your computer. If you don't see Solver on the Tools menu, click Tools ➤ Add-Ins, choose Solver Add-In from the Add-Ins dialog box, and click OK. Excel may prompt you for the Office 2000 CD to install this feature.

Solver's *Target Cell* is the same as Goal Seek's Set Cell—the cell that the final result should appear in. In the Equal To section, choose the Max, Min, or Value option to indicate whether you are looking for the largest or smallest possible number, or a set value (as you did with Goal Seek). As in Goal Seek, the By Changing Cells is the cell that Solver is to change to find the solution. Click the Guess button, and Excel will add cells that contain values reflected in the Target Cell results in the By Changing Cells control. Unlike Goal Seek, Solver can change more than one cell value to create an optimal solution.

NOTE In the WellBilt worksheet, Excel will "guess" cells B5 and B10–the only non-formula cells in column B. The value in B10 can't change in our model, so we would need to change this to B5 only.

After you have made choices for these three controls, clicking the Solve button instructs Solver to find a solution. Like Goal Seek, Solver will try 100 iterations before reporting that it cannot find a solution. The results of a successful optimization are shown in Figure 4.13.

NOTE With Excel 2000, you can save and load Solver models and add constraints that provide upper and lower limits to changing values. See Excel's Online Help for more information on Solver.

FIGURE 4.13: The Solver Results dialog box

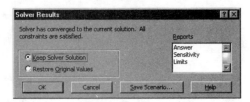

You can choose to place the Solver solution in the worksheet, or restore the original values.

WARNING If you choose Keep Solver Solution, the original values will be deleted. You cannot undo this change.

Using Solver

1. Open the worksheet with the data you want to analyze.

2. Choose Tools ➢ Solver to open the Solver dialog box.

3. Select a Target Cell.

4. Choose an Equal To option.

5. Enter the cell to be changed in the By Changing Cells control.

6. Click Solve.

7. Choose Keep Solver Solution (to replace the original values) or Restore Original Values, and then click OK to discard the solution.

Creating Scenarios

Wouldn't it be nice if you could create multiple sets of values to simulate the best case/worst case/most likely case scenarios? Excel has just the tool for this type of "what if" analysis! Create and save different groups of values using Excel's Scenarios feature, then view the results of different scenarios with just a couple of clicks.

Objective XL2000E.11.4

We used Solver to find the maximum gross profit. Given the current assumptions and fixed costs, WellBilt can maximize their gross profits by producing 31,875 CD organizers at a unit price of $13.63. The Solver solution is shown in column D in Figure 4.14.

FIGURE 4.14: WellBilt data

	A	B	C	D
1	**WellBilt Manuracturing**			
2	**CD ROM Disk Organizer Production**			
3				
4	Income	High	Medium	Low
5	Units Produced & Sold	50,000	45,000	31,875
6	Unit Price	10.00	11.00	13.63
7	Total Income	500,000	495,000	434,297
8				
9	Expense			
10	Fixed Expense	80,000	80,000	80,000
11	Labor Expense	306,000	270,000	191,250
12	Material Expense	62,500	56,250	39,844
13	Total Expense	448,500	406,250	311,094
14				
15	Gross Profit	51,500	88,750	123,203

Now that we know how good it can get, let's take a look at WellBilt's gross profits in a worst-case scenario. We can create a scenario that projects gross profits for a bad month where production delays cause the Units Produced & Sold to fall to 15,000. It's easiest to begin by clicking in the cell that contains the variable you are changing. Since we're experimenting with Units Produced & Sold, cell D5 needs to be selected.

Click Tools ➤ Scenarios to open the Scenario Manager. Click the Add button to open the Add Scenarios dialog box:

Type a name for the scenario (like Worst Case Production) and then enter the changing cell's address. If you selected the cell in advance, the address is already entered. Enter additional details about the scenario in the Comment field. If you're sharing the workbook with other users, you may choose to protect the scenario by preventing changes or hiding it. Click OK; the Scenario Values dialog box opens:

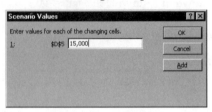

Enter the value that "fits" your scenario. In this example, we entered 15,000, a number that represents a very low production rate. Click OK to return to the Scenario Manager, and create additional scenarios as needed.

When you're ready to view the results of a particular scenario, open the Scenario Manager if it isn't already open and choose the scenario from the list. Click the Show button to display the scenario results in your worksheet. To display another scenario, choose it from the list and click Show.

Creating and Displaying Multiple Scenarios

1. Click Tools ➢ Scenarios to open the Scenario Manager.

2. Click Add to create a scenario.

3. Type a name for the scenario in the Scenario Name field.

4. Enter the references for the cells that you want to change in the Changing Cells field. Enable protection options if desired.

5. Click OK to proceed to the Scenario Values dialog box. Type the values you want for the changing cells, and then click OK to finish creating the scenario.

6. To create additional scenarios, click Add, and then repeat steps 3–5.

7. When you're ready to view one of your scenarios, choose it from the list in the Scenario Manager dialog box, then click Show.

Creating a View

A *view* is a specification for the appearance of an Excel workbook. You can define custom views for a workbook, allowing you to quickly switch, for example, between a view that includes all the columns in a worksheet and a view with hidden columns that you print for customers. View settings include:

- Size and position of the Excel window and child windows, including split windows
- The hidden/displayed status of each worksheet in the workbook
- The active sheet and active cells when the view is created
- Column widths, zoom ratio, and other display settings

You can specify whether print area and other print settings and hidden rows, hidden columns, and current filter settings should be included in a view.

Creating a Custom View

1. Set print options, hide worksheets, set column widths, zoom, and other display options, and activate the worksheet and cell that should be selected when a user opens the view.

2. Choose View ➤ Custom Views to open the Custom Views dialog box.

3. Click the Add button to add a new view.

4. In the Add View dialog box, enter a name for the view. Choose whether to include the current print settings and hidden rows, columns, and filter settings in your view.

5. Click OK to create the view and add it to the Custom Views dialog box.

To open a view, choose View ➤ Custom Views, select the view in the Custom View dialog box, then click Show.

Using the Report Manager

Objective XL2000E.5.2

The Report Manager, another Excel add-in, creates reports that can include views and scenarios. You create a report by combining sections (worksheets) in the order in which you want them printed. Reports are saved within the workbook.

To create a new report:

1. If you want to use a view and/or scenario in your report, create them first.

2. Choose View ➤ Report Manager to open the Report Manager.

NOTE   If Report Manager doesn't appear on the View menu, choose Tools ➤ Add-Ins and install the Report Manager add-in.

---

3. Click the Add button to open the Add Report dialog box:

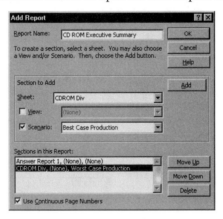

4. Enter a Report Name.

5. Select a sheet (and, optionally, a view and/or scenario within the sheet) to add to the report.

6. Click Add to add the section to the report.

7. Repeat steps 5 and 6 until you're finished adding sections.

8. Use the Move Up, Move Down, and Delete buttons to rearrange the report sections.

9. Enable the Continuous Page Numbering checkbox to print the report with page numbers.

10. Click OK to add the report to the Report Manager.

11. Click OK again to close the Report Manager dialog box.

Printing Reports

To print a report, choose View ➤ Report Manager to open the Report Manager dialog box. Select the report then click Print to open the Print Report dialog box. Select the number of copies you wish to print, and click OK.

Deleting and Editing Reports

To delete or edit a report, open the Report Manager and click the Delete or Edit button.

Hands On

Objectives XL2000E.11.2, E.11.4, and E.11.5

1. Recreate the WellBilt data model shown in Figure 4.14 or, alternatively, develop a worksheet model using your own data.

    a) Use Goal Seek to determine unit price and production numbers for a gross profit of $90,000. (Use Ctrl to enter two changing cell values.)

    b) Use Solver to determine maximum gross profit.

    c) Create a best-case and a worse-case scenario by changing fixed expenses. View each scenario after you create it.

CHAPTER

5

Working with Objects and Graphics

The power of Microsoft Office 2000 is most clearly demonstrated by its ability to exchange data between applications. Adding objects and graphics created in other applications to spreadsheets not only makes the spreadsheets more interesting, but it can make them more functional, too. From Excel's new Web query feature to old standbys such as OLE, Excel's object and graphic tools help you to grab the attention of your coworkers and make a lasting impression!

Converting, Linking, and Embedding in Excel

▶ *Objectives XL2000.1.7 and E.1.2*

An *object* is data that can be embedded or linked in another application. Object Linking and Embedding, or *OLE*, is a protocol that allows applications to communicate with each other to create or update objects. Pictures, charts, Access tables, Word text, and PowerPoint slides are all examples of objects you can convert, embed, or link in Excel 2000 worksheets. As you'll see below, you can also embed or link graphics, sounds, video, and virtually anything else you can select and copy to the Clipboard.

Before you can decide whether you want to convert, embed, or link an object, it's important to understand how the object works after it is imported:

- *Converting* an object changes it from its native format to a format used in the destination document. For example, an Excel chart pasted in Word can be converted to a graphic or text. From the time of conversion, you'll use Word's tools to work with the converted selection.

- *Embedding* an object makes a copy of the object that is then saved within the destination document in its native format.

- *Linking* means that each time you open the destination document, the application will reload the object from its native application file. If you double-click to edit the linked object, the source document will open; you can't change the linked object, only its source. If a linked file is moved or renamed, opening the destination document results in an error message, and the destination document loads without the linked object. You can only successfully open a linked document on a computer that contains both the native application and the source document.

Linking has two advantages over converting or embedding: it saves disk space and, more importantly, it is *dynamic*. If the object's source changes, the change is reflected in all linked documents.

The easiest way to convert, embed, or link data is to use a modification of the standard copy-and-paste operation:

1. Open the *source application* (also called the *native application*) that contains the text, picture, or other object you want to embed or link in the *destination application*.

2. Select and copy the object to the Clipboard.

3. You can close the source application if you wish; in some programs, you'll be asked if you want to retain the contents of the Clipboard. Choose Yes.

4. Open the destination document and place the insertion point where you want to paste the selection.

5. Choose Edit ➢ Paste Special to open the Paste Special dialog box, as shown in Figure 5.1, where a paragraph from a Word document is being pasted into an Excel spreadsheet.

F I G U R E 5.1: Paste Special dialog box

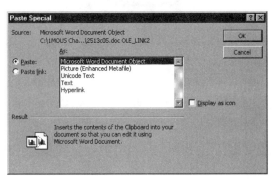

From the Paste Special dialog box, you can choose to convert, embed, or link the selection in the destination application, depending on how you want to use the selection after it arrives. The source for the object is displayed at the top of the Paste Special dialog box. The As box allows you to select a format for the pasted information:

- Microsoft Word Document Object creates an embedded Word object in the Excel spreadsheet that you can edit using regular Word tools.

- Picture (Enhanced Metafile) converts the selection into a Windows Metafile graphic.

- Unicode Text inserts the text with formatting.

- Text inserts the text without formatting.

- Hyperlink inserts the text as a hyperlink.

If you choose the Microsoft Word Document Object option, you can click the Display As Icon checkbox in the Paste Special dialog box to insert an icon rather than text. If you prefer to change the Microsoft Word Object icon that is inserted in the worksheet, click the Change Icon button, which becomes visible when you click the Display As Icon checkbox. You can choose from Word's icon library or click the Browse button and select other icon files.

To link, rather than embed, the selection, choose the Paste Link option. You can link any of the converted file types listed.

NOTE From the computer's point of view, OLE is a complex operation. Give the destination document a moment to accept and place the new object.

Editing an OLE Object

To edit an OLE object, click once on the object in the worksheet to select it. Use the object's handles to size it, or click Delete to delete it. The real magic of OLE occurs when you double-click the object. After you click, wait a moment.

If the object was embedded, the toolbars from the object's native application will open in the destination application. The embedded object is a copy. Changing the object doesn't change the original document, and changes in the source document have no effect on the object.

With a linked object, double-click, and you'll be transported to the source document to edit the object.

Importing from PowerPoint, Access, and Outlook

PowerPoint creates slide and presentation objects, which can be embedded in Excel spreadsheets. Convert, embed, or link a PowerPoint slide just as you would any other object. Copy the slide in PowerPoint, then switch to Excel and click at the destination location. Choose Edit ➤ Paste Special to adjust the settings in the dialog box. PowerPoint also accepts embedded objects from Excel, including charts, if you want to go the other way.

OLE requires a source application that can create an OLE object (an *OLE server*) and a destination application that can accept OLE objects (an *OLE client*). Access and Outlook are OLE clients, but not OLE servers, so they cannot create OLE objects. You can paste Access tables, fields, or records and Outlook items in Excel or Word, but the result will be an Excel worksheet or a Word table, not an OLE object.

TIP To work with live Access data in Excel, you can use Microsoft Query. To access Microsoft Query, choose Data ➤ Get External Data ➤ Database Query. For more about using Microsoft Query, refer to "Querying a Database" in Chapter 3, *Beyond Excel Basics*.

Exporting Excel Data

Objective XL2000E.1.4

Since Excel is an OLE server *and* client, you can link or embed Excel data in other applications. The only difference between exporting Excel data and linking and embedding into Excel is that when you export data, Excel is the source application.

To export Excel data:

1. Select the cells or objects you want to export.
2. Click the Copy button on the Standard toolbar.
3. Switch to the destination application and position the insertion point.
4. Click Edit ➤ Paste Special.
5. Select the type of object you want to use from the As list.
6. Choose whether you want to link or embed. Enable the Display As Icon feature if desired, and then click OK.

Depending on the choices you make in the Paste Special dialog box, you can edit the worksheet in one of the following ways:

- If you choose Paste As A Microsoft Worksheet Object, double-click the object to open a worksheet window and Excel toolbars within the destination application.

- If you choose Paste Link As A Microsoft Worksheet Object, double-click the object to launch Excel and work with the object in the source file.

- If you choose Paste As HTML Format, you can edit the worksheet as you would any other table in Word or PowerPoint.

OLE with Files

If you want to embed or link an entire file instead of a selection, it is often easier to insert the object. Choose Insert ➤ Object ➤ Create From File to open the Create From File page of the Object dialog box, shown in Figure 5.2.

F I G U R E 5.2: Inserting an object with the Object dialog box

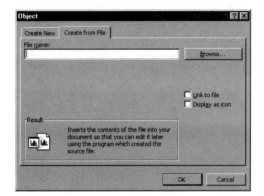

Select and open the file you want to embed or link, and set the other options as you did in the Paste Special dialog box. Click OK to insert the object in the destination document. Some files are inserted as icons, whether or not you choose Display As Icon. Sound files, for example, place an icon in the destination document. Double-clicking the icon plays the sound file.

Embedding or Linking a File

1. Open the destination document and place the insertion point where the object is to be inserted.

2. Choose Insert ➤ Object from the menu. Click the Create From File tab.

3. Browse to select the file you want to embed or link.

4. Click the OK button to embed the file, or choose Link To File, and then click OK to link the file.

Creating New Objects

You can use the Object dialog box to create a new OLE object. For example, you might want to have a PowerPoint slide in an Excel spreadsheet. You don't have to open PowerPoint and create the slide; you can create a PowerPoint slide object in Excel. Because new objects don't exist as separate source files, they cannot be linked, only embedded.

Office 2000 includes other programs—such as Microsoft Graph—that are OLE servers. You probably have other non-Office applications on your computer that also create objects. Choosing Insert ≻ Object from the menu opens the Object dialog box. The scroll list in the Create New page displays the objects that can be created using applications installed on your computer, as shown in Figure 5.3.

F I G U R E 5.3: Creating a new object

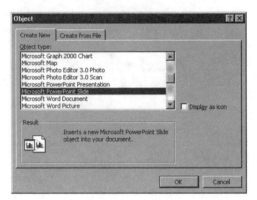

Select an Object Type and click OK. The appropriate OLE server will open within the current spreadsheet. Create the object, then click in the destination window (outside the object) to close the OLE server.

Creating a New Object

1. Position the insertion point in a spreadsheet and choose Insert ≻ Object from the menu bar.

2. Click the Create New tab. Select an Object Type from the scroll list.

3. Click the OK button to insert the newly created object.

The Object Type list is amended as you install new applications. Applications may remain on the list, even if they have been removed from the computer. If you select an application that has been moved or removed, the destination application provides an error message:

Importing a Text File

Objective XL2000E.1.1

There are several ways to import a text file into Excel. If you simply want to import the data and you don't care whether the data may later change in the source file, just open the text file in Excel. Click File ➤ Open and browse to the drive and folder that contains the text file. You'll have to change the Files Of Type control in the Open dialog box to see text files. Select the file you want and click Open. Proceed through the steps of the Text Import Wizard as described below.

However, if you want linked data (and the ability to refresh the data in Excel when the original data changes), you want to follow a slightly different procedure:

1. Click the cell where you want to place the imported data. If you don't want to overwrite existing data, make sure the worksheet has no data below or to the right of the selected cell.

2. Choose Data ➤ Get External Data ➤Import Text File.

3. Locate and select the text file you want to import.

4. Click Open to activate step one of the Text Import Wizard (see Figure 5.4).

F I G U R E 5.4: Step 1 of the Text Import Wizard

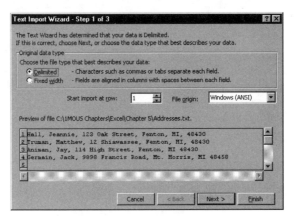

The Text Import Wizard attempts to determine whether your data is delimited (separated by tabs or commas or some other character) or of a fixed width (like columns in a Word table.) If Excel guesses wrong, change the file type option to match your data. Use the spin box to set the Start Import At Row control. You can look at the data preview to see the row numbers Excel has assigned. Set the spin control to 1 if you want all the data. Choose a file origin if your data comes from a location other than the one Excel has selected. When you are finished, click Next to move to step 2 of the Wizard.

Step 2 looks different depending on whether your text file is delimited or fixed-width. Figure 5.5 shows options for delimited files. Your goal in step 2 is to specify how Excel divides the text into columns. So choose a delimiter or, in the case of fixed-width files, create the column breaks as specified in the dialog box for step 2. Click Next to proceed to step 3, where you choose the format for your data.

F I G U R E 5.5: Step 2 of the Text Import Wizard (delimited files)

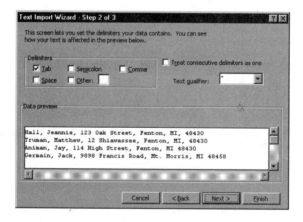

Click Finish at step 3 of the Wizard, and the Import Data dialog box opens:

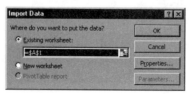

The default is to place the data in the selected cell, but you can collapse the dialog box and select another cell, or choose to insert the data in a new worksheet. Click the Properties button to set additional formatting and layout options. Click OK to close the dialog box and import the data into Excel. The External Data toolbar will open.

Importing a Text File Using the Text Import Wizard

1. Click Data ➤ Get External Data ➤ Import Text File.

2. Locate, select and open the text file you want to import.

3. Choose a file type and enter a number to specify which row of data you want to use as a starting point for the data import. Choose a data origin from the list and click Next.

4. Specify how you want to divide the text into columns. You'll choose a delimiter if you're importing a delimited file. You'll set column divisions if you're importing a fixed-width file.

5. Set data format options in step 3 of the Wizard and click Finish.

6. Choose a location for the imported data in the Import Data dialog box.

7. Click Properties in the Import Data dialog box to set additional formatting and layout options.

8. The External Data toolbar opens when the data import is complete. (Click View ➤ Toolbars ➤ External Data if it doesn't.) Use the tools on the External Data toolbar to edit the import setup and refresh the data as needed.

Importing with Drag and Drop

Another method of importing text into Excel is by using old-fashioned drag and drop. To drag and drop text into Excel, follow these steps:

1. Launch Excel and the source application. Open the file that contains the text you want to import.

2. Resize the two application windows so you can see both of them on the screen.

3. Select the text and drag the selected text with the right mouse button to the desired location in the worksheet.

4. Release the mouse button and choose Copy or Move from the shortcut menu.

Importing a Table from an HTML file

> ## Objective XL2000E.1.3

One of the exciting features of Excel is the ability to use a Web query to import a table directly from a Web page and refresh the data when the content of the table changes. You can import a table from a Web page by inserting it, copying and pasting it, and using drag and drop, as discussed earlier in this section. However, to be able to refresh the data, you must create a Web query to import the table.

TIP To help you get started with Web queries, Excel comes with a number of saved Web queries that you can run to see how they work and to get ideas for queries you may want to create. You can find these queries in `C:\Windows\Application Data\Microsoft\Queries`, the default folder that opens when you choose Data ➤ Get External Data ➤ Run Saved Query.

Creating a Web Query

To create a Web query, first locate the Web page that contains the table you want to import. Then, to design the query, choose Data ➤ Get External Data and click New Web Query. This opens the New Web Query dialog box, shown in Figure 5.6.

F I G U R E 5.6: Use the New Web Query dialog box to import a Web table into Excel.

Follow these steps to import the file:

1. Enter the address of the Web page that contains the table you want to import; either type the URL or click the Browse Web button.

2. When you locate the page you want, select the address in the Address box of the browser and minimize the browser window; Excel automatically enters the URL for you.

3. Choose the part of the Web page that contains the data you want to import:

   - Choose The Entire Page if you want all the text, formatting, and tables on the page.

   - Choose Only The Tables if you want all tables and preformatted sections of a page.

   - Choose One Or More Specific Tables On A Page if you want to specify the table you want. If you want the first table on the page, enter 1 in the text box. If you want more than one table, enter the number of each table in quotes, separated by commas: "1", "3".

4. Indicate how much formatting you want:

   - None strips all formatting and displays text only.

   - Rich Text Formatting Only keeps the Web page formatting but ignores advanced formatting, such as hyperlinks.

   - Full HTML Formatting preserves all of the page formatting.

5. To save the query so you can run it again, click Save Query. Enter a name and location for the query in the Save Query dialog box. Saved Web queries use the file extension .iqy.

6. To change how Excel retrieves preformatted sections and dates, click the Advanced button.

7. Click OK to retrieve the data from the Web page into Excel.

TIP Because Web pages are often designed using tables to help with page structure, the page may contain invisible and nested tables. If you do not get the desired table on your first attempt, choose Data ➤ Get External Data ➤ Edit Web Query and enter a different number in the One Or More Specific Tables On A Page text box based on how many tables you think the page contains.

Refreshing Query Data

To refresh Web query data in an open query, choose Data ➤ Refresh Data. Excel goes out to the Web site and brings in the most current data in the table.

Running a Saved Query

After you save a query, you can open it to refresh it anytime:

1. Choose Data ➤ Get External Data ➤ Run Saved Query.

2. Locate and select the query in the Run Query dialog box.

3. Click Get Data.

If you have a dial-up Internet connection and are not connected, Dial-Up Networking launches to connect you.

TIP If you want to apply formatting, including conditional formatting, to the query, save the query, and after you have the worksheet formatted the way you like it, save the workbook. Rather than running the query in a blank worksheet to retrieve new data, open the saved workbook and refresh the data. The worksheet retains the formatting you apply to individual cells.

Inserting and Creating Hyperlinks

Objective XL2000.1.11

The unprecedented growth of the World Wide Web has contributed to an expectation that software users will be able to jump from one document to another when they want more information about a particular topic.

Office 2000 includes the ability to create hyperlinks within documents, between documents on your network or local drive, and between local documents and the World Wide Web. In Excel, you can create links to named ranges, to worksheets, to other Office documents, and to the Web.

Pasting Text as a Hyperlink

When you paste text into a spreadsheet, one of the options available in the Paste Special dialog box is Paste As Hyperlink. (You can also find Paste As Hyperlink on the Edit menu.) By choosing this option, you insert a link to the document that contains the text rather than the text itself. To use Paste As Hyperlink, follow these steps:

1. Select and copy a word or a phrase in the source document that describes the document you are linking. For example, if you are linking a Word document that contains details on the 2001 budget projections to the 2001 Budget Projections worksheet, select the 2001 Budget Details heading in the Word document and copy it.

2. Switch to the destination worksheet and position the cell pointer where you would like the link to appear.

3. Choose Edit ➤ Paste As Hyperlink. Excel inserts the copied text and underlines it to show it is a hyperlink.

When you point to the first cell containing underlined text, the mouse pointer changes to a hand with a pointing index finger, and a screen tip appears describing the link. Click the link to switch to the linked document.

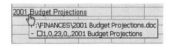

Creating a Hyperlink within a Worksheet

If you would like to create a hyperlink to another location from text within a worksheet, follow these steps:

1. Select the text in the worksheet you want to link and right-click it. Choose Hyperlink from the shortcut menu.

2. From the Link To box in the Insert Hyperlink dialog box (see Figure 5.7), choose a destination for the hyperlink:

   - Existing File Or Web Page: Enter the file path, Web page, or bookmark (worksheet or named range), or browse to locate the destination.

   - Place In This Document: Select a worksheet or named range within the document.

   - Create New Document: Create a new document that you can edit now or later.

   - E-Mail Address: Link to an e-mail message form to send an e-mail to the identified address.

3. Click the ScreenTip button if you want to enter a custom screen tip for the user.

4. Click OK to create the hyperlink.

F I G U R E 5.7: Create hyperlinks within and between documents using the Create Hyperlinks dialog box.

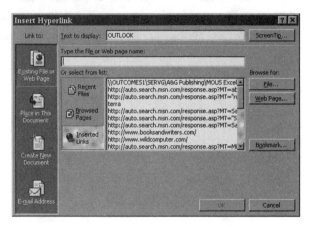

To make changes to a hyperlink in a spreadsheet, right-click the hyperlink and choose Hyperlink from the shortcut menu. Make your choice from the shortcut menu:

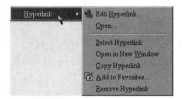

TIP To provide users with additional help on a worksheet you've created, you can include hyperlinks to appropriate topics in the Excel Help files. Open the Help file and then use the Create Hyperlink dialog box to link to the Browse page.

Hands On

Objectives XL2000.1.7, 1.11, E.1.1, E.1.2, E.1.3, and E.1.4

1. Create or open a Word document. Select and copy a paragraph and place it in an Excel spreadsheet:

a) As regular text in a cell using Paste

b) As a picture using Paste Special

c) As an embedded Word object using Paste Special

d) As a linked Word document object

e) As a linked picture

2. Double-click either of the linked objects and make changes to the Word document. Return to the Excel spreadsheet and notice the differences between the converted, embedded, and linked objects.

3. Place a sound or video file in an Excel spreadsheet using Insert ➤ Object ➤ Create From File. Play the media file.

4. Create a small database in Excel using names and addresses of people you know.

a) Save the newly created data as a text file.

b) Open a blank workbook and import the text file.

5. Open another Office application such as Word or PowerPoint. Select a range of cells in an Excel worksheet and paste them in the open application as a linked worksheet object.

6. Create a new Web query based on data you are interested in on the Web (for example, financial data, sports standings, collectible prices, and so on).

a) Save the Web query and refresh the data.

b) Close the workbook, open a new one, and then run the saved query again.

7. Copy text in a Word document and insert it as a hyperlink in an Excel spreadsheet. Follow the hyperlink to make sure it takes you back to the Word document.

8. Create a hyperlink from a named range in an Excel worksheet to another worksheet. Test the hyperlink after it is created.

Inserting Clips and Graphics

Objective XL2000.7.4

If you're thinking of clip art as being too "cutesy" for the office, think again! With thousands of clips from which to choose, you're sure to find the right piece of art to enhance your work in a professional way. Whether you're inserting a clip, WordArt, scanned image, or another type of object, begin by choosing Insert from the menu. If the type of media you want to insert is listed on the Insert menu, select it. If not, choose Object and select the media type from the list in the Insert Object dialog box.

Adding Clips to an Excel Document

The Microsoft Clip Gallery, included with Office 2000, has a broad selection of media clips. When you add other media files to your system, you can add them to the gallery for easy selection. Click Insert ➣ Picture ➣ Clip Art to open the Insert ClipArt dialog box, as shown in Figure 5.8.

F I G U R E 5.8: Microsoft's Clip Gallery

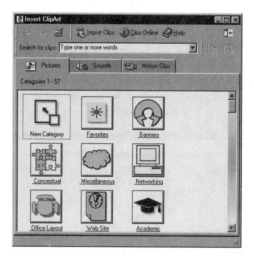

NOTE Even though the Insert ➣ Picture menu choice says *Clip Art*, you can also insert photographs and sound and motion clips from the Clip Gallery. Motion clips, including the animated photographs, are designed for viewing in a Web browser.

The Clip Gallery is arranged in categories. Click one of the icons displayed in the gallery to choose a category, and then locate the thumbnail for the clip you want to insert.

Not all clips in a category are displayed at once. If you wish to see additional clips, click Keep Looking at the bottom of the scroll list. Shift+Backspace will also display more clips when the Clip Gallery is open. Continue to choose Keep Looking until you locate the exact clip you are looking for.

Use the Back and Forward buttons at the top of the Insert-ClipArt dialog box to navigate between current and previous screens.

Click once on the thumbnail for a clip to select it and open a shortcut toolbar with choices to Insert Clip, Preview Clip, Add Clip To Category, or Find Similar Clips.

Choosing the Preview option enlarges the thumbnail so you can see more detail. Close the preview and choose Insert Clip if you decide you like it. You may decide to include this clip in another category. Choosing this third option on the shortcut toolbar allows you to reference the clip in an additional category you select from a list.

The Find option allows you to search for similar clips. You have the option to search for clips by artistic style, by color and shape, or by keyword. Click one of the buttons or click a keyword to move to a page of similar clips.

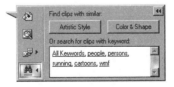

Your search history is kept on a drop-down list at the top of the Insert Clip-Art dialog box. If you wish to duplicate a past search, simply choose the keyword from the list and press Enter to perform that search again.

When you choose Add To Category or Find Similar Clips, the pane that opens stays in view until you click the Hide Pane button at the top-right corner of the dialog box or close the dialog box.

You can choose to insert multiple clips at one time, since the Gallery stays open until you close it and return to your spreadsheet. If you change your mind and wish to delete a clip, click it once to select it, then press Delete on your keyboard. Once you insert a clip, you can resize it by selecting it and dragging the clip's handles. (See "Moving and Resizing Clips" later in this chapter.)

Inserting Clips from the Clip Gallery

1. Position the insertion point where you want to insert the clip.

2. Choose Insert ➢ Picture ➢ Clip Art to open the Clip Gallery.

3. Click the tab to browse Pictures, Sounds, or Motion Clips. Select a category and use the scroll bar to see thumbnails of clips.

4. Preview a picture by clicking it and then clicking the Preview icon from the pop-up menu. With video and sound clips, select one, and then click the Play Clip icon to see or hear a preview.

5. Choose a clip, and then click Insert from the pop-up options or double-click the sound, video, Clip Art, or picture to add it to the document. Close the dialog box when you're through.

6. Delete Clip Art by selecting it and pressing Delete. Resize by dragging a selection handle.

Importing Clips

If your company has a logo or other clip art you want to import into Excel, you can use the Import Clips feature in the Clip Gallery window to store them in an easily accessible place.

To import clips from other locations, click the Import Clips button to open the Add Clip To Clip Gallery dialog box shown in Figure 5.9. Change the

Look In location and locate the file. Then set an import option: Create a copy of the new clip art by checking Copy Into Clip Gallery, or select Move Into Clip Gallery to move the original file. To create a shortcut to the file, choose the third Clip Import Option.

F I G U R E 5.9: Importing a clip

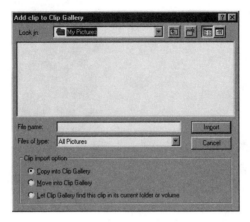

NOTE   You can also import new clips directly from the Web by clicking the Clips Online button in the Insert ClipArt dialog box. Your browser takes you to the Microsoft Clip Gallery Live Web site. Search the site for additional clip art you want to import into the Clip Gallery.

Moving and Resizing Clips

Use the mouse to drag a selected clip to move it. Drag the clip's handle to resize the clip. You can resize a motion clip as you can any other object by dragging a sizing handle. Use caution, however; badly resized motion clips are blurry and difficult to see.

TIP   If you insert motion clips, choose File ➤ Web Page Preview to launch your browser and see the clips in action.

Inserting Other Pictures

If the picture you want to insert isn't in the Clip Gallery, choose Insert ≻ Picture ≻ From File to open the Insert Picture dialog box, shown below. Locate and select the file to insert the selected picture in your document.

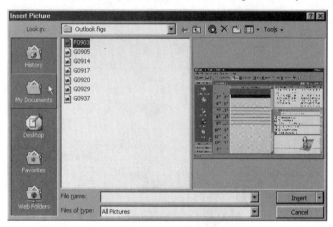

TIP To preview pictures, choose Preview View from the View button on the Insert Picture dialog box's toolbar.

Modifying Pictures

After you've placed a picture from a file or the Clip Gallery, you can adjust the picture using the Picture toolbar. Right-click the picture and choose Show Picture Toolbar from the shortcut menu. (If Hide Picture Toolbar is an option on the shortcut menu, the toolbar is already turned on.) Table 5.1 describes the buttons on the Picture toolbar.

T A B L E 5.1: Picture Toolbar Buttons

Button	Name	Use
	Insert Picture	Insert another picture from a location you specify
	Image Control	Choose from Automatic, Grayscale, Black & White, or Watermark

TABLE 5.1: Picture Toolbar Buttons *(continued)*

Button	Name	Use
	More Contrast	Increase color intensity
	Less Contrast	Decrease color intensity
	More Brightness	Add white to lighten the colors
	Less Brightness	Add black to darken the colors
	Crop	Trim rectangular areas from the image
	Line Style	Format the border that surrounds the picture
	Text Wrapping	Choose if and how text wraps
	Format Picture	One-stop shopping for picture properties
	Set Transparent Color	Use like an eyedropper to make areas of the picture transparent; used extensively for Web graphics
	Reset Picture	Return the picture to its original format

NOTE   The Crop and Set Transparent Color buttons are used with areas of the picture. All other buttons affect the entire picture.

Hands On

Objective XL2000.7.4

1. Start Excel with a blank workbook or open an existing spreadsheet.

   a) Insert a clip from the Clip Gallery.

   b) Size and position the clip.

   c) Insert a motion or sound clip.

   d) Play the motion or sound clip. View motion clip in Web Page Preview.

2. Open the Clip Gallery:

   a) Download a picture from the Microsoft Clip Gallery Live.

   b) Insert the downloaded picture into a document.

   c) Use the tools on the Picture toolbar to retouch the picture.

   d) Insert a picture from a file. Select and resize it. Move it to a different location in the worksheet, and then delete it.

Doing It Yourself with Draw

Microsoft Draw is a built-in Office application that lets you create line art and other objects, such as WordArt. In Excel, there are two ways to create your own graphics: as a single object or as individual drawing objects. To create an object, begin by selecting Insert ➤ Picture ➤ New Drawing, or by clicking Insert ➤ Object and choosing Microsoft Draw object in the dialog box. Because the new object is placed in a separate layer in front of the spreadsheet, you can create complex objects that contain more than one element. While working with the object, you have access to all the available drawing tools described in this section. When you complete your drawing, simply click outside the object's frame to return to the worksheet layer.

Objective XL2000.7.5

The other option, which is probably easier and more efficient for simple graphics, is to start with the Drawing toolbar and use those tools to create graphics directly in your worksheet. Access the Drawing toolbar by clicking the Drawing button on the Standard toolbar.

The Drawing toolbar includes two broad categories of menus and buttons. The first set, beginning with AutoShapes and ending with WordArt, is used to create drawing objects. The buttons to the right of WordArt are used to format existing objects. (More on WordArt in the next section.)

Inserting AutoShapes

Clicking the AutoShapes drop-down button opens a menu of categories:

Choose a category, and a menu of AutoShapes opens. Select an AutoShape by clicking it, and then click or drag to insert the shape in the document. If you intend to add a lot of AutoShapes (for example, when creating a flow chart), you can drag the bar at the top of the menu and place the menu in the document as a freestanding toolbar.

NOTE   Callout AutoShapes are used for annotating other objects or elements, so when you place a callout, the insertion point will automatically appear. To place text in any other AutoShape, right-click the AutoShape and choose Add Text.

Inserting Line Art Objects

  To draw a line or an arrow, click the Line button or the Arrow button, respectively. Move the crosshair pointer to one end of the line you want to draw. Hold the mouse button and drag to draw the line. Release the button to create the line and turn the Line or Arrow tool off. (With the Arrow tool, the arrowhead appears at the end of the line where you release the mouse button.) If you want a line that is absolutely horizontal or vertical in relation to the page, hold the Shift key while dragging the line. If you want a line that is diagonal across the page, hold the Ctrl key while dragging the line.

The Line and other object buttons work like the Format Painter button: When you have more than one object to draw, begin by double-clicking its button. The button will stay depressed, allowing you to draw more objects, until you click any button.

 With the Rectangle and Oval buttons, drag from one corner of the object to the opposite corner, then release the mouse button. Hold the Shift key while dragging to create circular ovals or square rectangles.

TIP   If you need a series of identical objects, create one object, and then use copy and paste.

 Use the Text Box tool to create text that floats on a layer above the worksheet cells. Draw the text box as you would a rectangle. When you release the mouse button, an insertion point appears in the text box. Select and format the text using the Formatting toolbar.

Adding WordArt

 WordArt is used to create a graphic object from text. You'll use WordArt to create logos and emphasize titles, and add excitement to a spreadsheet.

To create WordArt, place the insertion point where you want the graphic and click the WordArt button on the Drawing toolbar to open the WordArt Gallery, shown in Figure 5.10.

F I G U R E 5.10: Microsoft's WordArt Gallery

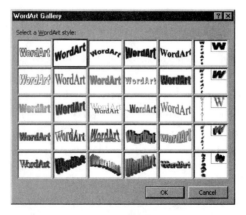

In the Gallery, select a WordArt style and click OK. (You can select a different style at any time.) When the Edit WordArt Text dialog box opens, enter the text you wish to create WordArt from. Use the Font and Size drop-down menus and the Bold and Italics buttons to format the text. Click OK to place the WordArt object in your document and open the WordArt toolbar. The toolbar buttons are described in Table 5.2.

T A B L E 5.2: WordArt Toolbar Buttons

Button	Name	Use
	Insert WordArt	Creates a new WordArt object.
	Edit Text	Opens the Edit WordArt Text dialog box.
	WordArt Gallery	Opens the WordArt Gallery.
	Format WordArt	Opens the Format WordArt dialog box so you can format colors, position, and wrap properties.
	WordArt Shape	Opens a Shape menu so you can select the basic shape the text should be poured into.
	Free Rotate	Changes the object handles to rotation handles so you can rotate the text. Click again to turn off.
	Same Letter Heights	Makes all letters the same height, irrespective of case.
	Vertical Text	Changes the WordArt orientation from horizontal to vertical. Click again to reverse.
	Alignment	Opens an alignment menu with standard options and unique WordArt options.
	Character Spacing	Opens an adjustment menu so you can change space between characters.

Formatting Objects

Use the Drawing toolbar's formatting buttons to format selected objects, including WordArt. To select a single object, just click it.

To select multiple objects, either hold Shift while clicking each object, or use the Select Objects tool and drag a rectangle around the objects you want to select.

Clicking the Fill Color button opens a menu of colors. If you just want an object without any "filling," choose No Fill. No Fill is *not* the same as the colorless sample on the bottom row of the palette—that's the color white.

Change the line color of the selected object by clicking the Line Color button to open a color menu.

The Font Color button changes the text color in a selected object like a text box or callout. With all three color buttons, if there is no object selected, the color you choose is the new default color and will be applied to objects you create in the future.

The Line Style button opens a line-style menu. Selecting More Lines from the menu opens a Format AutoShape dialog box, where you can set other line widths and object attributes.

The Dash Style menu includes solid lines, dotted lines, dashed lines, and other combinations thereof.

In the Arrow Style menu, select the style that should appear at the ends of the selected line from arrowheads and terminators of various types. If the combination of line endings you desire isn't in the menu, choose More Arrow to open the Format dialog box and set a beginning and ending style for the line.

Special Shadow and 3-D Effects

Shadow and 3-D effects are designed to give the selected drawing object more depth. You must choose one or the other; if you apply a 3-D effect to a shadowed object, the shadow is removed, and vice versa.

From the Shadow menu, you can choose a shadow style for the selected object. To format the shadow, choose Shadow Settings from the Shadow menu to open the Shadow Settings toolbar. The toolbar includes a Shadow Color menu and buttons to nudge the shadow up, down, left, or right.

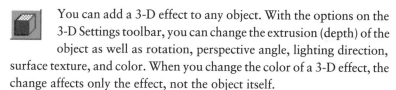 You can add a 3-D effect to any object. With the options on the 3-D Settings toolbar, you can change the extrusion (depth) of the object as well as rotation, perspective angle, lighting direction, surface texture, and color. When you change the color of a 3-D effect, the change affects only the effect, not the object itself.

Arranging Objects

The Draw menu on the Drawing toolbar includes other options for manipulating objects. Drawing objects are placed in separate *layers* on top of the text in a document. To move objects from layer to layer, choose Draw ➤ Order to open the Order menu.

  Bring To Front and Send To Back move the selected object(s) in relation to text and other graphic objects. If you draw an oval and place a rectangle over the right half of it, the rectangle covers part of the oval. If you want the entire oval to show, covering part of the rectangle, either send the rectangle to the back or bring the oval to the front.

  If you're working with more than two layers, use the Bring Forward and Send Backward buttons to move the selected objects one layer at a time.

You can adjust individual objects in a drawing using the Nudge, Align And Distribute, and Rotate Or Flip options on the Draw menu.

Grouping and Ungrouping Objects

When your drawing is complete, you can *group* all of the drawing objects so that they are treated as a single object.

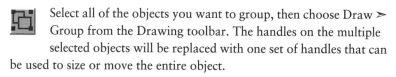 Select all of the objects you want to group, then choose Draw ➤ Group from the Drawing toolbar. The handles on the multiple selected objects will be replaced with one set of handles that can be used to size or move the entire object.

If an object contains more than one element, you can *ungroup* it into separate objects, each of which can be individually moved, sized, formatted, or deleted. This is the easiest way to format Clip Art images. Ungroup the image, then change fills and line colors, or delete portions of the image. When you have finished editing, select all the objects and group them again so you can move or size the entire image.

Hands On

Objective XL2000.7.5

1. Start a new workbook or open an existing one:

   a) Use the Drawing tools to draw a simple picture that includes AutoShapes and lines.

   b) Use the formatting tools on the Drawing toolbar to format individual objects in the drawing.

   c) Select and group all the drawing objects.

   d) Create and format WordArt.

   e) Place an AutoShape.

   f) Apply 3-D effects to the AutoShape.

   g) Use the 3-D Settings toolbar to format the 3-D effects.

CHAPTER

6

Internet Publishing with Excel 2000

In previous chapters, you've learned how to create the entire spectrum of Excel spreadsheets, from simple one-sheet workbooks to complex analysis workbooks with databases, pivot tables, and charts. This chapter focuses on using Excel with the Web, including saving and publishing Web pages.

We'll begin with saving and publishing simple Web pages, and then add advanced features that are more typically used on an intranet. In this chapter, we will use the Traverse Tree Sales workbook we've used in previous chapters (see Figure 4.1).

Saving Worksheets and Workbooks for the Web

Web pages—documents that can be displayed on the World Wide Web—are pages of HTML code. *HTML*, or *Hypertext Markup Language*, is programming code that a browser program like Internet Explorer or Netscape Navigator can interpret and display.

When you publish Excel 2000 worksheets as Web pages, you can create *interactive* or *noninteractive* pages. Noninteractive, or static, pages let browser users view and print published pages. Interactive pages let users manipulate the page data using some of the same tools they would in Excel 2000. Interactive pages can take the place of printed reports, because they allow users to sort, filter, and print the spreadsheet data from their browser.

Objective XL2000.2.6

To create a Web page, begin by opening the spreadsheet you want to save for the Web. Then choose File ➢ Save As Web Page to open the Web page version of the dialog box, shown in Figure 6.1.

F I G U R E 6.1: Use the Save As dialog box to create Web pages in Excel.

The default title displayed for your page in a browser is the workbook's filename. To create a new title, click the Change Title button in the Save As dialog box to open the Set Page Title dialog box, shown here:

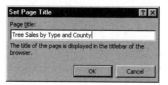

As shown in Figure 6.1, you can either save your entire workbook as a Web page, complete with sheet tabs, or you can save only the active sheet. To save an entire workbook as HTML, enter a location and a filename, then click the Save button to create the Web page and close the dialog box. Excel will create a master HTML page in the location you specify and place images and other files used in the page in a folder named *yourfilename_files* in the same directory. To open the page in your browser, use My Computer or Windows Explorer to locate the HTML file. Double-click the file to launch your browser and open the file.

To save only the active sheet as a Web page, choose the Selection: Sheet option in the Save As dialog box, and then click the Save button.

The easiest way to save a range of cells is to select the range before you choose Save As Web Page. In the Save As dialog box, the Selection option will list the selected range.

NOTE The HTML page is a copy of the data in your workbook or worksheet. If the data in your workbook changes, you have to save the workbook or worksheet as a Web page again to update the HTML page.

Saving a Range, Worksheet, or Workbook for the Web

1. Open the workbook that contains the items you want to save. Select a sheet or range to save part of the workbook.

2. Choose File ➤ Save As Web Page.

3. Choose a Save option: Workbook or Selection.

4. Click Change Title to open the Set Title dialog box. Enter a title that will appear in the browser window.

5. Click OK to return to the Save As dialog box.

6. Enter or browse to select a location and a filename.

7. Click Save to save the workbook or selection as a Web page.

Using Web Page Preview

Objective XL2000.4.2

You don't have to create a Web page to see what your workbook will look like in a browser. Excel's Web Page Preview lets you preview the HTML version of your workbook. Choose File ➤ Web Page Preview to launch your browser and open a preview of the active workbook. Use the tabs at the bottom of the browser window (see Figure 6.2) to move between pages.

FIGURE 6.2: A Web Page Preview of the Traverse Tree Sales workbook

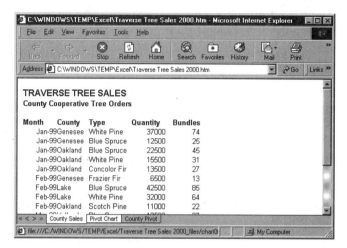

Publishing Interactive Web Pages

Interactive pages are a new feature in Excel 2000. You create interactive pages using one or more of the Office Web Components. There are three Web Components: the Spreadsheet Component, the Chart Component, and the PivotTable Component. You can use the same components in Access and FrontPage to present information from other data sources.

But don't run out and create a bunch of interactive pages yet. The Office Web Components require Office 2000. For a person to use the interactive features in a Web page, they have to have an Office 2000 license on their computer. And Web Components require Internet Explorer, and the newer version you have, the better:

- You can't even see Office Web Components in browsers other than IE, and versions of IE prior to 4.

- With IE 4, you can see and use the page and component, but some features aren't available.

- With IE 4.01 and later, all features are available, but the page is reloaded each time you open it, even within a browser session.

- With IE 5, all component features are enabled. If you modify the component (for example, sorting or formatting cells), the changes will still be there if you return to the page in the same browser session.

If you can't predict or dictate the Desktop environment for your users, you can't rely on interactive pages as your primary means of communicating data. However, for companies or workgroups moving to Office 2000, interactive Web pages are seeing immediate application, because they're a fast and easy way to let end users create reports.

TIP When you save an entire workbook as a Web page, the resulting page is always static. Web Page Preview previews your entire workbook, so the preview is the static versions of your pages.

To create interactive pages, you have to publish rather than save the pages. Begin as you did when saving a page: Choose File ➤ Save As Web Page. Change the page title if you wish. In the Save section, change the option from the default Entire Workbook to Selection. This enables the Add Interactivity checkbox. Click the checkbox before clicking the Publish button (see Figure 6.1) to open the Publish As Web Page dialog box, shown in Figure 6.3.

F I G U R E 6.3: Specify a sheet or range to publish in the Publish As Web Page dialog box.

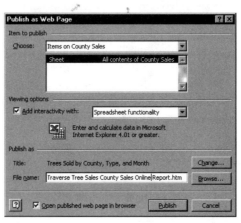

In the Items To Publish section, use the Choose drop-down list to indicate whether you're publishing a specific sheet, something that was previously published, or a range of cells in the workbook. (The range does not need to be named; use your mouse to select the cells you want to publish.)

If you enabled interactivity in the Save As dialog box, choose the component you wish to use from the drop-down list by selecting the kind of functionality you want browser users to have: Spreadsheet, PivotTable, or Chart. Click the Change Title button to supply a title that will appear above the component in the Web page. You can't preview an interactive page, but you can have it open in your browser as soon as it's created by enabling the Open Published Web Page In Browser checkbox at the bottom of the Publish As Web Page dialog box.

Click the Publish button, and Excel creates the Web page including any interactivity you have specified. A Web page that includes the Spreadsheet Component is shown in Figure 6.4. The same sheet without interactivity is shown in the Web Page Preview in Figure 6.2.

F I G U R E 6.4: The interactive Excel worksheet displayed in IE 5

The second Office Web Component, the Chart Component, includes the chart and the data table the chart is based on. Users can change the data in the table to change the chart, just as you do in Excel. However, they can't choose a different chart type or do extensive chart formatting.

Objective XL2000E.11.7

In Figure 6.5, we've published the County Sales worksheet using the third component, the PivotTable Component, which creates a PivotTable List. We selected the PivotTable interactivity in the Publish dialog box. The component works like the Excel PivotTable Report with areas for row data, column data, and page data (filter data).

F I G U R E 6.5: A PivotTable List lets users interactively analyze data.

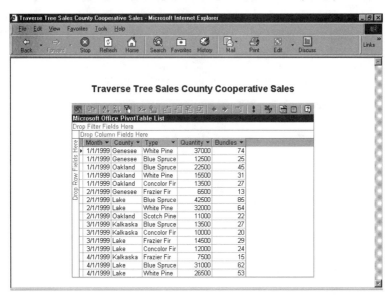

NOTE See Chapter 4, *Taking Excel to the Max*, for more information on working with Excel's PivotTable feature.

Creating an Interactive Pivot Table, Spreadsheet, or Chart for the Web

1. Open the workbook and select the database, sheet, or chart you want to publish for the Web.

2. Choose File ➢ Save As Web Page to open the Save As dialog box.

3. In the Save options, choose Selection: (the sheet or selected range will be listed here).

Creating an Interactive Pivot Table, Spreadsheet, or Chart for the Web *(continued)*

4. Enable the Add Interactivity checkbox.

5. Click the Publish button to open the Publish As Web Page dialog box.

6. Select the type of Item To Publish from the drop-down list.

7. Choose a type of functionality (PivotTable, Spreadsheet, or Chart) from the Add Interactivity Using drop-down list.

8. In the Publish As section of the dialog box, click the Change Title button to enter a title that will appear above the component and in the title bar of the browser window.

9. Select or enter a filename and location for the Web page.

10. To preview the completed page, leave the Open Published Web Page In Browser checkbox enabled.

11. Click Publish to create the interactive Web page.

Browsing an Interactive Page

Each of the Office Web Components supports specific kinds of interactivity. With the Spreadsheet Component, users can add formulas, sort and filter, and format the worksheet. The Charting Component is linked to a data table so users can change the chart display by changing the table data. The PivotTable List lets your users analyze database information using most of the sorting, filtering, grouping, and subtotaling features of Excel lists and PivotTable Reports. We'll examine the PivotTable List we created earlier in this chapter to see how the interactive page works in the Internet Explorer browser.

The interactive page opens with a toolbar above the list. Most of the buttons are familiar from Excel's Standard, Formatting, and PivotTable toolbars:

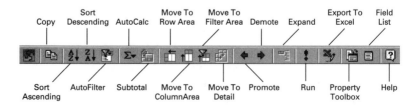

The Export To Excel button saves the worksheet data from the page in a user-specified location (like a user's hard drive). The Properties Toolbox button displays tools that let your users format the data in the list (for example, prior to printing), as shown in Figure 6.6.

F I G U R E 6.6: Users can change the properties of cells in an interactive page using the Properties toolbox.

Objective XL2000E.11.8

Users can sort and filter a PivotTable List using the toolbar buttons. The List has drop-down areas like an Excel PivotTable Report:

- Row
- Column
- Filter
- Detail

To rearrange the List and create a pivot table, in Internet Explorer, drag buttons from one drop area to another. To remove a field from the component, drag and drop its button out of the component onto the page background. Fields in the Column, Row, and Filter areas have drop-down arrows that open a list of the values in the column or row. Use the list to filter the values displayed in the table.

Select a field in a column or row area and click the AutoCalc button on the toolbar to choose a summarization method for the data area (choose COUNT, SUM, MIN, or MAX for value fields; COUNT is the only option for text or date fields). When you add totals, the details will still appear. Use the Expand and Collapse buttons on the Row and Column fields to display or hide the details. Select a Column or Row field and click the Subtotals button to add column or row "grand" totals to the PivotTable List.

To add fields that aren't currently used in the table, click the Field List button on the toolbar to open the Field List, shown in Figure 6.7. Fields in the Field List that are in bold are already displayed in the PivotTable List, and other fields can be added from the Field List. If there's an expand button in front of a field name, click the button to display additional fields.

F I G U R E 6.7: Add fields or dimensions of a field from the Field List.

TIP You can remove a field from the PivotTable List and the Field List. Simply right-click the field and choose Delete.

Some of the fields in the Field List don't actually appear in the data source. For example, fields you've added to the table (like subtotals) are included in the Field List. For date fields, Excel includes different time dimensions. The Traverse Tree Sales worksheet includes a Month field. In Figure 6.7, the Month field appears three times—Month, Month By Week, and Month By Month. Expand the Month By Week field, and you see three different date divisions: Years, Weeks, and Days fields. Expand Month By Month, and you can choose Years, Quarters, Months, and Days fields.

Why are there three different lists? When Excel sees dates in a PivotTable List, it allows you to regard each unique date as an item, or group them into one or more logical divisions. There are 12 months in a year, and 52 weeks, but the weeks don't fall evenly into months or quarters. If you want to display more than one type of date unit, choose all the units from the same group.

Adding Fields to a PivotTable List

1. Open the pivot table page in Internet Explorer.

2. Click the Field List button on the toolbar to open the Field List.

3. Select the field you want to place in the PivotTable List.

4. Drag and drop the field in the PivotTable List, or select the field in the Field List.

5. Choose the area where you want to place the field in the drop-down list.

6. Click the Add To button to place the field in the drop area.

Hands On

▶ *Objectives XL2000.2.6, 4.2, E.11.7, and E.11.8*

1. Open an existing workbook.

   a) Use Web Page Preview to view the workbook in your browser.

   b) Save the workbook as a static Web page with an appropriate page title.

   c) Select a range of cells and save the range as a static Web page.

   d) Save a worksheet as a static Web page.

2. Open an existing workbook that contains a database.

   a) Use the PivotTable Component to create an interactive Web page.

   b) Preview the page in Internet Explorer.

   c) Use the toolbar command buttons to sort and filter the Pivot-Table List.

   d) Open the Properties Toolbox. Format the column and row headings.

   e) Remove all the fields from the PivotTable list.

   f) Open the Field List. Add fields to the Column, Row, and Detail areas.

   g) Use AutoCalc to summarize the results in the detail area.

   h) Hide and display details.

   i) Use the Field List to remove a field from the PivotTable List and Field List.

C H A P T E R

7

Customizing and Automating
Excel 2000

After you have developed a number of workbooks, you may find that you're executing the same commands over and over again. Macros and customized menus and toolbars can help simplify your life and take the drudgery out of your workbooks.

A *macro* is a set of instructions that a program executes on command. The instructions can be simple keystrokes or complex menu selections. If you have tasks you regularly complete that include the same series of steps, creating a macro to automate the task saves time and effort. If you're creating worksheets for others, adding a few macros can make the worksheets more user-friendly. In this chapter, you'll learn how to create, run, and delete Excel macros, as well as how to customize menus and toolbars.

Creating a Simple Macro

Objective XL2000E.8.1

Most macros complete repetitive tasks that involve several steps. You create (record) the series of steps you want to repeat. The next time you need to carry out the operation, you can run (play back) the macro to repeat the steps.

Before creating a macro, you should practice the steps you want to record, because once you begin recording, all of your actions are recorded—mistakes included. Then determine and set up the conditions under which your macro will operate. Will you always use the macro in a specific document? If so, open the document. Will the macro be used to change or format selected text or numbers? If so, have the text or numbers selected before you begin recording the macro, just as you will when you play the macro back at a later time.

When you have practiced the steps and set up the same conditions the macro will run under, select Tools ➤ Macro ➤ Record New Macro to open the Record Macro dialog box shown in Figure 7.1.

F I G U R E 7.1: Create macros in the Record Macro dialog box.

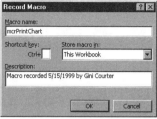

The default name for the new macro is Macro1. (Microsoft didn't waste a lot of imagination here.) Enter a more descriptive name for the macro, like the one shown in Figure 7.1, in the Macro Name text box. Macro names can be up to 255 characters long; can contain numbers, letters, and underscores (but not spaces or other punctuation); and must begin with a letter. Also enter a new description. If other users will have access to the macro, include your name for reference.

Storing a Macro

From the Store Macro In drop-down list, select which workbook you want the macro stored in. In Excel, a macro's storage location determines how you'll be able to access it on playback:

- If you select This Workbook, then the macro will only be available in the current workbook. If you want the same macro somewhere else, you'll have to copy or re-create it. You can also store the macro in a new workbook and then add other functionality to the workbook. Macros that are stored in a regular workbook are *local macros*.

- Storing a macro in the Personal Macro Workbook creates a *global macro*, available to all workbooks created in Excel.

From the description, you'd think that you should save every macro as a global macro, but all the global macros will be loaded each time you launch Excel. They'll take up space in memory, and any macro names used globally can't be reused in individual workbooks. Unless a macro is going to receive wide usage, it's best to store it in the current workbook.

You can assign a shortcut keystroke combination to macros, but use caution if you do. Most of the Ctrl+*key* combinations and many of the

Ctrl+Shift+*key* combinations are already in use. It's safer to assign frequently used macros to a toolbar. You don't have to make this assignment when you record the macro; you can always add a macro to a toolbar later (see "Adding Macros to a Toolbar," later in this chapter).

Recording a Macro

Once you've set the options in the Record Macro dialog box, click the OK button to begin macro recording. The message "Recording" is displayed at the left end of the status bar to show that you are recording a macro, and the Stop Recording toolbar opens.

The macro recorder records the actions you take, but not the delay between actions, so take your time. If you want the macro to enter text, enter the text now. Type carefully—if you make and correct a mistake, the mistake and correction will be included when you replay the macro until you edit the mistake (see "Examining and Editing Macros" later in this chapter). Make menu selections as you normally would to include them in the macro.

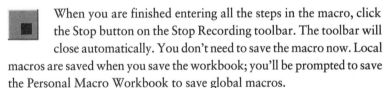

When you are finished entering all the steps in the macro, click the Stop button on the Stop Recording toolbar. The toolbar will close automatically. You don't need to save the macro now. Local macros are saved when you save the workbook; you'll be prompted to save the Personal Macro Workbook to save global macros.

Formatting Options in Macros

Whenever possible, don't use buttons on the Formatting toolbar in macros unless you can guarantee that the text you select when you play back the macro will be formatted exactly as the text was when you recorded the macro. If you use the buttons, the playback results will be unpredictable. If, for example, selected text is already italicized, clicking the Italics button will turn italics off.

If you want to format text in a macro, choose the formatting options from a formatting dialog box, such as Format ➣ Cells, rather than choosing the font, font style, size, and alignment by clicking toolbar buttons.

Cell References in Macros

All macro cell references are absolute references by default. If you click in a cell during macro recording, the macro selects that exact cell each time you play it back. Let's say for example that you want to format a range of cells and then move to the cell below the selection. When you record the macro, the cell below the selection happens to be J22. But each time you play the macro, you don't want Excel to select J22; you want to select the cell below the cells you just formatted.

 To instruct Excel to use relative cell references, click the Use Relative References button on the Macro toolbar. The macro will record references relative to the current cell until you click the button again to turn relative references off. Then you can record other actions using absolute references.

Creating a Macro

1. Create the same conditions that will be in effect when you play the macro.

2. Choose Tools ➤ Record Macro ➤ Record New Macro to open the Record Macro dialog box.

3. Enter a Macro Name and Description.

4. Choose a storage location from the drop-down list.

5. Click OK to begin recording the macro.

6. Perform the steps that you want included in the macro. If you want to include relative cell references, click the Use Relative References button on the Macro toolbar. Click again to turn relative references off if you need to include absolute references.

7. Click the Stop button on the Stop Recording toolbar when you have finished recording the steps of the macro.

Opening a File with Macros

A *macro virus* is a computer virus written as a macro. When you open a document that contains a virus, the virus copies itself into the default template. From that point forward, every workbook you save using the default template will be infected, which means that every file you give to someone else on a disk or via the Internet will also contain the virus.

WARNING Office 2000 does not include virus detection software. You should install some unless you *never* receive files from another computer by disk, network, or Internet connection.

Excel Macro Protection

Excel notifies you if any macros exist in a workbook you are trying to open. You can decide whether you want to open the workbook with macros enabled or to disable them. Disabling the macros gives you an opportunity to look at them in the Visual Basic Editor without endangering your computer. If you decide you want to enable the macros, just close and then reopen the file.

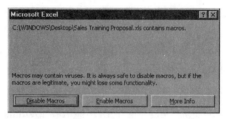

If you know that the workbook contains macros that you or a coworker put there, choose Enable. If, on the other hand, you received the workbook, unsolicited, from someone whose Internet name is HackU, you should consider disabling the macros or not opening the file.

Updating Macros from Previous Versions

Some earlier versions of Excel used a macro programming language called XLM. Visual Basic for Applications (VBA) replaced XLM as the programming language beginning with Excel version 5. Excel 2000 supports both macro programming languages: If you have workbooks that contain XLM macros, Excel 2000 will let you play them. However, you cannot record XLM macros in Excel 2000. All Excel 2000 macros are recorded in VBA.

Running Macros

Objective XL2000E.8.2

It's always a good idea to save anything you have open before you run a new macro. If you make a mistake during recording, the playback results may not be what you expected. (If there was an error, you can record the macro again using the same name. You might also have to click Undo a few times to back out of any problems the macro created.)

To run a macro, choose Tools ➤ Macro ➤ Macros to open the Macro dialog box, shown in Figure 7.2. Select the macro below the scroll list of macro names in the Macro Name/Reference control, and then click the Run button. The macro will execute one step at a time. You can't enter text or choose menu options while the macro is executing. When the macro is done playing, the application will return control to you.

F I G U R E 7.2: Excel's Macro dialog box

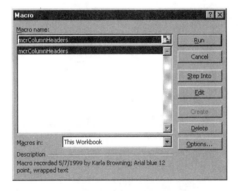

Running a Macro

1. Choose Tools ➤ Macro ➤ Macros.

2. Select a macro from the list of available macros and click Run.

Examining and Editing Macros

> ### Objective XL2000E.8.3

Excel 2000 macros are stored in Visual Basic *modules* and edited in the Visual Basic Editor. To examine or edit a macro, choose Tools ➤ Macros ➤ Macros to open the Macros dialog box, select the macro you want to examine, then click the Edit button to open the Visual Basic Editor, shown in Figure 7.3.

F I G U R E 7.3: Edit macros in the Visual Basic Editor.

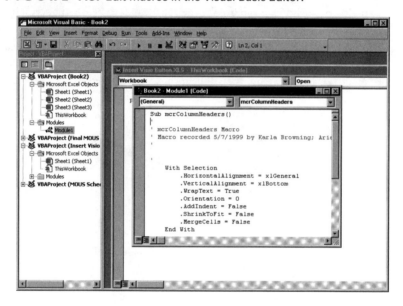

The Visual Basic Editor may contain a number of windows. In Figure 7.3, a Properties window is open on the left and a Code window on the right. You can scroll through the Visual Basic Code window to see the information recorded in a macro. The macro, beginning with the word "Sub" and the macro name and description, includes Visual Basic programming code. If you know VBA programming language, you can create macros and other procedures directly by typing Visual Basic code into a module's code window. If you want to learn about Visual Basic, recording macros and studying the resulting code is a good way to begin. Even if you don't understand Visual Basic, you can do some simple editing here. For example, you could edit the Excel macro shown in Figure 7.3 by entering a different font size or color. When you are finished editing a macro, save, and close the Visual Basic Window.

Editing a Macro

1. Choose Tools ➤ Macro ➤ Macros to open the Macros dialog box.

2. Select the macro you would like to edit and click the Edit button.

3. Make the changes you desire in the Code window.

4. Save the macro and close the Visual Basic window.

Deleting Macros

You can delete a macro in two ways. If you have recorded a macro and are not pleased with the way it executes, you can record the macro again, using the same name. You will be asked if you want to overwrite (delete) the existing macro.

You can also choose Tools ➤ Macro ➤ Macros, select the macro from the macro list, and click the Delete button to delete the macro from the template.

NOTE   If you delete a macro that has a toolbar or menu command, you also need to remove the macro's command from the toolbar or menu bar. See "Adding Macros to a Toolbar" later in this chapter.

You can copy macro modules from one workbook to another, add pauses for user input or the insertion of specific information, and otherwise customize macros. When you have mastered the information in this skill and want to learn more, choose Help ➤ Contents And Index from the menu bar and enter **macros** in the Index to find more information.

Customizing Toolbars

You may have already noticed that all Office users do not use applications the same way. Features that are important to you may be wasted on your colleague in the next office.

It used to be rather challenging for Office users to customize the command bars, i.e. toolbars and menus, that helped them access the features they wanted to use. Office 2000 changes all that with an easy-to-use interface that lets you add and remove toolbar buttons, change menu options, and even add macros to command bars for quick access. In this section, you'll learn about hiding and displaying the toolbars you want, customizing toolbars, and assigning macros to command buttons.

Hiding and Displaying Toolbars

▶ *Objective XL2000E.7.1*

In addition to the Standard, Formatting, and Drawing toolbars that are visible by default when you launch Excel, you can access eleven other pre-defined toolbars: Chart, Clipboard, Control Toolbox, External Data, Form, Picture, PivotTable, Reviewing, Stop Recording, Visual Basic, and WordArt. Any or all of these toolbars can be displayed or hidden at any given time.

Displaying Toolbars

1. Choose View ➤ Toolbars.

2. Click to select a toolbar you want to display. The menu closes automatically and the toolbar is displayed.

Hiding Toolbars

1. Choose View ➤ Toolbars.

2. Clear the check mark by selecting the toolbar you want to hide. The menu closes automatically, and the toolbar is hidden.

Customizing Menus and Toolbars

▶ *Objective XL2000E.7.2*

To customize a toolbar, right-click any toolbar and choose Customize, or choose View ➤ Toolbars ➤ Customize to open the Customize dialog box. Click the Commands tab to open the Commands page, shown in Figure 7.4.

F I G U R E 7.4: The Commands tab of the Customize dialog box

Drag menu items or buttons to new locations to rearrange them, or drop them in the document window to delete them. To add a command, scroll the Categories and Commands lists until you find the command you want. Drag the command onto a menu or toolbar. If you mess things up completely, you can always select and reset the menu bar and the toolbars on the Toolbars page of the Customize dialog box. You can also create your own personalized toolbar that contains only the buttons you use.

Creating a New Toolbar

1. Right-click any toolbar and choose Customize.

2. Click the New button on the Toolbar tab.

3. Enter a toolbar name of your choice. Excel opens an empty toolbar outside of the dialog box.

4. Click the Commands tab of the Customize dialog box and drag any buttons you wish onto the toolbar.

5. To copy a button from an existing toolbar, hold Ctrl while dragging the button.

6. To remove a button or menu item from a toolbar, drag the item off the menu or toolbar.

7. When you have all the buttons you want, click Close on the Customize dialog box.

8. Point to the title bar of the toolbar and drag it to the desired location in the application window.

Adding Macros to a Toolbar

Objective XL2000E.7.3

To add an existing macro to a toolbar, right-click any toolbar and choose Customize, or choose View ➤ Toolbars ➤ Customize to open the Customize dialog box. Click the Commands tab to open the Commands page, and select Macros from the Categories list. Two options appear in the Commands List: Custom Menu Item and Custom Button. If you want to add the macro anywhere on the menu bar, choose Custom Menu Item. If you'd prefer a button (with a picture, text, or both), choose Custom Button.

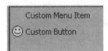

To add a menu item, select Custom Menu Item from the Command List. If you want to place the custom menu item on an existing drop-down menu, drag the menu item to the menu and hover a moment until the menu opens. Drop the menu item where you want it on the menu—a guideline shows you where the item will be inserted.

To add a toolbar button, select Custom Button and drop it on the appropriate toolbar. If you drop it on an existing button, the other buttons move right to make room for the new button. (Be careful here—buttons move to the right, so you can't see them on the screen unless you scroll the toolbar.)

After you've placed your button or menu item on the toolbar, with the Customize dialog box still open, right-click the item to open the shortcut menu:

In Excel, you must assign the macro to the button. Choose Assign Macro from the bottom of the menu and the familiar Macro dialog box opens. Select the macro you want to assign from the list, and then click OK.

WARNING   You must open the Customize dialog box to customize an existing macro on a toolbar. If you don't open the Customize dialog box first, you get the View Toolbars menu when you right-click the macro.

Changing Toolbar Item Options   The default toolbar button picture is the yellow smiley face. With the Customize dialog box open, right-click a button and choose Change Button Image to open a menu of icons you can assign to a command item.

If you prefer, you can label the button or menu item by changing the contents of the Name box on the shortcut menu. After you change the contents of the Name box, click the Text Only option on the shortcut menu to get rid of the button icon. The ampersand (&) is used on menu items and appears before the letter that a user can press along with the Alt key to choose the menu item. The letter is underlined on the menu bar like the *F* in File and *E* in Edit.

For the artistically inclined, Office 2000 offers an opportunity to create your own button images. While you are still in the Customize mode, select the button, right-click to get the shortcut menu, and then choose Edit Button Image to open the Button Editor to edit the button image.

When you are finished adding menu items, assigning macros, and sprucing up your button images, close the Customize dialog box. Now you can play the macro by clicking a toolbar button or making a menu selection.

Adding a Macro to a Menu or Command Button

1. If the macro is not global, open the workbook that contains the macro.

2. Right-click any toolbar and choose Customize. Click the Commands tab.

3. Choose Macros from the Categories list.

Adding a Macro to a Menu or Command Button *(continued)*

4. Drag Custom Menu Item or Custom Button from the Commands List to the toolbar or menu and drop it in the desired location.

5. Right-click the new item and select Assign Macro from the short-cut menu.

6. Choose the macro in the Macro dialog box.

7. Click OK to assign the macro to the button, then close the Customize dialog box.

Hands On

Objectives XL2000E.7.1, E.7.2, E.7.3, E.8.1, E.8.2, and E.8.3

1. Record a global macro that checks the spelling in the active worksheet and then sends the document to the printer. Name the macro SpellPrint, add it to the Standard toolbar, and test it.

2. Record a global macro that:

   a) Opens the Page Setup dialog box

   b) Inserts a header with your name and the current date

   c) Sets all four margins at 1 inch

   Name the macro StandardPageSetup. Execute the macro to see that it works the way you designed it.

3. In any Excel workbook, create individual macros to complete the tasks below. Create your own macro names. When all macros are recorded, create a new toolbar and add all the macros to the toolbar.

   a) Create a macro to format a range of cells for currency, no decimal places, Arial 12-point, dark blue.

   b) Record a macro that creates a footer that includes "All rights reserved, *your company name* (or *your name*)," and the current date.

   c) Record a macro to change the paper orientation to landscape.

4. Hide the Formatting toolbar and create your own customized Formatting toolbar to replace it.

APPENDIX

A

A Microsoft Office User Specialist (MOUS) is someone who has passed an exam administered through a Microsoft Authorized Testing Center on one of the Office 2000 products. Introduced in 1997 as the Microsoft Certified Office User Program, users today can receive designation as Microsoft Office User Specialists at the core level in Word, Excel, PowerPoint, Access, and Outlook (FrontPage and PhotoDraw core exams should be available soon). For those who really want to demonstrate their skills, exams are also available at Expert and Master levels.

Although the Office certification process is relatively new, Microsoft is experienced at certification. It currently offers several highly respected certification programs such as the Microsoft Certified Systems Engineer (MCSE) and the Microsoft Certified Professional (MCP) programs. Up until now, all of these certifications focused on networking, systems, or programming skills. They were not intended for end users, but rather they were designed to establish recognizable standards for computer professionals—those people whose life's work revolves around computer systems.

The MOUS Difference

The Microsoft Office User Specialist certification is fundamentally different from other certifications that Microsoft offers. People who pass the MOUS exams are just as likely to be employed in professions outside of the computer field. They are real people performing real jobs. Whether in a large corporation or in a small office, a MOUS is using applications such as Word and Excel to function effectively as an administrative assistant, a secretary, a manager, an account representative, or a myriad of other positions that require day-to-day problem-solving skills. The Microsoft Office family of products has helped this person accomplish the impossible to meet a deadline, impress their bosses, and perform their job more efficiently. MOUSs are interested in improving their skills and increasing their opportunities. As more and more employers begin looking for verification of a person's software skills, there is no better way to stand out from the crowd than to show your credentials as a specialist in the software the job requires.

NOTE   Although the MOUS program got off to a slow start, over 900 testing centers around the world have now delivered well over 30,000 exams.

Should You Become a Microsoft Office User Specialist?

If you were applying for an office job only a few short years ago, probably the only test you had to take was a typing test to document your speed and accuracy at a typewriter. It didn't matter if you understood what you typed or if you could create a similar document from scratch; all you had to be able to do was re-create what someone handed to you and do it in an acceptable amount of time.

With the infiltration of personal computers into large and small workplaces everywhere, the expectations placed on office workers have increased significantly. Typing speed and accuracy may still be important, but even more valuable is knowledge about how to make the most efficient and effective use of new office technology.

Microsoft Office 2000 is the fastest growing office suite on the market today. Knowing how to apply this group of powerful applications to the demands of your work environment can clearly put you ahead of the pack. You immediately stand out from the typists and become recognized as a problem-solver and, in some cases, even as a lifesaver to those who are in a position to help advance your career.

If you are in business for yourself, you may not care about whether you can prove your skills to someone else, but being able to influence potential clients with the quality of your written and verbal presentations may make the difference between your business's success and failure. With little validation available from co-workers, the small businessperson has to find other ways to feel confident in their skills, to know they are effectively using state-of-the-art technology to impress their clients.

The Microsoft Office User Specialist program provides a mechanism for all types of users, regardless of their motivation, to prove their competency in the family of Microsoft Office 2000 applications. Whether you are a student with little real-world experience or a highly trained professional with a top-level staff position, you may find that it is beneficial to add the Microsoft Office User Specialist designation to your portfolio.

Getting Your Employer to Foot the Bill

Companies that place a high value on employee education and training may very well agree to pay for you to take one or more of the MOUS exams. As the credential is becoming more widely known, more and more employers are looking at the MOUS credential as a mark of excellence in their company. Certainly, there is no hard-and-fast rule about this—employers are by no means required to pay for them. However, it certainly doesn't hurt to ask your boss or your Human Resources department. Some companies may agree to reimburse you only if you pass an exam—it doesn't pay for them to spend money for someone to fail it.

Unless your company has issued a statement about paying for the exams, do your homework before approaching your employer. It helps if your company has already adopted or plans to adopt Office 2000 as the company standard. Visit the Microsoft Office User Certification Web site (`www.mous.net`) and other Office certifications sites, such as the site offered by Quick Start Technologies (`www.officecert.com`), for more information (ammunition) to convince your employer of the benefits to the company of having certified employees.

If you decide to give your employer the opportunity to demonstrate his or her commitment to quality improvement and staff development, here are a few tips for you to consider when you are preparing a proposal to give to your boss:

- Plan to study for the exams on your own time. If you spend an hour after work or at lunch time working through this book three or four times a week, you'll be ready to take one or even two of the exams after just a few study sessions. By doing it on your own time, it shows that you can take initiative and that you are committed to personal improvement. Even if this doesn't impress your employer, you will have improved your skills to help you in other areas of your job (or to get a better job!).

- Become familiar with Microsoft's requirements and the process for taking the exams so that you are prepared to answer any question your employer may ask you about how the exams work.

- List at least three specific benefits to the company for having certified employees. Be able to point out the financial savings resulting from fewer technical support calls and from less downtime figuring out how to do something.

- Develop an argument that ties your getting certified into the company's overall quality initiative. Having certified employees in every field helps a company demonstrate to their current and potential customers that they are committed to quality. It makes the company look good, and that goes a long way in today's competitive market.

- Offer to be a mentor to other employees—individually or as a group. If work time is too precious, organize a weekly bag-lunch of Office users and have someone present a different topic each week based on a project they just completed. However you approach it, show your employer you are a leader, and it may be easier to make a case for the value of the certifications to the company.

If all else fails, pay for the exams yourself. Being certified makes you a more valuable commodity and may make your employer think twice when he or she sees you using Word to update your resume!

Microsoft Office 2000 User Specialist Designations

Once you've decided to pursue certification, you have to determine if you want to take all of the exams or pick and choose among them. Unless you plan to train other users or you have a technical-support-type job, you probably don't have a need to take all of the exams available. However, if you want a comprehensive knowledge base and you want the new plum of Office Specialist that Microsoft has placed on the platter, you may want to set up a plan of attack and go after them all.

It's possible to receive designation as a MOUS in each of six applications that are a part of the Microsoft Office family. These include Word, Excel, PowerPoint, Access, and Outlook. Because Word and Excel are the most popular of the six products and have the most widespread application, two levels of designation—Core and Expert—have been developed for these applications; that means that there is a separate test for each level.

Microsoft expects that a Microsoft Office User Specialist at the Core level is able to complete the everyday tasks that arise in a typical office setting.

For example, a Word Specialist should be able to format text and paragraphs, create tables and columns, manage files, and work with pictures and charts. An Excel Specialist should be able to format cells and worksheets, enter formulas and basic functions, work with multiple worksheets, create charts, and insert objects.

In order to become an Expert Specialist, you are expected be able to create more complex documents. For example, a Word Expert should be able to conduct mail merges to create personalized form letters with envelopes and mailing labels, work with master documents and subdocuments, add references, and use collaboration features. An Excel Expert should be able to use templates, work with multiple workbooks, create macros, use analysis tools, and use collaboration features.

The eight Specialist designations currently available are:

- Microsoft Office User Specialist: Microsoft Word 2000
- Microsoft Office User Specialist: Microsoft Word 2000 Expert
- Microsoft Office User Specialist: Microsoft Excel 2000
- Microsoft Office User Specialist: Microsoft Excel 2000 Expert
- Microsoft Office User Specialist: Microsoft PowerPoint 2000
- Microsoft Office User Specialist: Microsoft Outlook 2000
- Microsoft Office User Specialist: Microsoft Access 2000
- Microsoft Office User Specialist: Microsoft Office 2000 Master

Under Development

The MOUS program is still relatively new, and administration of the program was only taken over by Nivo International in late 1998. As a result, not all of the anticipated exams have been developed as of the publication of this book. Exam objectives, however, have been released for the following anticipated designations:

- Microsoft Office User Specialist: Microsoft PowerPoint 2000 Expert
- Microsoft Office User Specialist: Microsoft Access 2000 Expert
- Microsoft Office User Specialist: Microsoft Outlook 2000 Expert
- Microsoft Office User Specialist: Microsoft FrontPage 2000
- Microsoft Office User Specialist: Microsoft FrontPage 2000 Expert

- Microsoft Office User Specialist: Microsoft PhotoDraw 2000
- Microsoft Office User Specialist: Microsoft PhotoDraw 2000 Expert

Check www.mous.net for updates on the availability of these additional exams.

The MOUS Exams

Taking a MOUS exam is a lot like completing the Hands On exercises in each chapter of this book. You will be expected to be able to apply your knowledge of an application to real-world tasks that you will complete using the application itself. Unlike other Microsoft certification exams, there are no multiple-choice questions. Instead, each user is expected to complete specific tasks, such as formatting a document in a certain way, creating a formula, sorting a list, and so on. The exams must be completed within the designated timeframe, which generally is under an hour, depending on the exam.

This is not a paper and pencil test. You will be working with a fully functional, live version of the product on which you are being tested. You can use all of the features of the product, including Help. However, if you access Help too often, you'll run out of time before completing all of the required tasks.

When you're ready to start, take a deep breath (be sure to exhale, too!) and click the Start Test button. You complete each task on the sample documents provided, so you don't have to spend time creating documents of your own. Each task has a set of instructions for you to follow. When you've completed one task, you click Next Task and move on to the next task.

WARNING   Be aware: There is no going back to a previous task. Once you've moved past a particular task, it's gone forever.

Preparing to Take an Exam

Before you start studying, review the objectives for the test you are interested in taking. If you're an experienced user, you may even want to check off those activities with which you are already pretty comfortable. Spend some time reviewing those activities, making sure you are 100 percent confident about completing each of them. When you are ready to tackle new ground, either follow the topics of this book in order or use the certification map in the very front of the book to jump to the activities on which you want to focus.

If you are a relatively new user, you will benefit most from following each of the topics in this book in order, completing the Hands On exercises, and then moving on to the next topic. When you have completed the book, review the objectives again, and make sure you can complete each activity comfortably. If you need to review a topic for a second time, refer to the certification map at the front of the book to find out where that topic is covered.

If you'd like to get a taste of how the exams work, download the practice exams from the MOUS site (www.mous.net). You'll find practice exams for Word, Excel, and PowerPoint. They help you get used to the format and the structure of the exams, so you'll know what to expect when you sit down to take the real ones.

Registering to Take an Exam

You can receive information about a local Authorized Testing Center (ATC) by calling 800-933-4493 or visiting the Web site of the company that is managing the testing, Nivo International, at www.mous.net. Not every city has a testing center, but the number of centers is growing rapidly—there is probably one within a couple hours, drive if not right in your city. Although some centers allow walk-in test-takers, it's best to call first to make sure.

Each test you take has a fee associated with it. You can usually pay by check or credit card—check out payment arrangements when you call to register. Be sure to bring a picture ID (driver's license, passport, credit card) to the testing center with you.

Taking More Than One Exam

You may want to take more than one exam in a day, especially if the testing center is a distance from your house. Be careful not to overload yourself, however. Some people may be able to handle taking three or four in a day—others may faint after taking one. Evaluate how long you can realistically concentrate without affecting your ability to think clearly. There's no point in paying for an exam and then not allowing yourself optimal test-taking conditions.

If you plan to take more than one exam, talk with the testing center about spacing them out a bit throughout the day. Take one or two, and then go to lunch before taking another one or two. You'll be fresher and have time enough to refocus on the new topic (and maybe even get in a little last minute cramming).

Getting Help When You're Stuck

You may not bring notes, books, or a laptop computer into the testing center. However, you may use the application's Help files for a quick refresher during the test. If you are concerned that you might have to look something up during the exam, extensively practice using Help before going in. You may find yourself failing the exam because you wasted valuable seconds searching through Help files. Find the most efficient ways to locate the steps you need to accomplish a task; try using the Index to search for what you need.

If you know there are a couple of areas you are weak on, look the topics up in the Index ahead of time so you'll know what you are looking for— and when you have found it.

TIP   Stay away from using the Office Assistant while you are taking an exam. Even though it may be cute, it takes up precious time just appearing and disappearing. Save it for when you have the time to be entertained!

The Moment of Truth

The MOUS tests are scored electronically, so you'll know your score immediately; you need to get about 80 percent correct to pass. If you pass, you'll receive a certificate of completion in the mail one to two weeks after taking the test. Take yourself out to dinner to celebrate or, better yet, have someone else take you out!

What Happens If You Don't Pass?   If you need to take a test again, ask the test administrator for a printed score report, which identifies where you need to focus your energy as you prepare for another round. Of course, you'll have to pay to take a test again, but it will probably be money well spent. You'll have learned some things and, although it would be nice to not be out the exam fee, being more experienced means you'll probably pass it next time.

If you thought you were prepared and still didn't pass the exam, you may just have test anxiety that probably won't be as bad the second time around. You'll be in familiar surroundings and know very clearly what you are expected to do. If you realize that you didn't know how to do certain tasks that were asked for, study up on those and then be sure to review all the material before taking the test again.

APPENDIX

B

Glossary

Numbers

3-D cell reference

A formula reference to a cell or range that spans worksheets.

A

absolute reference

Used in a formula to refer to a specific cell; does not change when the cell containing the formula is copied or filled.

active cell

The cell that is currently selected.

align

To place text or numbers either to the left, center, or right, relative to the boundaries of a cell or selection.

application window

A Windows container that displays a program.

applications (apps)

Programs that allow you to complete specific tasks such as creating budgets, lists, or letters.

arguments

Parameters for a function enclosed in parentheses.

array

A special type of database in which one column or row contains unique values.

ascending (order)

A to Z (text); 1 to 10 (numbers).

AutoCalculate

A sum (default), count, average, min, or max displayed in the status bar when two or more cells are selected.

AutoComplete

A feature that completes a text entry based on other entries in the same column.

AutoCorrect

A feature that automatically corrects commonly misspelled words based on entries in a dictionary.

AutoFill

An Excel feature that allows you to copy a formula, weekday, or month name to other cells.

AutoFilter

Displays drop-down arrows next to the field names in a database so you can set criteria for the records you want to display.

AutoFit

An Excel feature that automatically adjusts column width to the widest value in the column.

AutoFormat

An Excel tool that allows you to choose from pre-designed worksheet formats.

automatic calculation

Excel's default calculation mode; all formulas are reevaluated after any cell is altered.

AutoShape

A collection of drawing objects such as arrows, clouds, stars, etc., accessible through the Drawing toolbar.

AutoSum

A button on the Standard toolbar used to create totals.

average (AVERAGE)

A function used to produce the statistical mean for a selection.

B

bar chart

A series chart where data points are represented by horizontal bars.

base field

The field used as a criterion in a pivot table custom calculation.

base item

The value used as a criterion in a pivot table custom calculation.

bold

Enhances the contents of a cell so they will print darker than non-bold cells.

border

A line above, below, to the left, to the right, or surrounding one or more cells; borders are visible on screen and in printed worksheets.

C

calculated field

A cell in a database that contains a formula.

cell

The basic worksheet unit; an intersection of a row and a column.

cell address

The column letter and row number that describe a cell's location.

cell selection pointer

The shape of the mouse pointer within the worksheet: a large plus sign or "chubby cross."

CellTip

A comment about cell contents or data entry; displayed when the user mouses over the red triangular comment indicator.

change history

Record of edits made in a shared workbook.

chart

A graphical representation of numerical data.

chart area

The area bounded by a chart's border, containing all the elements of the chart.

Chart Wizard

A program that walks you through the process of creating a chart.

circular reference

An error in a formula caused by including the answer cell, directly or indirectly, in the formula's range.

clip art

Commercially available graphics and other images, such as those contained in the Microsoft Clip Gallery, that can be imported into applications and then positioned, resized, and edited for use in various documents.

Clipboard

Part of the computer's memory reserved by Windows for cut, copy, and paste operations.

click

Press the left mouse button to select an object or command.

close

To remove a window and its contents (application or document) from the computer's memory when you are finished working with it; does not remove programs or files from your disks or hard drive.

collapse

Reduce an outline or outline level so all detail is hidden, or reduce the size of a dialog box so you can see the data behind it.

Collect and Paste

A new feature in Office 2000 that lets you copy multiple items to the Office Clipboard and paste one, several, or all of them in any order you want in any Office 2000 application.

column

A vertical unit within a worksheet referenced by letter.

column chart

A series chart that uses vertical bars to represent data points.

column header

The gray button at the top of a column labeled with the column's letter.

column width

The amount of space between the left and right boundaries of a column.

command bar

A menu or toolbar in an application window that allows access to the features in that application.

comment

A pop-up text box that displays a message when the user mouses over the red triangular comment indicator.

condition

An expression that can be evaluated to true or false.

conditional formatting

Formatting applied to selected cells based on whether or not the cells meet the criteria you set.

consolidate

Summarize data from one or more worksheets.

consolidation table

An Excel table created by summarizing information from multiple worksheets.

constraint

A rigid, externally imposed boundary in an analysis, such as the number of hours in a day.

context button

The non-primary mouse button; for right-handed users, the right mouse button.

context menu

A menu that pops open in response to clicking the right mouse button.

contiguous

Next to each other.

copy

Transfer a duplicate of selected cells to the Clipboard for later use.

criteria

User parameters that guide filtering or selecting records.

criteria range

In advanced filtering, the field names and user-defined criteria for each.

custom format

A string of placeholders that determines how values will be displayed in a cell.

custom lists

Lists maintained for AutoFill, such as the names of days of the week and months of the year.

customize

Change settings for a program to reflect user needs or preferences.

cut

Move selected cells to the Clipboard for later use.

D

data

Facts and figures to be entered in a worksheet.

data form

A dialog box used to enter, edit, delete, or select records in an Excel database.

data labels

In a chart, the description of each data point.

data map

Maps that illustrate numbers related to geographical areas.

data points

Numbers in a worksheet selected for representation in a chart.

data series

A group of related data points.

data validation

Business rules attached to a cell that establish a range of valid values that a user can enter.

database

A worksheet that includes columnar fields and records contained in rows.

database management system (DBMS)

Software like Microsoft Access that allows you to create and relate multiple sets of records.

default

Pre-existing settings for hardware and applications that the user can choose to accept or change.

delete

Remove a cell, selection, column, or row from a worksheet; clear the contents of a selected area.

delimited

Separated by a specified symbol or character.

dependent workbook

A workbook containing linked values stored in another workbook.

dependents

Cells that contain formulas that refer to the current cell.

depreciation

The reduction in the value of an asset over time.

descending (order)

Z to A (text); 10 to 1 (numbers).

Desktop

The control center for Windows.

destination

The application on the receiving end of an OLE object.

dialog box

A window that appears when a Windows-based program requires more information from the user to complete a task.

double-click

Press and release the primary mouse button twice in rapid succession without moving the mouse between clicks.

dpi

Dots per inch; used to measure the resolution (clarity) of printed copy.

drag-and-drop

A method for copying or moving cells.

drill down

Display additional levels of detail from a summary or consolidation.

drop-down list

A control that displays a list of choices when you click it.

drop shadow

A graphic technique for borders and boxes that looks as if the object is casting a shadow.

dynamic

An object, field, or contents of a cell that is linked to and changes in response to another object, field, or cell.

E

elements

Individually formattable parts of a chart.

embed

Copy a file or object and paste it into a document as a non-linked OLE object.

execute

Run a program.

expand

Change the view of an outline or outline level so additional layers of detail are displayed.

explode

In a pie chart, to pull one or more slices away from the center.

export

Transfer data for use in another application or at a later time.

extension

A three-letter designation following a period at the end of a filename used to relate a file to the application used to open it.

extract

To filter a subset of records from a database.

F

field

A category; a column in an Excel database.

field button

A button that represents an individual database field in a pivot table layout.

field name

The column heading in an Excel database worksheet; field names must be unique within a database.

file

A collection of data saved on a computer system.

filename

A unique name assigned when a file is saved.

fill

To copy a formula or other contents from the selected cell to additional cells; in an object, the shaded background.

fill color

Background shading in a cell, range of cell, or objects.

fill handle

The square box at the lower-right corner of a selection used to copy the contents of the selection to other contiguous cells.

filter

In a database, to use criteria to display specific records; a group of settings used to convert an object created in another application for use in the current application.

find

The Windows and Office feature that locates files, text strings, formatting, or special codes in a document or folder.

fixed expense

In a business or household, an expense that is the same each month for a length of time: rent, a vehicle payment, or a lease contract.

folder

A container for organizing and storing files and other folders.

font

A complete set of characters in a specific typeface, including design, weight, size, and style.

font color

The color assigned to the characters in a cell or object; default font colors are set in the Windows Control Panel.

font size

The height and width of characters, normally measured in points.

font style

Within a font, variations such as italic or boldface.

footer

Text or fields that appear at the bottom of every printed page.

forecast

Predict future values for one or more variables.

format

Change the appearance but not the contents or value of cells, worksheets, text, or numbers.

Format Painter

A tool used to assign the formatting in the selected cell to other cells in a workbook.

formula

A calculation.

formula bar

An area of the Excel application window that displays cell contents, including text and formulas.

Formula Palette

An Excel feature that appears when you click the = sign on the formula bar; used for entering functions.

function

A small program that uses one or more arguments to produce a result, often a calculation.

function name

Excel's specific name that is used to designate a function.

G

global macro

A macro stored in the Personal Macro Workbook available to all worksheets.

Goal Seek

An Excel tool used to determine the values of underlying variables required to meet a specific target.

graphics

Pictures or other images added to a worksheet.

gridlines

Non-printing lines that show the boundaries of rows, columns, and cells; in a chart, the background lines that display divisions on a value axis.

group

To simultaneously select more than one sheet for editing.

group (objects)

Unite two or more selected objects so that they are treated as one for purposes of moving and resizing.

H

handles

Markers that appear around a selected object; used to resize the object.

hardware

The physical parts of the computer, including the monitor, drives, micro-processor, printer, and other devices.

header

Text or fields that appear at the top of a printed worksheet.

header row

In an Excel database, the row at the top of the worksheet that contains field names.

HLOOKUP

A lookup function that returns a value from a specified row index.

home cell

Cell A1.

HTML

Hypertext Markup Language; the programming and formatting language of the Web; native document type for Office 2000.

hyperlink

Text or object in a document that, on mouse click, takes the user to another location in the current document, another document, a Web site, or e-mail message.

I

icons

Small pictures that represent programs and files; used in a graphical user interface.

IF

A logical function that completes one of two possible actions based on the value of a logical test.

import

Open or place a file created in one application in a different application.

indent

To offset the contents of a cell from its left boundary.

insert

Place a blank cell, row, or column in a worksheet and adjust the existing columns or rows.

interactive page

An Excel document published to the Web that allows users to enter and manipulate data.

Internet

The worldwide series of connected computers, for posting and accessing information about most any topic imaginable.

intersection

Where two ranges overlap.

intranet

A series of connected computers, generally within one company, displaying information by, about, and for the benefit of the company and its employees.

italics

A font enhancement that leans letters and numbers to the right.

iteration

One attempt to solve a problem including one or more variables.

L

landscape

A printing orientation with the long side of the paper at the top.

launch

Start a program.

layering

Placement of objects "on top of" text or other objects in a document, as if the objects were on printed transparency sheets.

leading zero

A zero to the left of other numbers and the decimal point, if any, in a cell.

legend

In a chart, the "key" that explains how a data series is displayed.

line chart

A series chart where data points are connected with a line.

linear programming

A sequential approach to problem solving that results in or clearly excludes the possibility of an optimal solution (also called linear analysis).

link

A dynamic reference to a cell in another worksheet, to another file, or to an OLE object.

list management

A term for working with Excel database records.

local macro

A macro stored and available in the workbook where it was created.

lock

Protect entries so they cannot be altered without first being unlocked.

logical function

A function like IF that is used to instruct Excel to choose between actions.

logical operators

Operators that return a value of true or false based on a comparison of two values or text strings: =, <>, <, >, >=, <=.

logical test

The decision-making condition for a logical function.

lookup function

A function that returns a value from an array.

lookup value

The cell that contains data used to select a row or column in a lookup function.

M

macro

A user-created program that repeats a series of keystrokes, menu selections, or other actions.

macro virus

Malicious code, written as a macro, designed to run automatically and replicate itself on your computer.

manual calculation

A calculation method that only recalculates worksheet formulas when the user requests calculation or saves a worksheet.

margins

White space that surrounds the top, bottom, and sides of a printed worksheet.

maximize

Make a window fill the entire screen.

maximum (MAX)

A function used to find the largest value in a range of cells.

menu bar

A command bar containing lists of options available in a program or window.

merge (cells)

Combine two or more cells into one.

microcomputer (PC)

A powerful computer designed to fit on a desktop.

Microsoft Excel 2000 (Excel)

A powerful, 32-bit spreadsheet program designed to run under Windows 9x/NT/2000; used to analyze and manipulate numbers: accounting, statistical, financial, and other numerical information.

minimize

To reduce an application or document window to a taskbar button, allowing it to continue to run in the background while another program has priority.

minimum (MIN)

A function used to find the smallest value in a range of cells.

mixed reference

A formula reference that includes relative and absolute cell references.

model

A worksheet that uses formulas to create a representation of some segment of the real world.

module

A unit of Visual Basic programming code; in Excel, macros are stored in Visual Basic modules.

mouse

An input device that allows entry into the computer by pointing to objects on the screen and clicking or dragging.

move

Reposition cells or an object from one location to another.

N

name

A string assigned to one or more cells (or to an entire sheet); used in place of a cell reference to refer to the cells or sheet.

name box

Area at the left end of the formula bar that displays the active cell's name or address.

navigation buttons

The arrows to the left of the sheet tabs; tools for scrolling through sheet tabs when there are too many to display at once.

noncontiguous

Not next to each other.

null set

An empty set; the results of a filter or select where no records meet the criteria.

Num Lock (or NUM LOC)

The toggle key on a computer keyboard that allows the calculator keypad to be used for numeric entry or insertion point movement.

O

object

Text, a graphic, or other artifact created in one application and placed in another.

Office Assistant

Microsoft's friendly help interface.

Office Shortcut Bar

The collection of Desktop buttons that provide one-click access to Office applications and features.

OLE

Object linking and embedding; a protocol for communication between applications.

OLE client

An application that can accept OLE objects.

OLE server

An application that can create OLE objects.

open

Retrieve a workbook or other file from disk so it can be used.

operating system

Software that allows application programs to run and manages computer resources such as memory, disk space, processor time, and peripherals.

operator/operation

A mathematical process represented by symbols like +, -, /, *, ^.

optimal solution

The solution that most efficiently uses the resources contained in a model to achieve a minimum, maximum, or target value.

options

A structured group of choices.

Order of Operations

Mathematical rules that govern the sequence in which formulas are evaluated.

orientation

The direction of print on a page: portrait or landscape.

outline

Displaying a range in levels, each of which can be expanded or collapsed to show or hide different levels of detail.

P

Page Break Preview

Allows you to see and adjust where printed pages will break.

page setup

The combined settings that direct how a worksheet or chart will appear when printed.

password

Secret word entered by a user to secure a workbook so that others can't open it.

paste

Copy the contents of the Clipboard beginning at the active cell.

path

The drive, folder, and subfolder(s) where a document is stored.

precedents

Used in resolving a circular reference, precendents are all cells involved in the formula containing the circular reference.

pie chart

A single-series chart used to show the relationship between points in the series.

PivotChart

A chart that displays values from a pivot table.

PivotTable

An Excel tool used to analyze the values in fields in a database or columns of worksheet data in relationship to other fields or columns.

placeholder

A field for date, time, or other variable that is filled with the current value when a worksheet is printed.

play

Run a macro.

plot area

The area of a chart used for graphical representation of data.

point

1/72 of an inch; used to measure font size.

point method

Entering parts of a formula by clicking or selecting cells.

portrait

A printing orientation with the short side of the paper at the top.

PowerPoint

A Microsoft program used to create electronic slide shows, overheads, and other presentation materials.

primary sort

The field that a group of records will be sorted on first.

print area

The area(s) of a worksheet that will be printed; the default print area includes all occupied portions of a worksheet.

Print Preview

A feature used to view a document's or a worksheet's printed appearance prior to printing.

R

range

One or more contiguous cells.

Range Finder

When a formula is open for editing, the Range Finder locates and marks cells that are included in the formula.

record

a) Information for one unit or individual; one row in an Excel database; b) To have Excel save a group of actions as a macro.

redo

A tool that restores the previously undone action.

relative reference

Used in a formula to refer to a cell; changes to reflect a copy or fill operation.

replace

An operation that substitutes one text string or formatting type for another.

right-click

Click the right mouse button (to open a shortcut menu).

row

A horizontal unit within a worksheet referenced by number.

row header

The gray button at the left end of a row labeled with the row's number.

S

save

Copy a workbook from the computer's memory to a more permanent location such as the hard drive or a floppy disk.

Save As

The command that always displays the dialog box where you can choose a location and name for a file.

scalable

Describes a font that can be resized; TrueType fonts are scalable.

scaling

Used to set the relationship between the worksheet's actual and printed sizes.

scenario

A set of possible circumstances with assumptions about certain values in a model, used to calculate other values in the model.

ScreenTip

An automatic informational pop-up message that appears when you mouse over certain items on the screen.

scroll bars

The horizontal and vertical bars to the right and below a document window that allow you to move to parts of a workbook that are not currently displayed on-screen.

scroll box

The rectangular box that appears between the arrows that mark the ends of a scroll bar; drag the scroll box to scroll quickly.

ScrollTip

The pop-up message that appears when you scroll through a worksheet; indicates your location in the worksheet as you scroll.

secondary sort

A field used to order records that have the same value in the primary sort field.

select

Choose one or more cells in preparation for a specific action.

series chart

A chart type that can illustrate more than one data series.

sheet tab

A feature on the bottom of a worksheet that contains the sheet's name; clicking the sheet tab activates the worksheet.

shortcut menu

The context-sensitive list of choices you see when you right-click the mouse.

shrink-to-fit

Reduce the size of the type so the contents of a cell fit its current size.

Shut Down

An option located on the Start menu that closes all applications and prepares your computer to be turned off or restarted.

simulate

Use a model to represent the results of changing variables.

size/resize

Reduce or enlarge a window or other object.

software

An application or operating system that provides specific instructions to the computer.

Solver

An Excel add-in used to find optimal solutions to multi-variable problems.

sort

Place in ascending or descending order based on the value in a field.

sort order

Ascending or descending.

source

A file that contains a value linked to a worksheet; an application used to create an OLE object.

Spelling

An Office tool used to check for misspellings in a worksheet.

spreadsheet

A program like Excel used to manipulate and analyze numerical information.

Start menu

Menu that appears when you click the Windows Start button to enable you to access Windows features and applications.

status bar

The bar at the bottom of a workbook window that gives you information about the current workbook; Excel also displays messages on the status bar.

style

One or more formatting specifications saved as a group within a workbook.

subset

A group of records within a database.

subtotal

A calculation for a group of numbers within a larger list of numbers.

syntax

The required and optional parts of a function.

T

Taskbar

Windows Desktop feature that contains the Start button and buttons for any current applications.

template

A pattern for the text, graphics, and formatting of a spreadsheet.

tertiary sort

The field used to order records that have the same values in the primary and secondary sort fields.

text string

One or more consecutive characters.

tick marks

Interval marks on a chart axis.

title bar

The horizontal bar at the top of an application window that displays the name of the application along with the Minimize, Maximize, and Close buttons for the application window.

toggle

A button or menu selection that switches between one of two values each time it is selected.

toolbar

A command bar containing buttons that carry out specific functions such as saving, formatting, and printing.

ToolTip

The ScreenTips you see when you point to a toolbar button; the button's name is displayed in a ToolTip.

track changes

A feature that allows you to see where others have edited a worksheet.

trailing zero

A zero to the right of the decimal point that is not followed by another number; does not affect the value of the number.

TrueType font

A font that appears on-screen exactly as it will appear when printed.

typeface

A font's design.

U

undo

Retract the last action taken.

ungroup

To select only one of the worksheets that had been simultaneously selected.

ungroup (objects)

To separate several objects or several parts of one object into smaller, distinct units.

union

All the cells in two separate ranges.

V

value

Contents of a cell; a number or date entered in a cell.

variable expense

In business, an expense that varies based on use, production, or some other business activity: labor expense, materials expense, and so on.

vertical alignment

The position of cell contents relative to the top and bottom boundary of the cell.

Visual Basic for Applications (VBA)

The programming language used with Microsoft Office applications; used to create macros.

VLOOKUP

A lookup function that returns a value from a specified column index.

W

What-If

Excel tools and add-ins used to provide support for decision making including Goal Seek, Solver, and the Scenario Manager.

wiffing

Using What If tools for decision-making support.

wildcard

Characters that can be used to replace unidentified characters.

Windows 9*x*/NT/2000
Microsoft's 32-bit graphical user interface operating systems designed to run on the newer, more powerful microcomputers.

WordArt
An Office program used to create special visual effects with text.

workbook
A document created in Excel.

workbook macro
A local macro saved in a regular workbook.

worksheet
A division of a workbook used for a set of numbers and labels; each Excel worksheet has 256 columns and 65,536 rows.

worksheet window
A window within the Excel application window that contains a worksheet.

workspace file
A file that retains all the window settings and arrangements when you're working on multiple workbooks.

wrap
Cause the cell contents to appear on more than one line.

X

x-axis
The label axis; horizontal axis in most 2-D series charts.

XLS
The file extension for an Excel workbook.

XLT
The file extension for an Excel template.

Y

y-axis

The value axis; the vertical axis in most 2-D series charts; the "depth" axis in 3-D charts.

Z

z- axis

The value axis in 3-D series charts.

Index

Note to the Reader: Page numbers in **bold** indicate the principal discussion of a topic or the definition of a term. Page numbers in *italic* indicate illustrations.

selecting data source, 138–139, *138*
software required for, 137–138
working with query results, 140
sorting, **124–127**, *125*, *126*
in ascending or descending order,
125–126
selecting all columns for
sorting, 126
date formats, Y2K compliance of, 121
date and logical functions, 91
date and time formatting codes,
119–120
default, **276**
Define Name dialog box, 79
defining, ranges, 79
Delete command, Clear Contents
command vs., 29
deleting
cells, 45–46, *46*
vs. clearing cells, 29
data series, 105
defined, **276**
macros, 253
ranges, 79
reports, 199
rows and columns, 43–44
styles, 114
worksheets, 50–51
delimited, **277**
dependent workbooks, **170**, **277**
dependents, **161**, **277**
depreciation, **277**
descending sort order, 125–126, **277**
Desktop, **277**
destination application, **203**, **277**
dialog box, **277**
displaying, toolbars, 254
double-click, **277**
dpi, **277**
drag-and-drop
copying cells with, 47–48

defined, **277**
importing text with, 211
moving cells with, 47–48
Draw. *See* Microsoft Draw
drawing. *See* Microsoft Draw
Drawing toolbar, 224–225, *225*
drill down, **277**
drop shadow, **278**
drop-down list, **278**
dynamic, **278**

E

editing
OLE objects, 205
reports, 199
styles, 114
templates, 168
Editing page (Share Workbook
dialog box), *176*
editing worksheets, **28–73**
changing worksheet layout,
42–52
adjusting column width and row
height, 42–43, *42*
copying and moving worksheets,
49–50
freezing and unfreezing rows and
columns, 52
hiding and unhiding rows and
columns, 51
inserting and deleting cells,
45–46, *46*
inserting and deleting rows and
columns, 43–44
inserting and deleting worksheets,
50–51
moving and copying cell contents,
46–48, *48*
naming worksheets, 48
selecting worksheets, 49

setting protection for, 183–184
zooming in and out of, 10–11, *10*
workspace files, 175, **297**
wrapping text, 57, **297**

X

X-axis, *98*, **297**
X-axis label, *98*
X-axis title, *98*
XLS, **297**
XLT, **297**

Y

Y2K compliance, 121
Y-axis, *98*, **298**
Y-axis label, *98*
Y-axis title, *98*

Z

Z-axis, **298**
zooming in and out of worksheets,
10–11, *10*

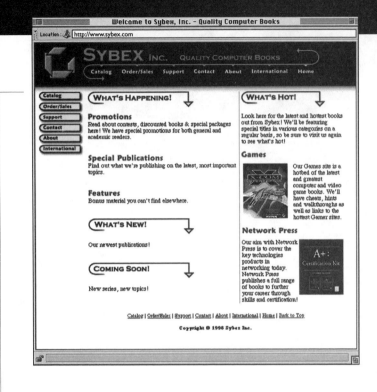

Microsoft Office User Specialist

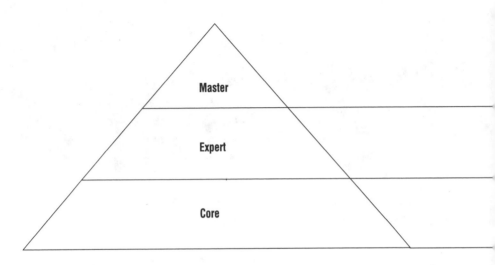

Level	Description	Requirements
Master	Becoming a Microsoft Office User specialist at the Master level indicates that you have a comprehensive understanding of Microsoft Office 2000.	Pass all FIVE of the required exams: Microsoft Word 2000 Expert Microsoft Excel 2000 Expert Microsoft PowerPoint 2000 Microsoft Outlook 2000 Microsoft Access 2000
Expert	Becoming a Microsoft Office User specialist at the Expert level indicates that you have a comprehensive understanding of the advanced features in a specific Microsoft Office 2000 application.	Pass any ONE of the Expert exams: Microsoft Word 2000 Expert Microsoft Excel 2000 Expert
Core	Becoming a Microsoft Office User Specialist at the Core level indicates that you have a comprehensive understanding of the core features in a specific Microsoft Office 2000 application.	Pass any ONE of the Core exams: Microsoft Word 2000 Microsoft Excel 2000 Microsoft PowerPoint 2000 Microsoft Outlook 2000 Microsoft Access 2000